"SWING THE SICKLE FOR THE HARVEST IS RIPE"

DAINA RAMEY BERRY

"Swing the Sickle for the Harvest Is Ripe"

GENDER AND SLAVERY IN ANTEBELLUM GEORGIA

UNIVERSITY OF ILLINOIS PRESS

URBANA, CHICAGO, AND SPRINGFIELD

FIRST ILLINOIS PAPERBACK, 2010
Frontispiece drawing by Michael Stevenson
© 2007 by the Board of Trustees
of the University of Illinois

⊗ This book is printed on acid-free paper.

The Library of Congress cataloged the cloth edition
as follows:
Berry, Daina Ramey.
Swing the sickle for the harvest is ripe : gender and
slavery in antebellum Georgia / Daina Ramey Berry.
p.   cm. — (Women in American history)
Includes bibliographical references and index.
ISBN-13: 978-0-252-03146-5 (cloth : alk. paper)
ISBN-10: 0-252-03146-6 (cloth : alk. paper)
1. Women slaves—Georgia—Social conditions—19th
century. 2. Slaves—Georgia—Social conditions—19th
century. 3. Sex role—Georgia—History—19th century.
4. Slavery—Georgia—Wilkes County—History—19th
century. 5. Slavery—Georgia—Glynn County—History—
19th century. 6. Slavery—Economic aspects—Georgia—
History—19th century. 7. Community life—Wilkes
County—History—19th century. 8. Community life—
Glynn County—History—19th century. 9. Wilkes County
(Ga.)—Race relations—History—19th century. 10. Glynn
County (Ga.)—Race relations—History—19th century.
I. Title.
E445.G3B47   2007
307.72086'2509758172—dc22   2006100938

PAPERBACK ISBN 978-0-252-07758-6

To the loving memory of my grandmothers:

Bertha Arlethia Houston &

Eleanor Louise Ramey and

To God Be the Glory

Contents

Preface

My interest in slavery started at an early age, when I was six and asked my father what it was like to be a slave. Although I grew up in a small northern California college town, my great-grandparents lived in Georgia and North Carolina before I ever had the opportunity to meet them or visit. When I was ten, my family moved to Georgia for the year and I connected with my southern roots. I remember meeting my great-great-uncle in Macon, Georgia, and feeling at home on his eighty-acre farm. I was particularly drawn to the fields and wanted to stay outside all day, soaking up the history and listening to stories about life in the past.

My formal introduction to history, however, came during my junior year at UCLA when I took an undergraduate African American history class from a visiting scholar. It was during his African American history survey class and after weeks of one-on-one discussions during office hours that I developed the urge to teach and research nineteenth-century U.S. history.

My experience that quarter was not always pleasant because it was the first time I was formally taught black history in a classroom setting, and the lectures and discussions were emotionally charged. This professor shared all kinds of stories about his childhood in the South and his African American servant, as well as his interpretation of the history of race in America. He also used the N-word on several occasions. When it was time for the midterm, I decided to write him a letter to tell him how I felt about the class, his discussions, and his personal stories. Needless to say, I did not pass the test; he asked me to come to his office hours for weekly meetings every Wednesday. At first I felt like I had been punished—what I referred to as "college detention"—but, as the weeks passed, it became clear to me that he and I had more in common than I realized, and I came to understand that we both loved history and were able to interpret it in different ways. I never dreamed I would become a historian until then. I am thankful to this professor for challenging me, questioning me, provoking me, and ultimately planting the seed that so many others have helped water, nourish, and grow.

Acknowledgments

I have been blessed to have the support of so many people, institutions, and sources of funding that have made this book possible. First and foremost I wish to thank Laurie Matheson, my editor, for believing in the project from my initial submission to the final page proofs. I am grateful that she dedicated so much time to reading several drafts and for always providing encouraging feedback.

My readers, Anne Firor Scott, Wilma King, Stephanie Shaw, and Deborah Gray White, deserve more that I can express in words for their comments, questions, criticisms, and suggestions. Anne Firor Scott introduced my work to the series editors after she and I met at a symposium in Arizona. From that point forward she has challenged me to write with clear and concise prose. How could I ever forget that first reader's report? I am thankful that she believed in this book and wanted to see it reach the shelves. I feel fortunate for the year I spent in North Carolina when she and I met regularly and read the drafts of the chapters out loud. My writing has improved because of her guidance. Wilma King provided detailed queries on sources that I had not previously questioned. She took the time to go over each chapter page by page and offer suggestions about how to make this a better book. She also generously shared primary documents and secondary literature that were instrumental to the argument. I am fortunate she has donated so much of her time to my professional development and growth as a scholar since our introduction at a Southern Historical Association Conference in Atlanta, Georgia. I would not have finished this book without her constant encouragement. Early on, Stephanie Shaw provided critical structural advice for the best way to organize the research, and she pushed me to transform the book in a way that made the material palatable. Toward the end of my writing, Deborah Gray White took the time to read this book and help me identify places that were unclear or unnecessary or that needed clarification. I am particularly grateful for her guidance in developing the discussions of family and community and for reminding me to maintain a sound structure. Working with her allowed me the opportunity to "clean up" the places that contained too much dust. I am thankful for each of these readers for their patience in reading more than one draft of this book, and I hope that it is something of which they all can be proud.

Thanks to Nwando Achebe, Pero G. Dagbovie, Laura Edwards, Farrell Evans, P. Gabrielle Forman, Wanda Hendricks, Jessica Millward, Leslie Schwalm, and Rosalyn Terborg-Penn for reading portions of this book and providing useful feedback. Joan Catapano at the press has always been supportive of this project; I am quite certain that I am unaware of all she has done "behind the scenes." I would also like to thank managing editor Rebecca Crist and assistant managing editor Angela Burton, copyeditor Drew Bryan, and the entire production staff at the University of Illinois Press. The talented Michael Stevenson kindly took time out of his busy schedule to create the image for the front matter, and I am truly honored. My family and I have been fans and supporters of his artwork for years, and I knew many years ago that I wanted him to design an image for my book.

I have been fortunate to have two personal copyeditors, Merrillee Burr and Anne Rogers. Both helped transform this book in ways I could not have done without their guidance. I am deeply indebted to Anne Rogers for working with me during the more time-sensitive stages of this process. Her guidance has been extremely helpful and she has contributed substantially to my development as a writer. It was comforting to know that I could always call her with technical questions that she would willingly answer.

Brenda Stevenson introduced me to slave women while I was an undergraduate student at UCLA. From her I learned how to conduct research in the archives and to think critically about enslaved families and communities. Her high standards in the classroom and in the archives have been invaluable. Since I left Los Angeles, Darlene Clark Hine has always been available as a mentor, colleague, and friend. It was a blessing to be in the same department as she for most of the time I worked on this book, and I often stopped by her office to ask her what she thought about a chapter or an idea. She has been extremely supportive and I am thankful for her professional advice and guidance along the way.

Acknowledgments   xiii

Several students at Arizona State University (ASU) and Michigan State University (MSU) contributed to this book. I am grateful for the research assistance of Terry Brock, Karen V. Carson, Andrew Dietzel, Dawne Curry, Jennifer Knight, and John Wess Grant. The graduate and undergraduate students from MSU History 870, History 800, History 201, and History 480 shaped many of the ideas that are expressed in this book. I am also particularly thankful for the ongoing conversations I've had with Sowande' Mustakeem and Kennetta Hammond Perry as this project has taken shape.

In addition to my students, I have been fortunate to have had wonderful colleagues at several universities. At MSU, David Bailey, Robert F. Banks, Peter Beattie, John Beck, Christine Daniels, Jualynne Dodson, Katie DuBois, Laurant DuBois, Kimberly Ellis, Kirsten Fermaglich, Lisa M. Fine, Randy Fotiu, Isaac Kalumbu, Mark Kornbluh, Bill Lawson, Patricia Lowrie, Pat McConeghy, Anne Meyering, Leslie Moch, Paulette Granberry Russell, Susan Sleeper-Smith, Curtis Stokes, Tom Summerhill, Ellen Vellie, David Weatherspoon, Erica Windler, and Wendy Wilkins have all supported my work. I was also able to complete drafts of several chapters and receive feedback thanks to the Women's Resource Center Writing Group.

My conversations with ASU colleagues T. J. Davis, Edward Escobar, Rachel Fuchs, Brian Gratton, Gayle Gullatt, Mernoy Harrison, Peter Iverson, Leanor Boulin Johnson, Peniel Joseph, Vicki Ruiz, and Noel Stowe were helpful and also contributed to this book in several ways.

Thanks to colleagues Josephine Beoku-Betts, Elizabeth Hughes, John Inscoe, Chana Kai Lee, Diane and John Morrow, and Melanie Pavich-Lindsay for making my many trips to the University of Georgia productive and for helping me feel at home when I visited the history department.

I appreciate the conversations I had with John F. Campbell while I did a summer study-abroad course at the University of the West Indies, Mona Campus. He challenged me to think critically about gender, enslaved families, and historical biases within the literature on U.S. and Caribbean slavery. I also want to thank Judith Carney and William Chancellor for our conversations about rice cultivation. Sue Morris shared her transcriptions of the Butler plantation records with me and I am thankful for her support. John and Novie Merchant were kind to help me with my computer programming and I am grateful for their support. Toward the end of my writing, Dennis Gardenmeyer introduced me to Philip and Anne Berolzimeher, who kindly invited me to spend time on Little St. Simons Island with their family. My time there was meaningful and I still hope we can make that trip to Five Pound and the slave settlement during low tide. I appreciate Bo Taylor and the staff for their support of my research.

I also want to thank the scholars who chaired, commented on, attended, and participated in the conference sessions where I developed many of the ideas presented in this book. In particular, I want to thank Victoria Bynum, Stephanie M. H. Camp, Catherine Clinton, Sharla Fett, Michael Gomez, Walter Johnson, Jennifer L. Morgan, and Margaret Washington. William Dusinberre and I had a memorable encounter at the Southern Historical Association meeting in Houston, Texas, and I have been blessed by our conversation ever since. David Barry Gaspar, although he may not realize it, has also contributed to this book, and our conversations at Duke University have truly shaped my thinking—I appreciate his wisdom.

The staff at several libraries and archives have been invaluable to the creation of this book. First and foremost, I would like to express my deepest gratitude to Dale Couch of the Georgia Archives for many years of support, guidance, and encouragement. He single-handedly directed my research as a graduate student and introduced me to sources, people, places, and libraries along the way. So many of the ideas and stories that appear in this book are because of documents he directed me to. I hope he knows how much his support is appreciated. I would also like to thank John Albert and Jewell Anderson of the Georgia Historical Society; Bob Wyllie, Mrs. King, and Pat Morris of the Coastal Georgia Historical Society; Mr. and Mrs. Hicks from the St. Simons Island Book Shop; Mrs. Celeste Stover from the Mary Willis Library in Wilkes County; Mary Ellen Brooks, Nelson Morgan, and Melissa Bush of the Hargrett Library at the University of Georgia; Laura Clark Brown of the Wilson Library at the University of North Carolina Chapel Hill; Elizabeth Dunn, Karen Jean Hunt, Linda McCurdy, and Janie Morris of the Duke University Rare Book, Manuscript, and Special Collections Library; Mike Unsworth from the MSU Library; John O'Shea of the Reese Library at Augusta State University; Ms. Linda Beck of the East Central Georgia Regional Library in Augusta, Georgia; and Sheri Kiaukaras of the Georgia Archives. Thanks also to the staff and researchers at the Robert Woodruff Library at Emory University, the Clements Library at the University of Michigan, the Library Company of Philadelphia, and the Atlanta History Center.

None of the research for this book would have been possible without the support of the following institutions and funding agencies. Thanks to Michigan State University for their support with an internal research grant, MSU dean Karen Klomparens's special research fellowship, the American Association of University Women for their postdoctoral fellowship, ASU's Faculty Grant-in-Aid and Women's Studies summer research awards, ASU's College of Liberal Arts and Sciences summer research award minigrant, and a travel grant from the history department.

Christine Conklin helped me by taking care of dogs Ella and Dizzy when I did not have time to walk them, run them, take them to the dog park, or bring them with me to the office. Thank you to the Michigan Weimaraner Rescue for blessing me with my canine children.

Thanks to Justin Austin, Cynthia Harrington, Dean John Kinney, Pastor H. Levi McClendon III, Dr. Carol Otis, Dr. Bill Parham, Dr. Hilton Thomas, Pastor Kenneth C. Ulmer, and members of the Intake Ministry at Mt. Zion Church for keeping my mind, body, and spirit in the right place. Thank you all for your support and constant prayers.

I am blessed with a large support network of family and friends, too many to name individually. Their interest, encouragement, patience, and support helped make this book possible. Jill Y. Allen, Alfiee Breland-Noble, Marian Ensley, Adriane Hopper, Andrea Lewis, Lisa Marovich, Tisa McGhee, Patricia Shropshire, Caryl Gilbert Smith, Iva C. Mills, Susan Steubing, and Lezlee S. Ware have called to check on me and sent nice cards of encouragement and well wishes; I thank you all for your prayers.

I owe a huge debt to Donna McIntosh for making so many of the research trips possible by allowing me to live with her for several summers. Donna, I thank you for your support and for your hospitality. I appreciate your coming to the archives and cemeteries with me and I promise that next time it won't take so long to find the slave gravesites. Your friendship, support, and sisterhood will always be remembered.

Thanks also to Dona C. Edwards for listening, praying, and caring about this book during so many difficult times. Thanks for the legal advice, word choices, and assistance with letters. I appreciate your always believing that I could get it done and for cheering me along the way.

Thank you to my family for allowing this book to be a part of so many family functions. I appreciate your care and concern, and I enjoyed your anticipation of this publication over the years. Thank you to all of the Rameys, Berrys, Houstons, Peelers, Bullards, Gordons, Simpsons, and Sains. Mamut—thank you for understanding my commitment to this project and for keeping me in your prayers. Dave and Felicia, thanks for asking about the book and for wanting to read it.

My parents, Melvin and Felicenne Ramey, saw the creation of this book from start to finish and have always been the cheerleaders I need. Thanks for learning about this process with me and for trusting my decisions. I appreciate your excitement and your assistance at every stage.

Because of you, I learned at a young age the importance of knowing one's history and for embracing it despite the pain and suffering; you taught me how to find the silver lining even when I had trouble seeing it.

The last person I wish to express my deepest appreciation for is my husband Lisbon. Without your guidance, support, agape love, and understanding, this manuscript would not have been finished. Thank you for staying up with me and for going through the day-to-day highs and lows of the research and writing process. I appreciate your company at the archives, cemeteries, slave cabins, wooded trails, coastal estuaries, cotton fields, rice marshes, conferences, meetings, and presentations. You are the minister, listener, advisor, friend, mate, and voice I needed to hear, and I will always be grateful for your spirit and truth. Finally, thank you Lord for guiding my way through this book.

This book is for my grandmothers, Bertha "Nanny" Houston and Eleanor Ramey. Despite your limited physical presence in my life, your spirits are always with me. Nanny, thank you for telling me to paint the perfect picture and for helping me select the frame, canvas, and colors. I pray that the ancestors are pleased with this work.

"SWING THE SICKLE FOR THE HARVEST IS RIPE"

Introduction

Swing the sickle for the harvest is ripe.
—Joel 3:13 NIV

One evening in the late 1840s on an upcountry Georgia plantation, Caroline, a bondwoman and the wife of an enslaved African American overseer, hosted a quilting. This couple "lived in good style in a
framed and well-furnished house" next door to their slaveholder. Caroline's husband was the "superintendent" and trusted "companion" of
their owner, and the relationship between the two men was character-
ized as having "equality and frankness and friendliness in expression."
Emily Burke, a northern educator who lived on this plantation for a few
months and considered Caroline one of her "best friends," commented
that it was hard to comprehend that "one was a master and the other
a slave." This unusual relationship produced frequent frolics, holidays,
and parties on the plantation "at the expense of their master." Thus,
when Caroline decided to host this quilting, she had permission from
her husband's trusted comrade.[1]

According to Burke, it was customary on Georgia plantations for
enslaved guests to attend such gatherings not only to work but also to
socialize. They came knowing that "the first part" of the night would be
devoted solely to "work on the quilt" and the "latter part to festivity and
dancing." In addition to Burke, Caroline had invited "field slaves, *both
men and women.*" To some, it might seem strange "to hear of men being
invited to a quilting, but . . . among the Southern field hands, the women
can hoe as well as the men and the men can sew as well as the women,
and they engage in all departments of labor according to the necessity
of the case without regard to sex." Burke observed that gender was not

used to divide bondpeople; rather, skill took precedence, regardless of the activity. As she sat and witnessed this scene, she was amazed at how men and women assembled themselves "around the quilt." Slightly amused by the sight, "the men and women were seated promiscuously around the frame, very quietly yet as expeditiously plying the needle to all sorts of lines . . . as if their lives depended upon having the quilt out before midnight." They worked diligently and with such expertise that Burke was astonished that they "executed very much as one would suppose it would be by hands much more accustomed to wield the spade and shovel than the cambric needle." With precision, these men and women "quilted with darning needles and traced their designs with charcoal" and "every one of them exhibited a width of distinctness worthy of a heavy hand!" After the quilt was completed, Caroline displayed her hosting skills and provided her guests with "deliciously prepared" chicken and ham; they drank fine tea and coffee and had a variety of pastries for dessert. It was a nice affair "that any ambitious landlady might be proud of."[2]

Burke's discovery that southern planters divided their workers according to skill rather than sex signals a disruption not only of her own expectations and understanding of enslaved labor, but also those of much historical writing on slavery. *Swing the Sickle* seeks to break down binary opposites such as house labor equals skilled work and field labor equals unskilled work to explore more subtle dynamics that involve skill, talent, seniority, experience, personal relationships, and circumstance. Building on recent scholarship on various aspects of slave labor from organizational structures to occupational hierarchies,[3] this book examines the intricacies of enslaved labor, family, community, and economy.[4]

Conveying the understanding that specialized, skilled labor crossed gender lines and that enslaved men and women used both agricultural and nonagricultural labor skills are the two primary goals of this book. Examining the daily lives, activities, and interactions of enslaved persons and slaveholders within their plantations and communities illuminates labor patterns and reveals both planters' and slaves' perspectives on skill and labor. It allows us to analyze how these perceptions about labor and skill affected the ways labor was organized and structured for both sexes. The concept of what constituted skilled labor was also influenced by the type of plantation or farmstead that the bondpeople lived on and by the particular type of crop that was grown. Some laborers worked on a single crop such as cotton, while others worked in a dual-crop system of rice and cotton. The size, location, and demographics of the plantation or homestead; the demands of the cultivated crop; and the specifics of the labor force all shaped the social system that either provided or precluded opportunities for the enslaved. *Swing the Sickle* explores the ways different crops created a social hierarchy among the enslaved and the effect of such power dynamics within the quarters.

Labor served as a defining component of slave life, but not only in bushels picked or acres plowed. Labor also offered opportunities for socializing, travel between plantations, and courtship. Burke's account of the enslaved experience highlights one such melding of labor and community in her description of a "working social," my term for public work environments where bondpeople labored to complete a task and used the balance of the evening for socializing.[5] Working socials involved repairing fences, fixing roofs, shucking corn—or quilting, as in Burke's vivid account. Once they finished the quilt, the participants enjoyed a good meal. Clearly, some slaveholders were lenient with their workforce because they understood the benefit of rewarding them with an evening of festivities.

Events such as working socials hint at the private lives of bondpeople, the lives that extended beyond the labor by which slaveholders measured and understood them. In plantation records, public documents, correspondence, and other sources, the shadowy traces of these private lives are discernible. They show the efforts made to keep together or reunite families, the informal economies where the enslaved traded or bartered for needed goods, the freedom to pass beyond the plantation gates on the trust of their slaveholders, and other demonstrations of enslaved humanity and independence.[6] Allowing a bondwoman like Caroline to host a working social indicates her elevated status within the enslaved community. Caroline reaped the benefits of a trusted relationship with her slaveholder and was given permission to host holiday parties, dances, and other celebrations.

Labor was central to enslaved life in antebellum Georgia, as it was in most states in the lower South. But slavery throughout the antebellum South was not simply about the work that Africans did for their slaveholders. It also encompassed survival, relationships, faith, hope, love, resistance, defiance, cooperation, negotiation, interaction, intimacy, exploitation, abuse, patience, dignity, strength, skill, and, most important, freedom. Planters primarily concerned themselves with forcing their chattel property to "swing the sickle"; during the past thirty years, historians have found that many slaveholders were completely unaware that bondwomen and bondmen fashioned lives of their own that had little to do with sickles, hoes, or plows. These enslaved laborers married, had children, attended social gatherings, worshiped at prayer meetings, and experienced the joys and sorrows of life with one another. *Swing the Sickle* builds on a body of scholarship that explores bondpeople's public and private lives.[7] Every aspect of enslaved people's private lives had some relationship to what was happening in the public world of their slaveholders, but the presence of planters did not deter bondpeople from shielding aspects of their public labor practices from their slaveholders. By the same token, even within their personal quarters where there was some ability to conduct "private" activities, enslaved women and men were always vulnerable to exploitation, interference, and intrusion.

Focusing on gender, labor, family, community, and economy in antebellum Georgia, *Swing the Sickle* draws on evidence from two representative regions, the upcountry/piedmont county of Wilkes, and the low-country/tidewater county of Glynn.[8] In these regions, open and closed systems of slavery developed.[9] The closed system prevailed in Glynn County, where, with the exception of a select few, slaveholders restricted bondpeople's geographic mobility. These "trustworthy" skilled slaves received permission to travel beyond the plantation boundaries to complete specific tasks or errands. Glynn County bondpeople resided on large estates with other family members that sometimes stretched across three generations. Even though this allowed for a modicum of family stability, all bondpeople were vulnerable to family separation through sale or as a result of the death or financial collapse of their owners.

Bondwomen and bondmen in Wilkes County lived in a community that supported an open system, which allowed them more freedom to move among nearby plantations or farms. This fluidity enabled bondpeople to socialize regularly with people from neighboring counties. Although this allowed for the creation and maintenance of relationships, enslaved men and women experienced family instability because many of them were rented out on a yearly basis. Such practices, also referred to as hiring, disrupted enslaved family formation and added to their constant fear of being separated and sold.[10]

This book employs both micro and macro levels of analyses to explore gender and slavery. At the micro level, what follows is the study of two counties in Georgia that differed in some salient ways yet shared underlying similarities. Many of the findings have larger (macro) implications that can be applied to other southern states and regions.[11] Wilkes and Glynn Counties make useful subjects of inquiry. Both contained black majorities during the antebellum era and both included laborers who cultivated cotton. These counties were part of primary economic trade

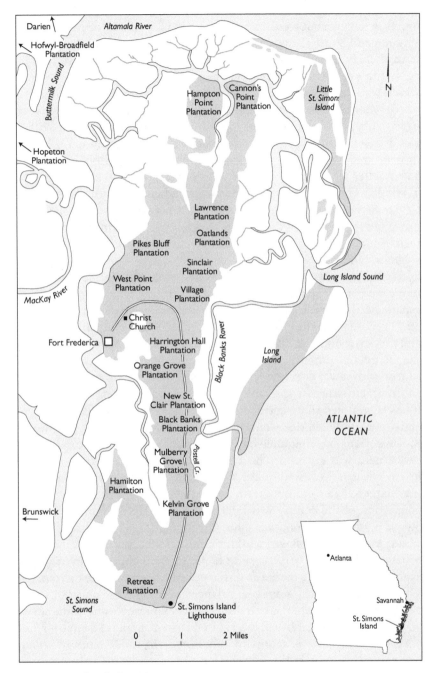

St. Simons Island, Georgia

routes in Georgia but were not the home of major trading centers. Several Virginia and South Carolina residents traveled through Wilkes County with their bondpeople before settling in other parts of the state. The coastal area of Glynn County served as a point of entry south of Savannah, which was the largest trading center and slave market in the state.

Slaveholders and occasionally bondwomen and bondmen traveled nearly fifty miles to exchange goods in a large market setting. Wilkes County residents went to Augusta to access this larger market, whereas those from Glynn County traveled to Savannah; in addition, each region had smaller local trading centers: Washington (Wilkes) and Brunswick (Glynn).[12] These locales represent understudied areas because scholars tend to focus on the social, political, and economic history of major trading centers where extant documents are available. Studying minor trading regions is also vital to our understanding of the intricacies of antebellum economic life.

Wilkes County, located 114 miles east of Atlanta in the lower piedmont area of the state, was one of the seven original Georgia counties established in 1777. It is often referred to as the "mother county of Georgia" because six additional counties were carved from its initial boundaries.[13] Bondpeople in this region resided on small farms common to the Georgia piedmont.[14] The typical bondwoman or bondman lived on a farm with fewer than ten workers. These slaveholdings created work environments that kept slaveholders and bondpeople in close contact. It has been noted that "cotton plantations [of the lower piedmont] generally outnumbered rice plantations [of the tidewater region]; however, they were smaller, contained fewer slaves per unit, and their total capital investment was lower."[15] The average slaveholding for Wilkes County in 1820 was a farm with eight bondpeople, and by 1857, the average was sixteen.[16] Despite the small size of the holdings, the total enslaved population of the county was large. In 1820, Wilkes County residents owned 9,705 slaves. A decade later, the population decreased slightly to 8,960. As the total enslaved workforce diminished, one aspect remained constant: the majority of those in bondage were children. In 1840, for example, more than half of the enslaved were twenty-three or younger. The male/female ratio remained balanced between 1820 and 1860.[17]

Like Wilkes County, Glynn County also represents one of the seven original counties established in 1777 and was the home of a large planter elite. Glynn County is approximately fifty-eight miles south of Savannah along the coast in the tidewater region of the state. In addition to the mainland, the county contains St. Simons and Jekyll Islands, which are part of a larger group of Sea Islands that stretches 120 miles along

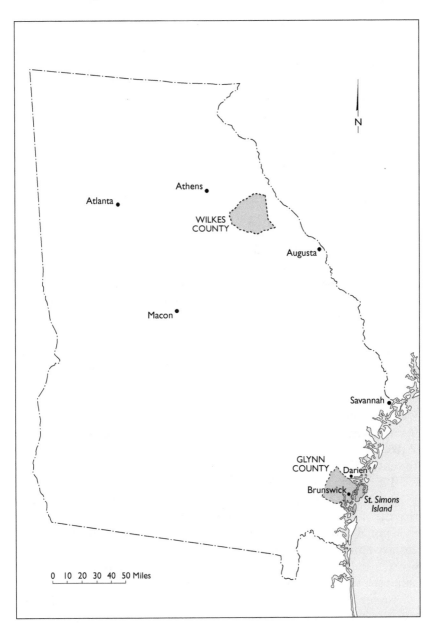

Wilkes and Glynn Counties, Georgia

the coasts of North and South Carolina, Georgia, and Florida.[18] Those who migrated to Glynn County came primarily from South Carolina and Virginia to capitalize on Georgia's lenient land policy and alluvial soil.

The enslaved population in this region represented approximately 80 percent of the total population for much of the antebellum period, and on some plantations, the enslaved outnumbered slaveholders ten to one.[19] A significant number of the planters on St. Simons Island owned more than fifty laborers and were considered large slaveholders. Many had estates on the island as well as the mainland, and they organized their workers around the cultivation of two crops, rice and Sea Island cotton. Most of the data relating to their daily lives in this coastal county come from the records of the fourteen large estates on St. Simons Island, which reflects the typical experience of bondpeople in the region. This large plantation setting and work regime shaped the personal lives of those in bondage.

Although enslaved women and men in Glynn County lived on plantations larger than those in the interior cotton belt, they were relatively isolated from whites because of the population demographics and the high incidence of absenteeism among coastal planters. "Absenteeism" is a term used to describe planters who did not live on their plantations year-round, but occasionally visited their property to make sure their overseers managed them properly. Unlike the Caribbean, where absentee slaveholders managed their plantations from Europe or the United States, Georgia planters served as "local absentees" because they "lived near their plantations, knew their people, and had strong personal ties with them."[20] The average slaveholding in Glynn County during 1850 was forty-one bondpeople per plantation.[21] Even though the total number of enslaved persons in Glynn County was approximately half that of Wilkes County, both counties had relatively balanced sex ratios during the antebellum era.[22]

Plantation and community demographics provide some clarity to local patterns of enslavement, but studying gender allows us to identify the numerous ways bondpeople experienced slavery in addition to regional variance. Like the guests who attended Caroline's quilting, enslaved men and women had a variety of talents that slaveholders recognized and utilized. We cannot understand slavery until we know more about the work that men and women performed.

Swing the Sickle begins with an exploration of agricultural labor, which occupied most slaves most of the time. Gendered divisions and the blurring of labor tasks between men and women reveal that slaveholders defined and assigned tasks according to skill, but historians disagree on the meaning and significance of specialized labor. This book provides a definition for skilled work that encompasses a variety of labor tasks in agricultural and nonagricultural settings. Moving away from binary categories and assumptions that reserve skill for male artisans, I argue in chapter 1 that women field hands, although traditionally considered "unskilled" by scholars, had specialized skills that their slaveholders valued and utilized.

Throughout this book, skill is defined as the ability to do any form of work well. For example, a bondwoman who works in the fields might be a skilled cotton picker—someone who regularly makes or exceeds her required quota for the day—whereas a fellow laborer who barely manages to complete his quota would be considered unskilled. A bondman may be a skilled carriage driver, whereas his carriage-driving friend—who regularly damages the horses and who once turned the carriage over—would be considered unskilled. In this framework, a person might develop skills because of natural talent, rigorous training, or continuous practice. Skilled labor, therefore, includes all activities and crafts that a person mastered with her or his hands or body, regardless of whether the work took place in the fields, barnyards, plantation homes, or enslaved cabins, or along creeks, in the woods, in provision grounds, at the spinning wheel, or in the kitchen. Skill in these settings appeared in complex and visible forms. The definition here accounts for agricultural and nonagricultural labor as well as the gender of the worker, and it does not limit skilled work to trades performed by men. This definition also includes tasks performed beyond the urban world of male artisans and incorporates rural plantation settings where both men *and* women displayed skilled labor.

Chapter 2 examines the ways skill manifested itself in nonagricultural work settings in and beyond the confines of bondpeople's home plantations and farms. Nonagricultural skilled bondpeople had the privilege of traveling to worksites away from their home estates, and some accompanied their slaveholders to the market, to social gatherings, and to vacation getaways in the North. The opportunities for geographic mobility were not reserved solely for skilled males, and contrary to the prevailing assumption, both men *and* women traveled to a variety of nonagricultural work settings. Understanding that off-plantation mobility and skilled labor crossed gender lines changes our perception of the enslaved experience; by adding women to the equation, we can no longer make the assumption that males dominated nonagricultural skilled positions.

Labor performed in public for their slaveholders or neighbors affected the private lives of the enslaved. In chapter 3, I suggest that working socials represent a space where public and private worlds functioned simultaneously. Therefore, labor and social interaction were inextricably linked. In this setting, enslaved women and men expressed themselves, shared coping strategies, and interacted with people from neighboring properties. They also used working socials for courtship, counsel, and camaraderie.

Life in the quarters differed from work settings as a place where women and men participated in religious activities, holiday celebrations, courtship rituals, and marriage ceremonies without constant scrutiny from their slaveholders. However, family and community interactions were not completely private. Slaveholders, both literally and figuratively, found ways to enter the quarters and exercise their control. By examining rape, domestic violence, and physical abuse, chapter 4 explores the impact of hard labor, the interference of slaveholders in relationships, and the effect of separation and sale on the stability of enslaved families.[23] Selecting certain bondpeople to form relationships with one another was one way planters tried to control the private lives of their human property for economic gain. Forced breeding represented a tactic slaveholders used to disrupt families even when the slaveholders were not present. This interference was one source of tension and stress that often resulted in domestic conflict among the enslaved. The constant threat of separation and sale marked the greatest challenge to family and community stability.

The practice of hiring out bondpeople created another source of family instability and is discussed in chapter 5.[24] Despite the temporary separation it caused, hiring affected families' access to geographic mobility and provided opportunities for independent economic activities. Even though enslaved families in Georgia strived for cohesion, they also did everything they could to improve their condition; one way involved participation in clandestine economic activities.[25] The chapter discusses how these two "secondary institutions"—the system of hiring and the clandestine informal economy—are directly related.

Examining the micro history of gender, work, family, community, and economic activities among the enslaved in Georgia allows a multifaceted portrait of slave life to emerge. Bondpeople in Glynn and Wilkes Counties led complicated lives that provided concurrent benefits and disadvantages. This study confirms some old ideas about family and community formation, but it also presents new interpretations of skilled agricultural and nonagricultural labor, family stability, slaves' public and private lives, slave owners' hiring practices, and informal economic activities.

The enslaved experience varied depending on several internal and external influences; this diversity can be explored in a number of settings. Antebellum slave life was dependent on a person's sex, age, location, crop type, skills, owner, population demographics, and myriad other variables. Bondpeople's lives were greatly affected by whether they were male or female, aged ten or fifty, healthy or sickly, picked cotton or grew rice, lived in the tidewater on a large plantation or in the piedmont on a small farm, had a flexible or uncompromising shareholder, lived with other relatives present or in isolation, and had special skills or not. Underlying these differences, however, was the shared environment of enslavement.

1 *"I Had to Work Hard, Plow, and Go and Split Wood Jus' Like a Man": Skill, Gender, and Productivity in Agricultural Settings*

As soon as the grain is ripe, he puts the sickle to it, because the harvest has come.

—Mark 4:20 NIV

Wilkes County bondwomen boasted about their mothers' talents. Former bondwoman Adeline Willis testified that her mother was a field hand who drove steers, was the best meat cutter on the plantation, and "could do all kinds of farm work." She was also a good spinner and one of "the best dyers anywhere 'round."[1] Willis expressed pride in her mother's agricultural and nonagricultural labor skills. Bondwoman Arrie Binns's mother worked in the fields by day and at the spinning wheel by night.[2] Most upcountry enslaved women "plowed alongside the men . . . [during the day, then] shared . . . [in] quilting parties and other feminine social-economic functions" at night.[3]

This chapter examines agricultural labor from the perspective of the enslaved worker, both male and female, and from the perspective of the planter. It also expands the concept of what constitutes skilled labor and develops a complex picture of women's contributions to the plantation economy. Equal consideration of female and male workers broadens our understanding of slave labor and reshapes discussions of the enslaved family, community, and economy; all are inextricably linked to work. By highlighting contributions of women and men to the plantation work-force, it becomes clear that the sex of the worker was connected to perceptions of "skilled" and "unskilled" labor.

In early March 1839, Sally, a mulatto field hand at Hampton Point Plantation on St. Simons Island, Georgia, approached her mistress Frances Kemble in hopes of changing her work status. According to Kemble, Sally complained about the difficulty of field labor and "begged" her to assign "some less laborious kind of work" because "hoeing in the field" was too hard. Exhausted from long hours in the cotton fields, Sally suffered from "incessant pain and weakness in her back." Therefore, she asked Kemble if she could "be allowed to learn a trade."[4]

Bondwomen like Sally understood that skilled labor, especially in the trades, provided certain physical and material privileges. But the idea of becoming a skilled cotton picker was not Sally's goal. Essentially, she wanted relief from agricultural labor altogether. From her perspective, bondpeople who learned trades—those who worked as carpenters, coopers, wheelwrights, blacksmiths, and shoemakers, among others, were nonagricultural laborers excused from the harsh rigors of agricultural work. However, most of these traditionally defined trades were reserved for men. Women utilized their nonagricultural skills as nurses, cooks, seamstresses, midwives, and washerwomen and their agricultural skills as cotton pickers, ginners, and rice threshers. They worked side by side in the fields with their male counterparts and were equally valuable to the plantation regime.

Whether Sally realized that the skills some field hands acquired set them apart from other workers is unclear. It is evident, however,

Table 1.1. Antebellum Slave Population

Total Slave Population	1820	1830	1840	1850	1860
Wilkes	9,705	8,960	6,501	8,281	7,953
Glynn	2,760	3,968	4,409	4,232	2,839

Note: The total slave population in Glynn County increased during the antebellum period, whereas the population in Wilkes County decreased between 1820 and 1840 and then fluctuated in the 1850s and 1860s as planters moved to other parts of the state. In 1820, the slave population for Wilkes was 3.5 times larger than Glynn; in 1830 it was 2.25 larger; in 1840 it was 1.5 times larger; in 1850 it was 2 times larger; and in 1860 it was 2.8 times larger. These statistics were compiled from the "Slave Population Census," by the Geostat Center, which is now part of the Geospatial and Statistical Data Center, University of Virginia Library: http://fisher.lib.virginia.edu/collections/stats/histcensus/.

that she wanted to learn a trade and knew that enslaved women were excluded from most trade positions. This exclusion forced larger numbers of women into the fields, where they were productive in terms of the volume, speed, quality, and endurance involved in completing their work. Many of the large estates in coastal Georgia included populations where bondwomen outnumbered men.[5] Labor skills and a female majority did not prevent Sally from making her request—but in the end she remained in the fields.[6]

Enslaved women worked in the fields because their slaveholders recognized the value of their agricultural skills. However, upon pregnancy, some women received a short period of rest. On 8 March 1845, when most of the 105 enslaved workers at Elizafield Plantation in Glynn County, Georgia, planted rice in the "Upper 20," two women were temporarily excused from the fields. While her husband Jack worked and worried, Cumsey gave birth to a girl named Sissy. Not far away, Catherine's labor brought Bella to her, her husband Henry, and the Elizafield community. Infants Sissy and Bella would not comprehend until much later what their parents knew from experience—that their newborn daughters would spend the majority, if not all, of their lives in bondage.

Hugh Fraser Grant, their slaveholder, made sure that all able hands planted rice that day because he operated under a tight agricultural schedule, despite the occasional diversions of childbirth in the quarters. His calendar demanded that laborers plant rice in March to ensure that it was ready for harvest during late August and early September for shipment to local markets. During the month Sissy and Bella were born, Grant worried about the health of his workforce because "whooping cough was on the place" and as a result he "lost 2 Negroe Children." He made particular note of women when they gave birth to new laborers and of men when they died. "Mulatto John" and "March a prime Man aged about 32 years old" died on the same day as two children, according to Grant's records.[7] No other deaths appear throughout the journal except for those included on the slave list. It is not clear that Grant, highly touted as one of the most successful rice planters in coastal Georgia, understood the interaction among gender, labor, skill, health, and family of his slaves, but his records provide scholars with a glimpse into the lives of those he owned.[8]

Despite the acknowledgment of families in his plantation journal and account book, Grant's primary concern was their labor. Though he was a fastidious bookkeeper who maintained detailed records for more than thirty years, when it came to his management strategies for his bondpeople, he was hardly consistent. Some of his work descriptions contained gender-specific assignments such as "women thrashing straw rice" and "men cutting wood," while others appeared as gender neutral, such as "hands collecting mud to replace canal trunk."[9] Gender neutrality in the historical record, however, does not necessarily indicate that gender was insignificant.

On plantations and small farms, planters utilized bondwomen's skills in the fields. Slaveholders noted that some women displayed greater dexterity than bondmen because of their small hands; this allowed some women to pick cotton faster without leaving excessive amounts of fiber in the boll.[10] Travelers such as John D. Legare, who visited the South in 1833, concurred. He witnessed weekly Glynn County cotton-picking competitions where slaveholders awarded victors with molasses and rice; many of the winners of these events were women.[11] Likewise, former bondman John Brown "observed that the women pick much faster than the men, their fingers being naturally more nimble."[12] In the rice fields, women workers displayed a variety of skills in their knowledge of rice cultivation and processing.[13] From the plantation records and other documents, it is clear that slaveholders had a complicated view of slave labor; they listed men and women with notes about their specific skills. Daily work in the fields might be done by men or by women, working separately or together. Because many of the required tasks on a plantation were performed by members of either sex, it is no surprise that enslaved women often boasted about being able to work hard "jus' like a man."

Defining Skilled Labor

If skill means that a person has the ability to do something well, then some cotton pickers and rice cultivators were certainly skilled. Slaveholders acknowledged that agricultural labor required training and practice. Commenting on this subject in a popular agricultural journal, Dr. Daniel Lee encouraged slaveholders to view the South as a "school" where "Africans may learn productive industry . . . to acquire habits of steady labor." By doing so, they could develop "knowledge of all the mysteries of skilful planting." Dr. Lee felt that "tillage and farm economy are so common, [that] the masses overlook their importance and erroneously assume that no bona fide apprenticeship is needed in rural arts." In his opinion, "instruction and experience are as valuable in agriculture as in any other occupation."[14] With this in mind, it is no surprise that slaveholders assigned various aspects of field labor, from thinning rice stalks to ginning and moting cotton, to specific bondpeople according to their skills. They seldom made the mistake that historians often do of equating "skilled labor" with men and "unskilled labor" with women. Planters, traders, and enslaved workers alike described various aspects of skilled labor with specific reference not only to certain bondpeople but also to gender, power, and productivity.

Lowcountry bondwomen represented the majority of the agricultural workers and contributed substantially to the plantation economy.[15] They labored alongside bondmen at similar tasks and completed traditionally gender-specific jobs at night. Women were the central figures in the agricultural workforce in this region because more women than men worked in the fields. This assertion does not suggest the insignificance of female labor in regions like Wilkes County where the ratios of men to women were more balanced. It does, however, confirm that some planters purchased women more frequently than men for a variety of reasons: cost, their capacity to bear children, and their labor skills.

The labor of enslaved men working as drivers, carpenters, shoemakers, bricklayers, or any of the other artisan skills that large slaveholders prized has been readily understood as skilled, but women's labor, whether in the house or in the field, has not. Agricultural workers (male and female alike) acquired skills crucial to the production of staple crops; therefore, in some instances, the connection between field and unskilled labor is inappropriate.[16] Field hands, of both sexes, "acquired a wide variety of *farm skills*" even though scholars found that enslaved males were the only group that earned the title and status of a skilled laborer.[17] Others referred to skilled slaves "not just [as] craftsworkers, but managers, transport workers, and household slaves—that is, the semiskilled and those with specialized roles."[18] In order to revise our understanding of these categories, we must begin with an exploration of labor systems and then examine labor patterns on specific plantations.

Productivity and Organizational Structure

Slaveholders organized their workers according to two labor systems: task and gang labor. Supervisors measured bondpeople's work with precision in the task system, which required that each full hand complete approximately 105 feet square of labor per day.[19] After enslaved workers finished their assigned task and any additional tasks, they had the remainder of the day to themselves. The gang system, by contrast, divided slaves in various groups based on their ability to complete a particular job. Often segregated by rows, the workers in the first gang controlled the pace of those that followed, and they remained in the fields from sunup to sundown.

Because some scholars maintained that tasking was used exclusively on coastal rice plantations and the gang system on upcountry short-staple cotton plantations, the association between rice and tasking and between cotton and gang labor became widely accepted. Contrary to these observations, a close examination of the daily activities of the enslaved through plantation records and agricultural journals reveals that variations of *both systems* occurred in upcountry and lowcountry Georgia.

Although it is true that most Sea Island cotton plantations utilized tasking, several short-staple cotton farms adopted tasking for some parts of the cultivation process. Task and gang labor operated at different ends of a continuum, which included an array of variations such as partial tasking—a method used to divide gang laborers between specific tasks.[20] On Sea Island cotton plantations, bondpeople worked either under the task system similar to the method used on rice plantations or under a combination of the gang and the task system. The latter was used particularly in the coastal communities of South Carolina and Georgia. The average bondperson in Wilkes County often labored in the fields with their slaveholders. Depending on the work structure, some planters put women to work in all-female gangs, while in other cases women worked alongside slaveholders and enslaved men. Reviewing lowcountry management strategies clarifies these patterns.

Kelvin Grove

On St. Simons Island in Glynn County, Georgia, James P. Postell inherited Kelvin Grove Plantation from his father-in-law, Benjamin Franklin Cater. On the 1,600–acre tract, 500 acres were used to cultivate Sea Island cotton and corn. Benjamin's father, Thomas Cater, migrated to St. Simons from South Carolina in the 1790s and purchased the plantation. He was murdered during the War of 1812 by his wife's lover, and their only son escaped with their house servant Denbrow. This loyal servant brought young Benjamin to Retreat Plantation, which at the time was the home of Major William Page, who later became his legal guardian. Benjamin F. Cater married Ann Armstrong and they had one child, Ann, who was the last Cater descendant. Ann married James Postell, and through this marriage he became the owner of the estate in the 1850s.[21] Despite the tragic murder of his grandfather-in-law, Postell spent the rest of his life maintaining the property and producing Sea Island cotton, corn, potatoes, and peas.

The enslaved population at Kelvin Grove included male and female workers of various ages.[22] In 1825, a local planter noted that ten people were engaged in agriculture at Kelvin Grove with two house servants, thirty-five acres of cotton, ten acres of corn, five acres of potatoes, and ten acres of peas.[23] In 1853, the population increased to eighty-one slaves, of whom forty-five (56 percent) were female. Postell noted that of this group, thirty-four worked in the fields, thirty-seven were children, and ten occupied nonagricultural positions.[24] His concern for productivity is evident in the way he listed each slave's value based on his or her physical capability. Like other planters, Postell rated his hands as 1, $\frac{3}{4}$, $\frac{1}{2}$, or $\frac{1}{4}$ based on the amount of labor a slave could perform in a given day. The first category of workers rated 1 were sometimes referred to as "full" or "prime" hands and often were between the ages of eighteen and thirty years. "Field laborers (both male and female) were rated at prime when they could perform the expected task in the usual working day of nine to ten hours" while "[b]oys aged 10 to 14 and women with little physical vigor were rated as one-quarter or one-half of a prime hand."[25] Some slaveholders rated their nonagricultural slaves, however, by focusing on the quality of their trade (i.e., carpentry, cooking, sewing) rather than on the quantity they produced in a given day.

At Kelvin Grove, more women worked in the fields than men. Twenty-three (62 percent) of the field hands were female, and they completed work equivalent to seventeen taskable hands. They cultivated Sea Island cotton and corn, worked in the plantation house, and, during 1853, gave birth to seven children. By contrast, only eleven men served as field hands, estimated as seven and one-quarter taskable hands. Such demographics indicate that women completed more work than men because their rates totaled a higher amount of taskable labor (seventeen versus seven and one-quarter). Male and female agricultural laborers planted ninety-seven acres of cotton in 1853.[26] Four years later, in 1857, Postell's workforce produced one hundred fifty pounds of cotton per acre and fifteen to twenty bushels of corn.[27]

Of all the tasks done at Kelvin Grove, Postell seemed most interested in the amount of cotton ginned each day. Ginning was sometimes a gendered occupation that required certain skills depending on the type of equipment available to enslaved workers. Women served as the primary ginners on this plantation, but in other communities young boys and girls ginned the cotton. There is little evidence to suggest that prime males ginned cotton in Glynn or Wilkes Counties. It is likely that planters reserved this work for women when field work posed a threat to their physical health, especially during and immediately following pregnancy. In order to measure the skill involved in ginning, one must first consider the methods used to complete this task.

There were several ways to gin cotton and each method depended on the equipment, proximity, and accessibility to a gin house. Bondpeople either ginned cotton by hand or they relied on a roller-, foot-, barrel-, saw-, animal-, or water-powered machine. Hand ginning was more challenging than field work such as picking cotton because it exposed slaves to dust and lint for several hours. Those who did not own a cotton gin required their slaves to "laboriously" pull "apart [the cotton] by hand," and in these instances, skill became extremely important.[28] When Charles Lyell traveled through the South in the 1830s, he "saw many women employed in separating the cotton from the seeds with their fingers, a neat and clean occupation."[29] Without the use of a machine, it took both skill and dexterity to separate cotton, maintain its cleanliness, and not ruin the fiber at the same time. "Effective ginners," according to one historian, "developed the dexterity needed to process the seed cotton without breaking the fiber or cracking the seed."[30]

Depending on the machinery, ginning required strength, skill, and precision. The quantity produced in a given day correlated to the pace or speed a ginner worked the equipment. It also depended on the quality of the cotton because nearly all Sea Island cotton was ginned by hand. Ginning by hand or using foot or barrel gins were the most arduous methods and required prime hands to complete the work.[31] Planters who owned foot gins deliberately selected men because the constant treading motions often induced miscarriages among pregnant women. Other health-related risks included severe abdominal strain and hernias.[32] A roller gin required workers to feed the cotton through a device that removed the "oily black seed from the lint without injuring the fiber."[33] James Hamilton Couper of nearby Hopeton Plantation noted that "[t]he essential points are to gin from six hundred to eight hundred revolutions of the rollers per minute, one hundred and twenty-five strokes of the feeding arm, and from twenty-five to thirty revolutions of the fan in the same time."[34] On his plantation, Hamilton and his brother supervised three girls and three boys—a total of one and a half hands—to complete this task. Because he used an Eve's (Eave) gin, which was self-feeding, animal-powered, or water-powered, Hamilton could assign this work to any slave regardless of skill. For the most part, individual bondpeople ginned an average of fifty pounds of cotton per day.[35]

Gender, productivity, and skill were clearly important to Postell. In the plantation records, he noted the specific ginning skills of five women: Jane, Sarah, Nanny, Hamit, and Hester. These women each ginned averages well above sixty pounds per day, probably using some type of roller gin.[36] During a twenty-eight-day work period, for example, Jane averaged seventy pounds per day (and on some occasions achieved eighty pounds in one day) while Sarah and Nanny each processed sixty-six pounds per day. While traveling through the South during the winter of 1832, J. D. Legare found that most Sea Island cotton plantations collectively averaged 400 pounds of ginned cotton per day; these figures depended on the size of the plantation, the quality of the gin, and the productivity of the workers.[37] It took slaves at least nine hours to gin approximately 400 pounds of cotton.

Looking at the work patterns of the five women at Kelvin Grove, it appears that Postell rotated the task of ginning between this small group of workers. Two women, Hamit and Hester, did not gin as often as the others. For slightly more than a month (between 10 January to 15 February 1853), Hamit and Hester ginned for four and eight days, respectively. They worked on the days that Sarah, Jane, or Nanny did not serve as ginners, suggesting that Postell preferred certain workers over others. Of the five women listed, all but Nanny were full hands.[38] They were in their late teens and early twenties, the common age of "prime hands," although strength and skill seemed more important criteria for most slaveholders.[39]

In addition to ginning, Jane, Sarah, and Nanny moted (cleaned) cotton on 8 February 1853. The estimated average for moting cotton on a given day was twenty-five pounds for a prime worker, and even though Jane and Nanny provided amounts that were slightly below average, they often ginned *and* cleaned at the same time. On this date, Jane and Nanny ginned forty-five pounds and moted twenty, while Sarah completed forty and fifteen, respectively.[40] Except for these women, Postell mentions only five other bondpeople by name in his records.[41] Such specific notation indicates that planters understood the importance of productive laborers. Since ginning, and possibly moting, cotton involved the ability to do something well, in this case Hamit, Hester, Jane, Sarah, and Nanny had skilled positions, and Postell, as he did for the skilled male slaves at Kelvin Grove, recognized these women for their special talents. The importance of these women to Kelvin Grove's productivity shatters assumptions about gender, labor, and skill and forces us to consider that certain aspects of the cultivation and production process were indeed skilled work. Similar patterns occur on lowcountry rice plantations as well.

Elizafield

Like James Postell, Hugh Fraser Grant inherited Elizafield Plantation from a family member; his father, Dr. Robert Grant, gave him the property in 1833. Dr. Grant and his wife Sarah Foxworth had migrated to St.

Simons from South Carolina after the American Revolution, where they left behind Waterfield Plantation. They retired from rice cultivation in 1833 and divided their land between their sons, Hugh Fraser (1811–1873) and Charles Grant (birth and death dates unknown). Each son received $12,500 and part of the plantation. At age twenty-four, Hugh Fraser became the owner of Elizafield, which included 105 slaves; his brother Charles received the adjoining property, "Evelyn" (aka "Grantly"), and 113 slaves.[42] Located on the south bank of the Altamaha River, seven miles inland from the mouth, Elizafield contained nearly 1,500 acres of cleared land, of which 300 acres were dedicated to rice cultivation.[43] Scattered tax returns from 1845 to 1856 illustrate that this estate maintained 1,768 acres of fertile land and 338 acres of marshes for more than a decade.[44]

The slave population at Elizafield was unusually stable and ranged from 105 slaves in 1834 to 143 in 1855. The estate contained a female majority, indicating that Grant utilized bondwomen's labor. In 1850, for example, the slave population consisted of 126 workers, of which 74 were female and 52 were male.[45] Grant was the second largest planter in Glynn County during the 1850s and 1860s.[46] He made special notation of "prime Negroes" by designating a "1" in front of their names. In 1855 he had 143 enslaved workers, and 69 of these individuals were listed as prime. Women were 58 percent of the prime workers while men totaled 42 percent. Drivers such as Prince, John, and Scipio represented the only bondmen listed with an occupational specialization.[47] Bondwomen with special skills included Nurse Jeany and Bella the plantation cook. The female majority at Elizafield was similar to patterns on other large estates, and most women worked in the fields.

This planter, like Postell, utilized women workers based on their skills and capabilities. Grant understood that women were capable of doing all kinds of labor; therefore, he put them to work, provided them with the necessary tools, and maintained meticulous records of his assignments. Elizafield bondpeople worked in gender-specific gangs and gangs mixed with members of both sexes; the former was a common practice on some South Carolina, Louisiana, and Mississippi plantations. When Grant and his overseer Benjamin Talbot used partial tasking, they allowed men and women to work together. For Grant, ditching and chopping represented tasks that men and women could do together. Enslaved women worked in ditches, threshed straw, and gleaned rice; they also tied, bundled, stacked, and dried sheaves. They gleaned rice on 26 September 1842 and threshed straw on 8 and 10 October 1855. Grant also noted that women were "tieing up Scipio [one of his rice fields] and drying rice on the creek" on 11 September 1854.[48] Even though it is believed that men engaged in the most laborious and skilled work, Grant assigned women several tasks that one might consider "men's work." On 26 November 1840, Grant sent seventeen women to work at the Point Fields' "Large Ditch" along with thirteen men. During the preceding eight days he had separated their labor, with a total of seventeen to eighteen women listed as "chopping" and ten to fifteen men listed as "ditching."[49] But on 26 November there was no separation by gender. Such practices contradict claims that "in ditching, 'none but the primmest *males* were employed.'"[50] Grant clearly utilized slave skills to complete rigorous work, and in some instances he assigned specific tasks based on gender.

On many occasions, there were more women in the fields than men, which is consistent with the plantation demographics. Some of these women were assigned to work in rice ditches slinging mud with their male counterparts. To aid them in their work, Grant provided field workers with axes, hoes, and rice hooks. Axes usually contained a foot-long wooden handle with a blunt rectangular blade attached. A typical hoe was five to six feet long with a small metal edge attached to one end. Rice hooks had a short wooden handle and a sickle-shaped blade. Grant made references to the distribution of forty-five tools during 1839, 1840, 1842, and 1853 in his journal. Of those distributed, twenty-four were given to bondwomen and twenty-one to bondmen. However, women such as Nelly, Mira, and Julatta received at least two of the three tools listed, perhaps indicating some agricultural prowess.[51] The number of tools given to women also suggests their important role in the lowcountry workforce, particularly on this rice plantation.

Enslaved males on this estate did much of the same work as their female counterparts, but Grant reserved a few tasks such as collecting and chopping wood for men only. On 26 September 1842, men spent their day "getting wood out of the New Ground," while the women spent the day "gleaning." Likewise, on 9–11 October 1843, Grant sent six men to get the mud out of a "break in New Ground," while six others spent the three days "cutting wood for the House." In October of 1851, Grant kept enslaved women busy "thrashing" rice, while men cut a "Canal through Johns square to the River about 15 tasks long."[52] Clearly, labor was so important to this planter that he measured distances in terms of his enslaved laborers' daily tasks; this was not a common measurement.

Grant's perception of enslaved labor enables us to understand that gender and skill were much more important than previously assumed. Planters in other parts of the South during the colonial and antebellum years recognized women's contribution to the economy; thus, "the invisibility of enslaved women in the iconography of early American slave labor is a modern omission."[53] Countless plantation records confirm the importance of gender and labor, but so did travelers who visited the South on short and lengthy trips.

During Emily Burke's nearly decade-long stay in Georgia, for example, she noticed the agricultural skills of bondwomen. Amazed by the way plow hands worked, she made the following remarks:

> I always observed that the females displayed the most agility and usually completed their tasks first. Every man and woman has the entire charge of the beast they drive before the plough, and there is not a little ambition excited among them to see who shall have the finest looking and most spirited animals, and they usually test their fleetness by running races with each other in going and returning from the scene of their labors, which they always do on the back of their mules. I have been an eyewitness of these sports a great many times and have generally had the gratification of seeing the women go a little ahead of the men![54]

Burke expressed pride in her observations of skilled female field hands. Yet the links between gender, agricultural labor skills, and livestock may be deeper than they appeared.

At Elizafield, Grant made interesting connections between his field hands and his oxen. In 1851, he owned twenty-three oxen, of which fifteen had the same name as an agricultural laborer on the estate. Eleven of the oxen had the same name as one of the enslaved women, and four were named after bondmen.[55] Burke had trouble interpreting this practice when she visited Georgia plantations: "I have often been puzzled to know, when I have heard old Peggy or Sally spoken of, whether the conversation referred to a mule, a cow, or a woman."[56] Perhaps slaveholders gave similar names to livestock and enslaved workers so they could maintain organized records, particularly on large plantations. It is also likely that slaves chose the names of their livestock and made special connections to them since they spent hours on end working in the fields. Regardless of the intended or unintended meaning of naming cattle and enslaved workers, slaveholders like Grant found unusual ways to record their human and animal property. Slaveholders in the upcountry utilized other management strategies because they had fewer workers, less livestock, and a much different crop.

Short-Staple Cotton: Upcountry

Gender patterns become even more pronounced when we broaden the discussion beyond individual planters to specific crops. Wilkes County enslaved women laborers were involved with virtually every aspect of cotton production, from planting the seeds to preparing the crop for the market. They helped clear the land, plant the seeds, hoe the fields, thin the stalks, pick the cotton, remove the dirt, gin the fiber, and package it for shipment. Looking specifically at this upcountry crop, it is clear that Wilkes County contained fertile soil perfect for the cultivation of short-staple cotton. "If ever a crop and a place seemed well suited to each other," one historian wrote, "they were short-staple cotton and the lower piedmont."[57] This variety of cotton had a growing season of approximately 200 days, which determined the rhythm of work on farms and plantations alike.[58] The fields were prepared for planting between January and March when bondpeople cut down and burned old stalks, repaired farming equipment, and mended fences. After the field preparation stage, in April workers listed the fields with plows, creating furrows approximately five to six feet wide so the plants would grow fifteen to twenty inches apart during full bloom.[59] This was extremely laborious work because it required constant hoeing and chopping with small axes that placed extra pressure on the shoulders, arms, and lower back muscles. Enslaved women and men planted the seeds in drills—small holes made by light plows—and with a "harrow," an instrument with spikes used to break up and level plowed ground. "When the cotton started coming up," one twentieth-century picker recalled, "we had to hoe it, chop it, and thin it out [so that] it didn't grow too close together." Weeds and grass "would get up in it and we had to get that out too."[60] Nine to ten days later, a young plant surfaced and slaves commenced to "scrape" or "thin" the stalk. Two weeks later, in mid- to late May, slaves hoed the fields a second time by "throw[ing] the furrow *on to the roots*." If a late frost occurred, the ground had to be replanted.[61] The last plowing occurred in July before the plant reached full bloom. This was followed by a "lay-by season." According to agricultural historian Lewis Gray, thinning the stalks required the "most skillful and intelligent hands."[62] On cotton plantations with partial tasking, women often served in the "hoe gang," where they spent time "scraping" weeds in order to thin the stalk, which required skill and dexterity. Hoeing did not represent the only agricultural task women performed, as some worked in gender-specific groups as part of "plow gangs."

Slaveholders did not excuse their enslaved laborers from work during the lay-by season, but their workloads decreased, providing additional time for bondpeople to devote to their families. Many bondwomen and bondmen continued to work on provision crops such as corn, potatoes, turnips, and peas, but the intensity was not the same as cultivating cotton. After this brief labor respite, picking season began in early August and ended around Christmas. The final process of preparing cotton for shipment included drying, ginning, moting, and packing. Slaves placed cotton on large scaffolds to dry and then took it to a gin house, where they ginned and moted the cotton and placed it into large bags for shipment to local markets.[63] "In packing cotton," Emily Burke observed, "the sack is suspended from strong spikes, and while one colored person stands in it to treat the cotton down, others throw it into the sack." Much of this work was done by enslaved women, and Burke "wondered how the cotton could be sold so cheap when it required so much labor to get it ready for the market."[64]

A typical workday for a field hand on a short-staple cotton plantation in the Georgia upcountry lasted from 4:45 A.M. to 7:00 P.M. in the summer, and from 6:15 A.M. to 7:30 P.M. in the winter.[65] However, one local newspaper reported longer hours: "the [evening] horn will be blown in the winter at 8 [P.M.], in the summer at 9 o'clock [P.M.] after which no negro must be seen out of his cabin." In case recalcitrant workers decided not to report to the fields, planters expected overseers to "visit every negro house at day light in the morning and see that all are out."[66] One former Wilkes County enslaved male, Henry Rogers, recalled being awakened by his uncle Alex Hunt, the plantation "bugler," who blew the horn "ev'ry mornin' at 4:00 o'clock . . . for us ter git up."[67] Whether Hunt enjoyed serving as the plantation alarm clock is unclear, but this daily task required tremendous responsibility because he had to make sure everyone woke at a designated time each day. Wilkes County bondmen Robert Henry remembered that each day "the field hands were at work at sun-up and were not allowed to quit until dark."[68]

Upon entering the fields, enslaved workers picked cotton until it was time for a meal break. Most slaveholders expected the average laborer to pick 150 to 200 pounds per day. Wilkes County bondwomen and bondmen were well aware of this requirement because of the severe consequences of unfinished work. "All the niggers worked hard," explained Marshal Butler. "De cotton pickers had to pick 200 pounds of cotton a day and if a nigger didn't, Marse . . . would take de nigger to the barn and beat him with a switch."[69] Twentieth-century cotton pickers used similar figures to denote their work progress. "It always bugged me that I couldn't pick 100 pounds per day," recalled one woman who picked cotton during the 1930s and 1940s. "Most people could do it with ease, but I never could."[70]

In order to maintain the rhythm of work, bondwomen and bondmen sang to control the tempo of cotton picking. One song contained the following verse:

De little bee suck de blossom,
De big bee make de honey.
De nigger make the cotton,
And de white folks tote de money.[71]

Bonded workers were clearly aware of their exploitation and resorted to singing as a coping mechanism. Planters and overseers alike supported this practice. As one who referred to himself as "Agricola" noted, "When at work I have no objection to their whistling or singing some lively tune, but no *drawling* tunes are allowed in the field, for their motions are almost certain to keep time with music."[72]

Working to the beat of various songs, women tied a bag around their waists in which to place the cotton until reaching the end of a row where they deposited it in straw baskets. Others carried a "long canvass sack" that went over one shoulder. "Imagine the homemade bag made of cotton with a strap that hooked over your shoulder," said a former cotton picker. "You had to pull this bag *all* day . . . it was heavy, backbreaking labor."[73] Another woman recalled that "the bags hurt your shoulders" and that "depending on the size of the bag, you could have as much as 100 pounds of cotton over *one* shoulder."[74] To release some of the pressure, Dorothy Brown said they "had a large bed sheet that we used to dump the cotton when the bags got too heavy," which enabled workers to move through the rows at a faster pace.[75]

In spite of their agricultural productivity, enslaved women rested at every available opportunity; their respite served as a form of resistance and survival similar to the melodies they sang. Mariah Callaway, a Wilkes County field hand, explained that women "often waited until the overseer got behind a hill, and then we would lay down our hoe and call on God to free us."[76] Circumventing the overseer's authority through rest and prayer enabled Callaway and others to reject their slave status and place their hopes for freedom on a higher power. It also gave them a modicum of control over their work and a break without supervision.

Wilkes County agricultural workers received their first meal break between the hours of noon and 2 P.M. Some slaveholders gave their laborers an hour-and-a-half break at midday, while others excused slaves for as many as three hours, particularly during the hot and humid summer months. Slaveholders who implemented the practice of an afternoon break during May through August often extended evening work hours until 9 or 10 P.M. to account for lost time during the day.

Twentieth-century cotton pickers experienced similar work patterns. It was so hot in the fields that "we left at noon to have dinner" remembered eighty-one-year-old Ursula Scott, "and we went back out der to pick again till almost dark, then we'd get up early in the morning and go back out to work."[77] Victoria Morris recalled that her mother was the *only* person who had the opportunity to leave the fields. "My mother left the fields during the afternoon to cook, and then she returned to continue picking cotton."[78] Their labor had dual implications because they not only had to work in the fields during the day, but they also had household responsibilities to their families at night. Female "domestic chores" in the quarters after labor in the field separated the work lives of male and female agricultural laborers because most women had to cook and clean for their families. Women were assigned night tasks such as sewing, weaving, and quilting that kept them up well beyond midnight.[79] Enslaved males did not have assigned chores at night but they did spend time in the evenings fishing, working in provision grounds, and visiting spouses and loved ones on other plantations.

Some slaveholders relied on overseers, foremen, and drivers to maintain a productive workforce. But supervisors sometimes abused the workers and took advantage of their elevated status. Dr. Ficklen, a prominent Wilkes County physician, was distressed about his overseer named Bullock and the exploitation of his slaves. Ficklen explained that another resident "has seen my hands sometimes before day ploughing and working on going [*sic*] and carrying a torch to see by and has heard them frequently at night at work in the fields."[80] Upon further investigation, Ficklen learned that Bullock worked the laborers in order to make profits for *himself.* Two other Wilkes County residents confirmed these allegations and noted "that the way Bullock pushed the negroes was not out of all character," suggesting that this occurred frequently. In addition to field work, Ficklen discovered that Bullock kept slaves busy "hawling of [*sic*] timbers for his own benefits . . . when he ought to have been attending to my business."[81] Slaveholders like Dr. Ficklen did not want to work their bondpeople at night, but many could not control their overseers' misuse of them. Gender was important to labor systems on short-staple cotton plantations in the upcountry. Slaveholders understood that skill took precedence over sex in terms of work assignments; similar patterns occurred in coastal communities on Sea Island cotton and rice plantations.

Sea Island Cotton: Lowcountry

Cotton workers in the lowcountry planted Sea Island cotton, which represented a finer quality of cotton than the strand cultivated on Wilkes County plantations. Planters first introduced this unique strain of cotton to St. Simons Island in the 1780s because they found the environment suitable for the long-staple variety. The origins of Sea Island cotton are debatable, but most agree that Georgia first exported the crop in 1788.[82] Sea Island cotton (often referred to as the black-seed variety) yielded a longer, stronger, silkier, and higher-priced variety than short-staple cotton (which contained green seeds and was called the green-seed variety).[83] By comparison, the price of short-staple cotton was approximately twenty cents per pound while Sea Island cotton was fifty cents per pound.[84] Planters and plantation mistresses throughout the region did all they could to sell their cotton at fifty cents per pound. Anna Page King of Retreat Plantation, for example, noted on Christmas Eve in 1855 that her son "just returned from shipping 44 bags of prime cotton," but she added that "if it would only bring 50 cts I would be at ease."[85] Retreat Plantation cotton brought the highest price in the region because of its fine quality, and it often sold for fifty cents per pound while cotton from neighboring plantations sold for forty cents.[86] The higher-priced variety had a staple that measured 1.5 to 1.75 inches as opposed to short-staple cotton, which measured 0.625 to 1 inch long.[87] Thus, Sea Island cotton "surpassed all other types of cotton in strength, fineness and silkiness and was often used in delicate laces and for cloth of fine quality."[88]

Although the field preparation and planting stages of the two crops were comparable, Sea Island cotton required greater attention during the cultivation and market procedures. Therefore, Glynn County enslaved workers exercised greater care in picking, ginning, and packing this variety of cotton than their upcountry counterparts working on tougher short-staple cotton crops. "The sea-island cotton industry developed a restricted geographic location and peculiarities of production and marketing so distinctive as compared with upland cotton," explained Gray, "that the two may be fairly considered different industries."[89]

Sea Island cotton cultivation required a yearly work cycle, with four to eight hoeings throughout the course of a year.[90] Those enslaved on two large plantations on St. Simons, namely Hampton and Hamilton Plantations, hoed five to seven times per year and six to eight times per year, respectively.[91] This meant that Glynn County enslaved workers did not have a lay-by season like their short-staple counterparts. Their labor was often under the task system, which slaveholders felt aided in the productivity of the crop. Some former planters noted that there were approximately thirty-four specific tasks used to cultivate Sea Island cotton along with daily requirements that varied according to the quality of the land.[92]

Because gender appeared important to only two of the thirty-four tasks, female and male work assignments rarely differed. Skill served as a key factor for most aspects of Sea Island cotton production. For example, threshing requirements for females totaled 500 sheaves, but males were expected to produce 600. Yet "a man and woman can put up 100 pounds [of wood or metal]" for "making worm fences."[93] Only two tasks appeared solely as "male" jobs—"getting staves" and "getting barrel heading."[94] These two tasks involved building, filling, and lifting large wooden barrels. Despite this evidence of a gendered division of labor, skill remained the primary determinant for work assignments, since "an experienced laborer" could mow hay and "an expert hand" could cradle oats or small grain, regardless of sex.[95] For example, Emily Burke witnessed women carrying heavy logs used to build fences:

> The fences are built of poles arranged in a zigzag manner. . . . In this work the women are engaged as well as the men. They all go into the woods and each woman as well as man cuts down her own pine sapling and brings it upon her head. It certainly was a most revolting sight to see the female form scarcely covered with one old miserable garment, with no covering for the head, arms, or neck, nor shoes to protect her feet from briers and thorns, employed in conveying trees upon her head from one place to another to build fences.[96]

Such work assignments suggest that women and men had similar agricultural skills, but some slaveholders did not permit women to carry heavy items such as barrels, casks, and staves. These gendered tasks indicate that slaveholders recognized that some enslaved workers, male and female alike, developed skills that denoted "expert" status. This designation was not limited to the work of male artisans. Instead, the quality of work rather than the sex of the laborer determined daily task assignments.

Despite equality of work in some instances, pregnant women had altered work assignments. During pregnancy, some women received lighter labor expectations if their slaveholders were sympathetic to their condition. "Suckling and pregnant women," explained a Wilkes County slaveholder, "must be indulged as much as circumstances will allow, and never worked as much as others." Those nursing, he continued, "must be allowed time to suckle children, and kept working as near the house as possible. No lifting, spinning or ploughing must be required of pregnant women."[97] This slaveholder clearly understood that harsh labor did not guarantee healthy progeny. But most slaveholders were reluctant to reduce female workloads until their pregnancies could be confirmed visually.

Harvesting represented the most arduous task as enslaved laborers completed ten to twelve pickings with daily averages of approximately 100 pounds. Like their upcountry counterparts, lowcountry bondwomen and men maintained the work rhythm through songs. On Georgia Sea Island cotton plantations, women and men worked to the following song:

> Way down in the bottom—whah the cotton boll's a rotten
> Won' get my hundred all day
> Way down in the bottom—whah the cotton boll's a rotten
> Won' get my hundred all day
> Befo'e I'll be beated—befo'e I'll be cheated
> I'll leave five finguhs in the boll
> Befo'e I'll be beated—befo'e I'll be cheated
> I'll leave five finguhs in the boll
> Black man beat me—white man cheat me
> Won' get my hundred all day
> Black man beat me—white man cheat me
> Won' get my hundred all day.[98]

Clearly, bondwomen and men felt pressured to pick 100 pounds of cotton per day, and references to drivers indicate that fellow slaves filled this gender-specific, male-dominated occupation. This song is also suggestive of a tense relationship between supervisors and laborers. Despite the interaction between laborer and supervisor, enslaved women and men completed a variety of tasks on short-staple and Sea Island cotton plantations "without regard to sex." Similar patterns emerge in the rice fields.

Rice: Lowcountry

In addition to planting cotton, lowcountry slaves cultivated rice. Nineteenth-century rice cultivation was labor-intensive and required slaves to work under strenuous conditions, often knee deep in water. The summer months were the most rigorous in that slaves worked barefoot in the fields with temperatures ranging from 90 to 100 degrees. Men rolled their pants to keep dry, while enslaved women pulled their skirts above their knees using a cord around the waist or hips to hold up the slack.[99] The procedures for planting, cultivating, harvesting, and preparing rice for the market included many tasks: clearing land, digging ditches, sowing seed, four floodings, five strenuous hoeings, threshing, and winnowing.[100] To complete this process, slaves worked under the task system.

Rice, like Sea Island cotton, required a yearlong work cycle. Enslaved laborers prepared the land between the middle of December and March, using implements such as plows, hoes, and harrows to turn the topsoil over and prepare for planting season. They also burned the stubble of the preceding crop, cleared excess mud, and dug ditches approximately two feet wide, three feet deep, and fifty to seventy feet long.[101] Referring to the work of slave women on his father's South Carolina rice plantation, Duncan Heyward recalled:

> Burning stubble was usually done by women, who dragged the fire with their hoes. When the stubble was thoroughly dry and a stiff breeze blowing, they sometimes had to jump across the quarter ditches to avoid the advancing fire. There was considerable excitement in this work, and the women seemed to enjoy it. Their dresses were tied up to their knees and did not hinder them from jumping the ditches when they were caught in a close place by the fire. 'Look out, Sister!' they would often call to each other. 'Don't let dat fire ketch 'ona. Jump across de ditch.'[102]

Certainly, Heyward's perception that women enjoyed their labor differs from the testimony of bondwomen. Perhaps jumping for these women represented their attempt to avoid injury rather than seek pleasure as their observer suggested.

From March to April and sometimes as late as June, rice laborers planted the seeds for the new crop. "The seed was sown by hand" and placed in trenches approximately "3 inches wide and 15 inches from center to center." Labor expectations at Elizafield Plantation included sowing "at the rate of three bushels per acre for new land, and from two to two and one-half bushels per acre for other fields."[103] Once again, women served as the primary sowers. "Women always did this work, for the men used to say that it was 'woman's wuk,'" explained Heyward, "and I do not recall seeing one of the men attempt it."[104] Cumsey, Catherine, Mira, Amey, and Sary, among other bondpeople, spent their days sowing seed at Elizafield. They often worked alongside their husbands, Jack, Harry, Andrew, and London. After placing the seeds in the ground, agricultural workers covered it with about two inches of soil by "dragging light wooden bats behind them."[105]

Cultivation began in May, June, and July as slaves flooded the fields on four occasions. The "sprout flow" represented the first flooding and lasted from three to six days.[106] Next, the "point" or "stretch flow," which enabled slaves to see the first seedlings, lasted from three to six days. Two weeks later, slaves flooded the fields again during the "long" or "deep flow," which was followed by several days of light hoeing. As they slowly drained the fields, female and male laborers occupied themselves by pulling trash and debris from the fields. The final flooding, referred to as the "lay-by" or "harvest flow," lasted seven to eight weeks and occurred after several weeks of rigorous hoeing. Late August and early September marked the beginning of harvest time. It was at this time that enslaved laborers used farm implements such as sickles (rice hooks) to cut down rice sheaves. In some instances, female laborers were more adept than males during the harvest.[107] In order to maintain the rhythm of labor while harvesting the crop, females and males worked to the following song:

> John say you got to reap in the harvest what you sow
> John say you got to reap in the harvest what you sow
> If you sow it in the rain, you got to reap it jus' the same
> You got to reap in the harvest what you sow.[108]

During the month of October, after the harvest, enslaved laborers processed rice through five different stages before it was prepared for the market. First, they cut, dried, tied, bundled, and stacked rice sheaves in bushels approximately seven feet wide and twenty feet long. The stacks reached heights of twelve to fifteen feet.[109] Bondpeople completed this task by "[g]rasping the stalks with their left hands, [then] they used the sticks with the right, [finally] laying the rice on the stubble behind them in order that the sun may dry it."[110] From November to December, slaves threshed, winnowed, and polished rice, completing the process of preparing it for market. Threshing required them to use a flail with which they beat rice grain from the stalks. Threshing was such a difficult task that many slaves dreaded harvest time, particularly on large plantations like those on St. Simons Island.[111] Finally, laborers polished rice by carefully pounding the grains with a mortar and pestle, a task that required great skill and dexterity.[112] During this stage of the rice cultivation, bondwomen and men sang songs like the following:

> Turn sinner turn—sinner wouldn't turn
> Turn sinner turn—sinner wouldn't turn
> My Lord call you—wouldn't come
> I know sinner too late, too late
> O too late I know, sinner, too late.
> Church bell ring—you wouldn't come
> Preacher preach—an' you wouldn't come
> My Lord call you—an' you wouldn't come
> I know sinner too late, too late
> O too late, sinner, too late.[113]

Another common song used by slaves to keep the rhythm while beating the rice went as follows:

> I gwine t' beat dis rice
> Gwine t' beat 'um so
> Gwine t' beat 'um until the hu'ks come off
> Ah hanh hanh (nasal)
> Ah hanh hanh.
> Gwine t' cook dis rice when I get through
> Gwine t' cook 'um so
> Ah hanh hanh.
> Ah hanh hanh.
> Gwine t' eat mah belly full
> Ah hanh hanh
> Ah hanh hanh.[114]

The postharvest process required a work regime that many argue was more rigorous than cotton or sugar plantation labor. Once bondpeople harvested the crop, planters like Hugh Fraser Grant breathed a sigh of relief, and in 1840 he noted that they completed "a very fine Harvest Season" because "not one day [was] lost from the commencement." Similar to Grant, slaveholders were also relieved when their slaves remained healthy: "Thank God . . . the Negroes [are] all very healthy."[115] Eight years later on September 22, he remarked, "It has been one of the finest harvests ever known"; therefore the next day he "Gave the Negroes to Rest."[116]

Summary

By expanding the definition of skill beyond that which has traditionally linked women to unskilled labor and men to skilled labor, male and female work patterns become more clearly defined. Plantation owners, whether they were growing cotton or cultivating rice, understood that skilled agricultural labor, much of which was done by women, was of the utmost importance to the plantation's economy. By examining various plantations that grew different types of crops and used different tasking systems, it becomes clear that skilled labor crossed gender lines and that the agricultural labor regime involved skilled work.

Dido, a field worker from Hofwyl Plantation, on the way to harvest rice. Note the water jug and the sickle. Brunswick, Glynn County, Georgia, ca. 1910. Courtesy of the Vanishing Georgia Collection, Georgia Archives.

Woman with an ax holding a cow by the chain. Robert Williams Collection, courtesy of Hargrett Rare Book and Manuscript Library / University of Georgia Libraries.

Two women on their way to the market in Augusta, Georgia. Note the milk containers and the cart full of produce. Robert Williams Collection, courtesy of Hargrett Rare Book and Manuscript Library / University of Georgia Libraries.

"Old Sibby," a midwife from Glynn County, Georgia. Courtesy of the Vanishing Georgia Collection, Georgia Archives.

Group of washerwomen in Glynn County, Georgia. Robert Williams Collection, courtesy of Hargrett Rare Book and Manuscript Library/ University of Georgia Libraries.

"Clarissa," a servant at the Hofwyl Plantation in Glynn, County, Georgia, ca. 1910. Courtesy of the Vanishing Georgia Collection, Georgia Archives.

Left to right: *Hope Powell (cook), Robert Powell (butler), Fanny Watch (maid) at the Hofwyl Plantation, Brunswick, Glynn County, Georgia, ca. 1910. Courtesy of the Vanishing Georgia Collection, Georgia Archives.*

Women working in the rice fields at Hofwyl-Broadfield Plantation, Brunswick, Glynn County, Georgia, ca. 1910. Courtesy of the Vanishing Georgia Collection, Georgia Archives.

A woman hulling rice with mortar and pestle, Sapelo Island, McIntosh County, Georgia, between 1915 and 1934. Courtesy of the Vanishing Georgia Collection, Georgia Archives.

Portrait of Anna Matilda Page King. Courtesy of the Coastal Georgia Historical Society.

Cotton pickers in 1875. Courtesy of the Kenan Research Center at the Atlanta History Center.

*A woman churning butter on the Hofwyl Plantation, Bruns-
wick, Glynn County, Georgia, ca. 1910. Vanishing Georgia
Collection, Georgia Archives.*

*Two elderly men in the cotton fields. Robert Williams Collection, courtesy of
Hargrett Rare Book and Manuscript Library / University of Georgia Libraries.*

Young children picking cotton. Robert Williams Collection, courtesy of Hargrett Rare Book and Manuscript Library / University of Georgia Libraries.

Former bondpeople gather for a party at Hofwyl Plantation, Glynn County, Georgia, ca. before 1915. Vanishing Georgia Collection, Georgia Archives.

Image of woman returning from the fields with a hoe over her shoulder and basket in hand. From Rudolf Eickemeyer Jr. and Joel Chandler Harris, Down South *(New York: Robert Howard Russell, 1900).*

Group in the cotton fields with large baskets of cotton on their heads. Robert Williams Collection, courtesy of Hargrett Rare Book and Manuscript Library / University of Georgia Libraries.

Daguerreotype of "Mammy Cynthy," ca. 1850. Cynthia Peters was a bondwoman who served the Gilbert family of Wilkes County, Georgia. Courtesy of the University of Georgia Press.

2 "Dey S'lected Me Out to Be a Housegirl": The Privileges and Pain of Nonagricultural Labor

> She sets about her work vigorously; her arms are strong for her tasks.
> —Proverbs 31:1 NIV

Nonagricultural laborers provided important services to planter families; slaveholders valued their skills and made frequent references to them in plantation records. Rhina, a twenty-seven-year-old house servant, for example, was so important at Retreat Plantation in Glynn County that Anna Page King, the plantation mistress, referred to her as "my right hand."[1] She certainly seemed to be—Rhina cooked, cleaned, sewed, nursed, and traveled with the King family as their personal servant. She had her own room "which she kept in very nice order," compared to the others.[2]

In addition to her multiple skills, Rhina knew how to read and write and even had some knowledge of French. Rhina wrote letters to her daughter Annie and to Clementine, another bondwoman at Retreat Plantation, when she traveled with Anna Page King in the early 1850s. She also received letters written by Mr. Dunham (the Retreat overseer) from Maria.[3] Literacy and the ability to speak a foreign language were skills that few slaves acquired. Being able to read and write enabled bondpeople like Rhina to communicate with her family and friends while she was away. For others, such as Frederick Douglass, literacy provided the catalyst for freedom.[4]

This chapter examines household workers, how gender and age affected nonagricultural laborers, the value slaveholders placed on their skills, and bondpeoples' perceptions of labor. Enslaved men and women used their talents in nonagricultural settings to secure material advantages unavailable to field hands. Their skills were more clearly defined than those of agricultural laborers, and nonagricultural laborers sometimes boasted about their superior abilities and privileges. Close contact with planter families afforded geographic mobility to a select few—they ran errands, accompanied white families on vacations, and administered or received medical treatment. Depending on the enslaved person's age and gender as well as the location and demographics of the plantation, nonagricultural laborers received advantages and disadvantages from the planter class in both upcountry and lowcountry locales.

Gender, Age, Skill, and Nonagricultural Labor

Although, as discussed in chapter 1, the link between skill and agricultural labor was not clearly defined, this was not the case for nonagricultural labor—these enslaved workers displayed a variety of skills. Like field hands, nonagricultural laborers started their day before dawn. Their activities, however, centered on the maintenance of their slaveholders' comforts rather than on seeding, planting, plowing, and hoeing according to the seasonal calendar commonly used for cotton and rice production. The sexual division of labor was more pronounced in the household than in the field.

Some enslaved males had several skills that earned them certain privileges. A large proportion of bondmen served as artisans. The work of artisans such as brickmakers, blacksmiths, boatmen, carpenters, coopers, ironsmiths, masons, sawyers, shoemakers, and wheelwrights required skill and dexterity. Former bondman Willis Cofer of Wilkes County described the role of brickmakers and blacksmiths. Brickmakers, he explained, "made all de bricks out of de red clay what dey had right dar on most all de plantations." "De blacksmith," he continued, "had to make all de iron bars and cranes for de chimblies and fireplaces."[5] Enslaved males in both counties served as blacksmiths without receiving financial compensation. In other parts of the South, white master craftsmen and free black artisans received wages for their skilled labor and are the subjects of most studies on skilled labor. Blacksmiths were not the only group of skilled bondmen in plantation and farming communities. Men also served as butlers, valets, messengers, coachmen, and, on some plantations, cooks.[6]

Women, by contrast, spent time feeding, cleaning, and caring for their slaveholders, serving as cooks, nurses, seamstresses, housemaids, and midwives. Nonagricultural workers were always "on call," but bondwomen spent the majority of their days nursing, ironing, washing, and doing a variety of other domestic chores.[7] On some large plantations, slaveholders assigned one or two enslaved women as personal servants for the overseer's family. Caring for their supervisors included direct interaction with mistresses in activities such as tying up their corsets, combing their hair, bathing their infants, and running errands for or with them.

The interaction between black and white women in the household included both compatibility and tension. While serving their mistresses, enslaved women might become their close companions because of the proximity of their working space and the great distance between other white women on neighboring plantations.[8] Mistresses often shared intimate secrets with their bondwomen and received medical attention from them during illnesses. Enslaved women nursed, played with, and made sure their slaveholders' children were well-fed. Despite evidence of compatibility, tension between black and white women surfaced when mistresses punished bondwomen for the sexual indiscretions of the mistresses' husbands. Bondwomen often fell prey to their slaveholders' sexual desires; they were raped, abused, and exploited under their mistresses' roof. Countless narratives provide striking details about the physical, sexual, and verbal abuse of bondwomen by their slaveholders.[9]

In addition to gendered divisions of labor, supervisors sometimes separated tasks according to age. Elderly women, for example, served as nurses and cooks and tended to the children while their daughters worked in the fields. When Emily Burke interacted with the "oldest" woman on a plantation she visited in Georgia, Burke noted that although "she was one of the field hands, she had free access to her master's house." This woman "possessed such a good share of common sense that her master and mistress always consulted her on important matters."[10] Former Wilkes County bondwoman Jane Mickens Toombs remembered that her "Grandma, Nancy, wuz de cook an' she fed all de little 'uns in de big ole kitchen whut sot out in de yard. She had a tray she put our victuals on an Uh, Uh, whut good things we had ter eat, an' er plenty of everything!"[11] Older bondpeople held caregiving positions primarily because they could no longer perform strenuous labor in the fields. Their other duties included feeding the chickens, fishing, cooking, and light housework. Slaveholders made personal decisions about the treatment of elderly bondpeople, which reflected concern in some cases and neglect in others.

James Postell of Kelvin Grove in Glynn County found that gardening represented a good nonagricultural (i.e., not working in the fields) occupation for aged males like Old Sam and Old Robin, although he did not assign them monetary values on his enslaved list. By contrast, elderly women like Old Elsy were not listed among either the agricultural or nonagricultural workers, but they did appear on the lists of bondpeople. Postell indicated that he had five superannuated bondpeople in 1857. Besides gardening, these older men and women in the last years of their lives and whose ability to work was no longer sufficient most likely helped serve as caretakers for the thirty-one enslaved children at Kelvin Grove (quite possibly including their grandchildren) while their daughters and sons labored in the fields.

On the tidewater Butler plantations at Hampton Point and Butler's Island, "no person, however old or feeble, was allowed to be altogether idle." Therefore, when Flora, age seventy-one, told Pierce Butler, her slaveholder, that she was too old and could no longer work, he instructed his headman to "get a goose, give her a line" so that she could lead his "goose to graze for an hour" each day. Ten years later, an observer noted that Flora and the goose "pasture[d] together" just as they were instructed.[12] The Butlers kept records for all elderly bondwomen and men by noting "superannuated" next to their names; they ranged in age from sixty-one (Sally) to eighty-seven (Amy, the oldest). In fact, despite age, bondwomen rarely received references to their skilled labor in the estate inventory of 1859 with the exception of forty-three-year-old Hetty, who was listed as a "house servant—but sickly"; twenty-six-year-old Phena, listed as a "good house servant;" and fifty-five-year-old Sinda and forty-seven-year-old Rita, who were both listed as "Nurse."[13]

Like their grandparents and the other elderly bondpeople, young enslaved boys and girls performed light housework. They filled wood boxes, lit fires in chilly bedrooms, helped make beds, churned butter, ironed clothes, set tables, fanned flies, swept, polished, dusted, fetched water, milk, and meat, and served their slaveholders' families and friends.[14] Emily Burke noted in her travels that some enslaved children served as "human scarecrows" in the cotton and corn fields, spending their days in the fields assuring that birds did not threaten the crop.[15] Jane

Harmon of Wilkes County recalled her work experiences as a child: "De fust work I done wuz churnin' an' I loved ter do 'hit kase I loved milk an' butter so good. I'd dance an' dance 'round dat ole churn, churnin' an' churnin' 'till de butter wuz come."[16] She also spent time entertaining the overseers' children: "I uster play dolls wid de overseer's chillun, an' look fuh aigs [eggs], an' tote in wood an' pick up chips. Us had good times togeder, us all little niggers an' de little white chilluns."[17] The interactions between blacks and whites in the nonagricultural realm involved constant contact.

Mariah Callaway, another Wilkes County bondwoman, recalled her work as a child. "I was a pet in the Willis household," she explained, "and did not have any work to do except play with the small children. I was required to keep their hands and faces clean."[18] Because she referred to herself as a pet, Callaway may have recognized the negative animal imagery planters associated with bondpeople, or it's possible that she viewed it as a term of endearment. Plantation mistress Frances Kemble found similar practices on the Butler plantations in Glynn County when slaveholders with children of their own allowed enslaved female caretakers to live in their houses. Kemble found that young boys and girls were "kept as a sort of pet animal, and *allowed* to pass the night on the floor of the sleeping apartment of some member of the family."[19] Anna Page King, also a plantation mistress in Glynn County, used positive pet imagery as a term of endearment when she referred to her granddaughter as "my little pet."[20] Regardless of the connotation of these references, Callaway set herself apart from the other household servants because of her "pet" status.

For young male laborers, working in their slaveholders' homes sometimes meant contact with their parents. Wilkes County bondman Robert Henry proudly declared that his "Pa wuz de butler at the Big House" and his mother was the head seamstress. At age eight, he learned from his father how to "wait on Master's table."[21] Henry was fortunate that his father taught him various household skills not only because of the value of obtaining household skills but also because so many children were separated from their fathers. The nature of slavery often obliterated paternal ties, with enslaved status being defined by the mother, clothing and food rations given to mothers, and children listed with their mothers in plantation records. Henry's testimony suggests that in some instances there was an enslaved male network where fathers and other men taught their sons how to work, act, and survive slavery with camaraderie similar to that expressed within female-dominated networks. Enslaved men and boys bonded during fishing excursions, in barns tending to livestock, on errands to and from the plantation, during religious services, on their days off, and as runaways.

In addition to the common references to elderly bondpeople on the Butler plantations, there were even more frequent references to skilled men. In 1849, the Butler family owned 840 laborers who worked on their plantations in McIntosh and Glynn Counties. Of these bondpeople, fifty-four males served as artisans occupying the following positions: drivers (eight), carpenters (eighteen), coopers (thirteen), engineers (two), smiths (four), millers (three), masons (two), shoemakers (two), gardeners (one), sawyers (one), and boatmen (one). The drivers were highly valued and mature in age as all eight men were over thirty years old. Carpenters ranged in age from eighteen to seventy-four years old, but coopers were slightly older, with age ranges from twenty-five to fifty-nine years old. The specialized labor of these enslaved men involved working with material such as metal, wood, stone, and grain, and it involved the use of specific tools. "Cooper's tools for 11 men, consisting of axe, 2 drawing knives, saw, c[?], compass, jointer, adze and bit," contained the description of "well worn" next to them. The chest of tools belonging to the "carpenter's gang" included "match planes, mould planes, angus, firmer, chisels, gouges, brace and bits, hand saw, tenant saw, panel saw, [and] sash saw."[22]

Besides noting specific occupations, the Butler family also recognized various levels of skill among their nonagricultural bondpeople. On 21 February 1859, James Hamilton Couper, Thomas M. Forman, and Thomas Pinckney Higer helped administer the division of John and Pierce Butler's estate. Many of the enslaved men listed had remarks added about their health and skills as well as their occupations. They received rankings from "rough," "ordinary," "fair," and "good," to "prime." Some of the most notable drivers such as Frank (age sixty-one) and Angus (age forty-six) received the description "Bedridden and Superannuated" and "Prime Rice Driver," respectively. Abram (age forty-seven) received the ranking of a "good" carpenter, while George (age fifty-seven) had the title "ordinary carpenter" next to his name. Because George was ten years older than Abram, it is likely that he was unable to complete carpentry work at the same level of expertise or that he never acquired advanced skills. London (age seventy-one), one of the estate coopers, was also recognized for his preaching skills. Others like "Firearm Billy" (age fifty-one) and "Raccoon George" (age fifty-one) probably had good hunting skills, which explains their descriptive names.[23]

On small landholdings, common in Wilkes County, a significant number of women who served in their slaveholders' homes also worked in the fields at harvest time. During harvest season, "all hands, regardless of age and sex, who were able to do any work, aided in picking cotton," and because of this, many bondpeople experienced "double duty" of both agricultural and nonagricultural labor.[24] Former Wilkes County bondwoman Arrie Binns recalled serving as a housemaid *and* a plow hand before the age of sixteen. She testified that she had to fan her slaveholder when he was ill. But after spending long hours on her feet, she sometimes fell asleep and the fan would drop and hit him in the face. When he awakened, he "crack[ed] my hand with the handle" she explained, "to wake *me* up. I wuz allus so sorry when I done, that, but I jest had ter nod." After her slaveholder died, Arrie served as a plow hand in the fields where she drove an old horse named "Toby." Her role as an agricultural laborer consisted of "pick[ing] er round in the fields."[25] She probably enjoyed this work more than household labor because her mother was also an agricultural laborer and spending time with family represented a primary concern among the enslaved.

Glynn County slaveholders usually had more bondpeople on their larger plantations and thus tended to restrict their agricultural and nonagricultural labor. At Elizafield Plantation, for example, Grant, his wife, and their six children benefited from the services of six nonagricultural workers. These bondpeople included "Maum Rebecca, the maid and head seamstress; Frederick Proudfoot, the coachman; his wife Maum Ann, the children's nurse; Sukie, cook superlative; her assistant Martha; and Caesar, the butler."[26] Aside from their names and skills, we know very little about these individuals—but we can assume that their skills gave them some power and privilege within the enslaved community. Rebecca, the head seamstress, for example, had authority over the other seamstresses because of her title, and Sukie had superior cooking abilities compared to other laborers at Elizafield. The husband and wife duo, Frederick and Ann, had the privilege of living and working in the same environment.

On Kelvin Grove in Glynn County, ten enslaved workers filled nonagricultural labor requirements in 1853. Of those listed, women occupied four positions—a nurse, a cook, a seamstress, and a housemaid. Molly, the sixty-year-old nurse, "minded the sick" on two dates in January; one of those days was when a field hand named Ally gave birth to one of her four children. Molly assisted Ally again three days later to help her recover from childbirth. Chloe, the forty-five-year-old cook, spent September through December of the same year preparing meals, while one person, perhaps Pender, the thirty-eight-year-old housemaid, spent time "washing" on 2 and 3 November. The only notation for sewing appeared on August 19, indicating the work of forty-year-old Peggy.[27] As women changed occupations and acquired additional skills, they took on new work responsibilities. In 1857, Chloe became the nurse, perhaps after Mary's death, and Pender replaced Chloe as the cook. Peggy continued seamstress work but had the assistance of Flora, and Liddy became the new housemaid.[28]

Even though we know very little about the specific activities these women performed, it helps to draw upon other detailed descriptions of nonagricultural labor. Emily Burke witnessed firsthand the way slaves in general, and washerwomen and laundresses in particular, "carry all their burdens upon their heads." Washerwomen transported large tubs of heavy "iron-bound trunks," which were full of water and a basket of wet clothes, on their heads.[29]

Enslaved males at Kelvin Grove in 1853 served in the following capacities: Sam (age forty) as the driver, Jacob (age twenty-five) as the carpenter, Cassious (age fourteen) as a houseboy, and Old Sam (age seventy) and Old Robin (age eighty) as gardeners. Twenty-eight-year-old Joseph worked "in town," but Postell decided to sell him that year. It is likely that Joseph worked as an artisan in Savannah, and because of his frequent absences and Postell's increasing financial hardships, there was no reason to keep him. In a letter addressed to "Mr. Benton" (date unknown, but most likely in the mid-1850s), Postell made the following remark: "If I had sufficient means to plant . . . my wish would be to live on my place the remainder of 'my life,' but I am too poor—I am compelled to sell." Anna Page King made several references to the Postell's financial woes. "Postells negros have not had an allowance of food for weeks," she wrote to her son Henry Lord King during the summer of 1854. "They are going all about begging & offering to buy with poor chickens a little food," she continued. Apparently she felt that some of his hardships were self-induced as she noted that "he has in the midst of this managed to put up a nice portico in front of his house & is making a fence round the yard with tabby pillars." However, in November, she notes that Postell was "in very bad health" and that she had "not seen him since July."[30] By 1857, Postell had only four male servants: Hanibal the driver, Jacob and Cassious the carpenters, and Caesar the new houseboy. Since Cassious served as the houseboy four years earlier, it is likely that Jacob shared his carpentry skills with the young apprentice so the two could work as a team and make room for Caesar, the new houseboy.[31] Upcountry and lowcountry Georgia slaveholders like Postell utilized their nonagricultural workers of all ages in a variety of jobs, and they assigned them work based on age, skill, and gender. On some estates, these individuals were rewarded for their good work.

Advantages and Disadvantages of Nonagricultural Labor

Nonagricultural laborers received material benefits from working in their slaveholders' homes. Some of the advantages included better food, clothing, and housing than field hands. Other house servants benefited from working indoors because they received less exposure to disease, heat exhaustion, frostbite, snakebites, or other injuries.[32] In addition to improved living conditions, female nurses and midwives and male artisans gained access to geographic mobility and occasionally to wages.

Some nonagricultural laborers boasted about their "privileged" positions when their slaveholders acknowledged their talents. Bondwomen and men often felt superior to their agricultural contemporaries because they received material benefits unavailable to field hands; therefore, they spoke of their occupations with great pride. Old Rachael, an enslaved woman at Broadfield Plantation in Glynn County, considered herself nobility when she told people "I am an estate-woman or sarvant."[33] Jeems, an enslaved male from the same estate, received high praise from his slaveholders because "he could open and throw a long tablecloth from one end of a dinner table to the other without a fold."[34] Another enslaved male at Broadfield Plantation, named Jack, came to the aid of his slaveholder's daughter when a fishhook was accidentally lodged in her hand. While everyone else present panicked because the plantation owner was not home and the nearest doctor was twelve miles away, Jack came to the rescue and "cut it out with his sharpened razor."[35]

Bondwoman Jane Harmon of Wilkes County proudly testified to the privileged positions held by nonagricultural workers: "Atter er while dey s'lected me out to be a housegirl an' den I slep' in de Big House."[36] Sleeping in the slaveholders' house provided enslaved individuals with better bedding, heat, and food. By contrast, bondwomen and men who slept in the enslaved quarters stayed in one- or two-room cabins with a group of other bondpeople. Their bedding consisted of a combination of moss and straw; their only heat came from a central fireplace or from each other.[37] One Georgia enslaved woman described the beds in her cabin: "De beds had high posties and some of 'em was nailed to de wall of de cabin. Dey didn't know nothin' 'bout no wire springs den, and dey strung de beds wid heavy cords for springs. Dey made mattresses ticks out of coarse home-wove cloth; some was striped and some was plain unbleached white."[38]

Slaveholders also treated their enslaved workers' talents as noteworthy; they described their skills in advertisements for sale as well as in
their plantation records and personal papers. Sometimes they expressed
concern about the ability of their workers, and on other occasions they
made no assumptions about gendered connections to their workers' occupations. On 17 November 1829, for example, Thomas J. Heard and Singleton W. Allen advertised the sale of "20 Likely Negroes" in a Wilkes
County newspaper. Among this group of bondpeople were "men, boys,
women and children," including "an excellent carpenter, and an excellent shoemaker." According to Heard and Allen, these bondpeople were
special because there "has never been such a likely lot of negroes offered
for sale in the county."[39]

Unfortunately, although there were obvious benefits to residing in
their slaveholders' homes, such sleeping arrangements left enslaved individuals, male and female alike, vulnerable to sexual exploitation, particularly if they were forced to sleep in the same room as their slaveholders.
Often, bondpeople felt ambiguous about whether nonagricultural labor
was advantageous to them. This was determined by the bondpeople's
perception of the work, their compatibility with their fellow workers
and slaveholders, and, most important, proximity to their own family.

Despite the perceived and actual benefits, enslaved workers were not
always happy to work in their slaveholders' homes, and many nonagricultural laborers ran away to escape close contact with their slaveholders or to find family members. Mariah and Beck, a mother-and-daughter
pair of runaways, appeared in Wilkes County newspapers in the 1830s.
Their slaveholder, David Murray, recognized both women for their skills
as nonagricultural laborers, indicating that Beck "was usually employed
as a cook and weaver." Beck's twenty-two-year-old daughter Mariah was
described as "a good seamstress, having been from her infancy a housegirl, [and because of her domestic work] there is a little more polish in her
manners than is commonly met with among negroes."[40] Murray stated
that Mariah was "well adapted to almost every species of house-work.
She was more dressy than usual for a servant, having fine articles of clothing of almost every description. In addition to her own clothing, which
were numerous, she carried off five of my daughter's dresses, viz: Shady,
black, Silk plain; figured Swiss Muslin, richly trimmed with thread lace
insirting; two French Muslin; plain rich Gold Ear-Rings; hair brade; silk
Apron trimmed with velvet."[41] Clearly, Mariah and Beck received material advantages like fine clothing, and they both were skilled in a variety
of nonagricultural crafts. Even with these added benefits, the two left to
unite with other family members said to reside in Augusta, Georgia, or

Columbia, South Carolina.[42] Mariah and Beck still desired freedom and the company of family members, so they took with them their many talents and items they likely believed were rightly theirs.[43] Along with this discussion of individuals like Mariah and Beck, it is also important to examine the experiences of those on specific plantations.

Nonagricultural Labor at Retreat Plantation

Adjacent to Kelvin Grove on the southwest tip of St. Simons Island, Retreat Plantation was the home of the Page and King descendants. In 1824, Thomas Butler King gained possession of Retreat from his father-in-law, William Page. Page and his wife Hannah Timmons had migrated to St. Simons in the late 1790s, leaving their plantations, Page's Point and Ottasee, in Prince William Parish, South Carolina. Like many other migrants, they believed they could make a better home for themselves because of Georgia's lenient land policy and alluvial soil. Prior to their arrival, the Pages suffered the pain and loss of twelve miscarriages. Therefore, when Hannah Timmons Page gave birth to Anna Matilda on St. Simons Island, the couple believed that there was something mystical about the island and decided to make it their permanent home. Anna Matilda Page later married Thomas Butler King, and they raised all ten of their children at Retreat Plantation.[44]

Anna Page King kept meticulous records of the plantation while her husband tended to professional obligations throughout the country. His frequent and extended absences during the 1830s and 1850s forced the young mistress to manage a plantation that always contained more than a hundred bondpeople, at least three horses, eight mules, twelve hogs, thirty-three cattle, an ox, and several chickens.[45] During the 1830s, Thomas Butler King purchased additional land and established "Waverly," a rice plantation along the Satilla River in Camden County, and "Monticello," a short-staple cotton plantation in Wayne County. These two purchases increased the total enslaved population to 352 in 1839. His success was short-lived, and by 1842 King had sold all but Retreat Plantation along with 246 bondwomen, bondmen, and children.[46] In addition to family matters concerning their ten children, Anna King managed the plantation's financial records, food rations, clothing, equipment, crop exports, and the daily activities of the house slaves.

The King family carefully tracked the enslaved population at Retreat, a tradition that William Page (Anna Page King's father) started when he owned the estate. In his 1827 will, for example, William Page listed the names, ages, skills, and sometimes the relatives of 140 bondpeople, of which sixty-six (47 percent) were female. Thirteen of the 140 laborers occupied nonagricultural positions, of whom five were women. There were seventy-four bondmen comprising 53 percent of the enslaved population. More than two decades later, the 1850 census listed Thomas Butler King as the owner of 112 bondpeople, of whom fifty-nine (53 percent) were women.[47] And in her 1859 will, Anna Page King provided information about 131 laborers, of whom seventy-seven (57 percent) were female.[48] These statistics show that by the late antebellum period, bondwomen at Retreat slightly outnumbered bondmen, which is similar to the ratios at Kelvin Grove and Elizafield.

Even though little was recorded about the planting, cultivating, or harvesting cycles on this estate, the value of nonagricultural labor is clearly articulated through the variety of skilled positions and comments made by Anna Page King. Nonagricultural females at Retreat in 1827 included "Old Sarah," the seventy-four-year-old nurse, and Ruthy (age nineteen), Polly (age twenty-six), Lady (age forty and a half), and Old Betty (age seventy-five), all appearing on the enslaved list as "housemaids." Two men served as drivers, four specialized in carpentry work, one worked in the garden, and another worked in the house.[49] Anna Page King discussed the talents of men and women through personal letters dating from 1827 to 1857. In several of the letters written to her children, she discussed the importance of Retreat Plantation's nonagricultural laborers, especially the women. Over the course of nearly thirty years, she mentioned by name more than fifty bondpeople.

She spoke favorably about the cooking and sewing skills of Rhina. She also made several references to Maria, who served as the washerwoman and tended to the bees, birds, and chickens. In 1839, King made special notation of enslaved male skills. Thomas Butler King owned a total of 352 bondpeople that year, and eighteen men occupied skilled positions (see table 2.1).

Anna Page King was pleased with "Old Peter's" carpentry skills even when he was seventy years old. During the summer of 1853, one of the plantation managers worked hard and "got more work out of Old Peter than has been extracted in years" as he finished a desk, lounge, work table, rocking chair, and footstool for one of the rooms at the main house.[50]

Nonagricultural laborers on this estate developed close relationships with their supervisors, and the Kings knew them well. On 21 April 1857, when Thomas Butler King Jr. contracted the measles, Anna Page King left Rhina "to wait on him until he is able to be removed."[51] Six days later she assured his sister Hannah that Rhina would "cook for & take

Table 2.1. List of Skilled Males at Retreat
Plantation, 1839

Name	Occupation/Skill	Age
Edward	Carpenter	37
Ishmael	Driver	30
Cupid	Driver	62
Toney	Driver	30
Neptune	Carpenter	43
March	Driver	33
Big Peter	Carpenter	56
Tom	Carpenter	61
Henry	Bricklayer	36
Isaac	Blacksmith	42
Lymus	Mason	41
Davy	Body Servant	26
Joe	Carpenter	?
George	Carpenter	31
Robert	Carpenter	25
Tom	Carpenter	25
Lewis	Once Driver	50
Boston	Blacksmith	29

Note: Compiled by the author from "Register of Negroes Belonging to Thomas Butler King, November 1839," in Thomas Butler King Papers #1252, Southern Historical Collection, Wilson Library, University of North Carolina, Chapel Hill.

care of him . . . she cooks up his little meals so nicely & attends to all of his comforts."[52] Clearly her son was in good hands.

Anna Page King was also satisfied with the services of Clementine, the plantation seamstress. "You will I hope be pleased," she wrote to her daughter in 1851, "with the Swiss muslin dresses Clementine had braided for you." Admittedly, she continues, "I think she does deserve some credit for doing them so nicely & so neatly." She closed asking her daughter how she likes her "skirts hetched" so that she can "set Clementine to work at them as soon as the warm weather approaches."[53]

Equally praised was the plantation nurse named Pussy [*sic*].[54] On 28 September 1851, Anna Page King stated, "I do consider myself very much blessed in having so good & faithful a nurse. . . . I have often thought what would I have done in all this sickness had she been taken from me."[55] The Kings relied on Pussy to take care of the sick at the plantation hospital. However, when Anthony and Maryann developed symptoms "which Pussy's skill cannot reach," Anna Page King became worried.[56] The services of these individuals marked the importance of nonagricultural labor at Retreat.

Geographic Mobility at Retreat Plantation

Although the majority of enslaved workers in Glynn County had restrictions on their movement, a select few had tremendous mobility and were allowed to travel off the plantation. Nonagricultural laborers at Retreat moved beyond the confines of the plantation house as they traveled with the planter family on vacations, ran errands to other estates on the island, and temporarily worked in the homes of other whites. Their skills provided them with the opportunity to travel to Savannah and even as far north as New Haven, Connecticut. It appears that other Glynn County planters let a select number of bondpeople accompany them during their travels. Fanny, a servant of the Troup family, went "back and forth" all over the South and after being manumitted (freed) "established herself in Savannah."[57]

Such extensive travel was atypical considering the closed system and "isolation" policy of many Glynn County plantation owners. In fact, one recent study of bondwomen and resistance suggests that antebellum plantations functioned as "geographies of containment" where planters restrained the movement of their enslaved workers.[58] Women in general rarely left their plantations, but those with special skills occasionally traveled. On 22 August 1837, for example, cook Mom Jane journeyed to Hamilton Plantation, the home of Anna Page King's eldest daughter Hannah and her husband William Audley Couper, where she helped prepare dinner for several guests. Mom Jane clearly had skills that set her apart from other bondpeople on Retreat Plantation—enough that she received permission to leave the estate. In a letter to her daughter Florence, King said that Mom Jane "left them all well in the evening." Remarking further on her services, the mistress stated, "What a perfect pattern of an old negro Old Mom Jane is. . . . I would [if] I could take 30 years off of her age."[59]

Nonagricultural bondpeople on this plantation traveled frequently. On 2 December 1839, for example, Anna sent the fifty-two-year-old housemaid Lady to deliver peaches to her friend Miss Jane Johnson of Savannah, but on the 31st of the month, Lady had not arrived. In a letter addressed to Miss Johnson, she explained: "Your unfortunate peaches I gave charge of Lady who was to go from W to WL [?] in a vessel hourly expected at the former place when she left here the first week in Dec—instead of which she was kept waiting there until two days before Christmas when she was sent down in a boat. I hope she will have the wit to send them to Cannon's Point [plantation] and let your friends have the good of them if you are not to get them."[60] Clearly, Anna Page King seemed more concerned about the location of the peaches than the whereabouts of her enslaved worker. Lady was absent for nearly a month, which suggests that nonagricultural bondpeople also found ways to resist their enslavement beyond the jurisdiction of their slaveholders. They took their time on errands and used their "momentary freedom" for themselves. Even though Lady's whereabouts during her absence are unclear, it is obvious that she used the time away to her advantage, and the Kings trusted that she would return.

In addition to running errands, the Kings also allowed certain bondpeople to travel unaccompanied for medical treatment. When Rhina suffered from an unknown illness, they gave her permission to trek more than twenty miles to see Dr. Sulivan, the family physician. Of this episode, King wrote the following: "Rhina is very much out of health—I sent her to Darien to Dr. Sulivan but he did not seem to think much was the matter with her. After she came back she expressed so great a desire to go to Amanda that I sent her off to Fancy Bluff last Tuesday."[61] That King allowed Rhina to travel unaccompanied to the mainland suggests that she was an exception to the rule. It appears that Rhina was so important to the family that they overlooked constraints on her movement throughout the region and did not even consider the possibility that Rhina was feigning her illness.

A few months after her doctor's visit, Rhina accompanied Anna King on a seven-month trip to the North because she was still in "bad health." King hoped that taking Rhina "will be the saving of her life" since the summer months often proved deadly in this region.[62] At the same time, Davy, another servant, traveled with Thomas Butler King Sr. and Thomas Butler King Jr. to California. However, in this case, travel proved troublesome. Davy ran away and the family never saw him again. Anna King was not only angry, but she began to question their lenient policy regarding geographic mobility among their house servants. "I am more mortified & hurt than I can express," wrote Anna King to her daughter. "It gives me a worse opinion of the race than I had before," she continued, "and [it] makes me really desire to part with every one of them." King thought of her husband and said she was certain that he "feels this keenly." Disgusted, she explained that she had granted Davy's request to go to California only because "he beg'd me so hard to let him go to wait on his master I little dreamed he would have deserted that kind master."[63] A few days later, she blamed her husband, saying that "had he been less *liberal* with Davy he may have continued faithful." Since Rhina was with her in New Haven, Connecticut, at the time, King also began to question her loyalty. "I can only hope she will be more faithful," she wrote to her daughter back in Georgia.[64] Despite her apparent concern, Rhina was in fact obedient, so Anna King allowed her to take a short trip with her friend Ellen S. five years later. On April 12, 1857, King recorded the trip in a letter. "I would not let [Ellen] go alone so sent Rhina with her—telling her to get back in the Everglade [steamboat] if possible," King wrote. "She barely had time to go from one bed to the other. . . ." Apparently, Ellen was not feeling well, so King sent Rhina to accompany her on the steamer.[65] A month later, the mistress praised Rhina for being ". . . a real triumph. . . . She is *used to traveling* you know & is not to be put out of her way by trifles."[66]

Middleton, an enslaved male at Retreat recognized for his skill as a fiddler, also traveled. During the summer of 1851, he accompanied a "Mr. Bourke" on a "pleasure trip to Florida," and when he returned, Anna King "could see Middleton playing . . . 'Oh! Susannah!'" and it made her "feel more melancholy" because it reminded her of all the other family members and bondpeople that were absent.[67]

Like agricultural laborers, enslaved workers in nonagricultural settings sang songs to maintain work rhythms and break up the monotony of their workday. Some female washerwomen sang the following song while ironing: "Do tu'key buzzard len' me y'u wing / T' fly ova yonda t' see Miss Geo'gia King."[68] The lyrics probably referred to Anna Page King's daughter who lived across the island. Hidden within this song is the notion of freedom, which bondpeople often expressed through bird motifs. These lyrics also suggest that enslaved workers longed to travel beyond the confines of their plantations because they wanted to see other women and men who lived on neighboring estates.

Retreat Plantation bondpeople such as Mom Jane, Lady, Rhina, Davy, and Middleton traveled throughout the island community by foot, steamboat, and carriage. They assisted their slaveholder's family and ran errands for them. Such privileges signified their important role within a restrictive community because a large majority of Glynn County bondpeople never traveled beyond the confines of their home plantations. In 1854 Anna Page King lamented the loss of one of her nonagricultural laborers named Hannah:

> She [Hannah] died on Thursday night. For years her sufferings have been greater than words could express—yet nevr [sic] a groan or complaint escaped her lips. Patiently she endured her sufferings. To her owners she was all we could desire in a servant—in fact as servant, daughter, sister, wife, she had not her equal. She was in her senses to the last & willing to leave this for a better world. . . . I can't but sorrow for the departure of so good, so faithful a servant as Hannah ever was to us.[69]

Despite such admiration and praise for her servants, two years before her death in 1857, Anna Page King stated that she was "worn out from the care of negroes."[70]

Summary

Nonagricultural laborers had several valuable skills that slaveholders often appreciated and utilized. As with agricultural work, gender and age influenced the tasks and occupations certain bondwomen and bondmen completed. Elderly bondpeople and children were assigned light housework, gardening, and yard work. Women usually did most of the cooking, cleaning, and sewing, while men generally worked as artisans or house servants. Nonagricultural laborers received benefits such as more desirable living conditions, privileges, and prestige than their agricultural counterparts. A select few had the opportunity to travel beyond the plantation, forcing us to re-examine the notion of "containment" and to ask questions about the geographic boundaries of skilled laborers. Despite these advantages, nonagricultural workers also had disadvantages. Working in close proximity to their slaveholders often resulted in sexual exploitation and abuse that few if any could escape. In order to combat these realities, enslaved laborers turned to their families and communities for emotional support.

3 "There Sho' Was a Sight of Us": Enslaved Family and Community Rituals

God sets the lonely in families . . .
—Psalms 68:6 NIV

On 26 November 1840, William Barnett of Wilkes County placed an ad listing "TEN or TWELVE likely NEGROES" for sale in a local newspaper. This group of individuals included three skilled bondpeople described as "a good wagoner and first-rate field hand; a first-rate Cook, Washer and Ironer; another good Cook and field-hand; and some very likely boys, girls, and children." Following the detailed reference to the slaves' skills, Barnett concluded, "The above Negroes are of *good families*, and can be well recommended by all persons who know them."[1] Assuring potential buyers that these laborers came from "good families"—whether the family of the former owners or the enslaved—served as an additional incentive for purchasing them besides their apparent labor skills.

Slavery as a whole negatively affected the development and maintenance of families. Since slavery was inextricably linked to work, it is almost impossible to develop a solid understanding of enslaved families without acknowledging the backdrop of labor in which families and communities evolved and interacted. Long hours of backbreaking labor in agricultural and nonagricultural settings restricted the time bondpeople had to spend with each other. Chapters 1 and 2 focused on labor; this chapter shifts the discussion to family and community life among the enslaved. Although studies of enslaved families have devoted considerable attention to the structural analysis which is useful and included here, the primary objective of this chapter is to define and explore the opportunities for the creation and maintenance of families and communities in antebellum Georgia.[2] To maintain family and social bonds, bondpeople interacted in work-related environments such as working socials, and in non-work-related environments such as religious services (in interracial settings) and holiday festivals (within the enslaved community). Of course, it is difficult to think of anyone enslaved as having an ideal family situation when the reality of their experience involved the constant fear of separation and sale.

Defining Slave Families and Communities

Enslaved Africans interacted within particular types of relationships that represented "family" and, in a broader sense, "community." Loosely defined, family units might be labeled "cohesive or functional families" because they included a mix of biological, extended, and fictive connections that all operated as a family unit. "Fictive kin" represent family connections not related by blood. In contemporary society, some people refer to these relatives as "play cousins" or "play aunts and uncles." As in Louisiana, South Carolina, and Virginia communities, these families were complex, adaptive, and ever-changing—constantly living with the loss and gain of their members.[3] Enslaved women, men, and children relied on their adaptive abilities to develop familial connections in order to cope with the daily hardships and challenges of enslavement.

Enslaved communities in antebellum Georgia were diverse, close-knit, and sometimes geographically removed from each other. Considering communities as any group of people living together in a particular place or local area with certain commonalities such as race, religion, social position, etc., this chapter suggests that bondpeople in upcountry and lowcounty Georgia functioned in communities that developed patterns of interaction based on the plantation size and attitudes of their slaveholders. In the lowcounty, enslaved women and men lived on large plantations with multiple communities on one plantation. There were communities of field hands, communities of seamstresses, communities of ginners, as well as boatmen, blacksmiths, and sawyers. Many of these individuals lived on plantations with fictive and blood kin, so their families were often intact. Upcountry bondpeople lived in an enslaved community that was broad and incorporated people from neighboring counties. Thus family and community life in the upcountry was not confined to a single plantation. In order to develop a solid understanding of family and community life, one must first explore the parameters of the social environment.

One way to comprehend life in the quarters is by delving deeper into the personal relationships of the enslaved, taking concepts beyond determining whether bondpeople developed nuclear, simple, or complex family structures. To fully understand the family and community structure within enslavement and the environment that was available for family development, one must enter the enslaved quarters, witness their courting and marriage rituals, join them at the dinner table, and participate in their holidays and religious services.

Social Environment

The social environment shaped the options available for bondpeople to form relationships. Although men usually initiated courtship, demographic constraints, such as age and gender distributions, influenced mate selection in significant ways.[4] Depending on the size of the plantation, the open or closed nature of the system, the demands of the crop, the access to geographic mobility, the visitation patterns established, and the disposition of the slaveholder, bondmen and bondwomen elected to or were forced to partner with each other.

In the upcountry, mate selection often transcended plantation boundaries because most slaveholding units contained fewer than fifteen slaves. On small farms and plantations, like those common in Wilkes County, bondwomen and bondmen looked to other holdings for prospective partners because mate availability on their home plantation was extremely low. Small slaveholders supported the practice because owners of females profited from the offspring of these unions. Slaveholders of males also benefited because they could use visitation privileges as a measure of control. Wilkes County bondpeople often found their mates on adjoining plantations by necessity, and sometimes by choice, which explains the preponderance of less stable, abroad marriages in this community.

In the lowcountry, large slaveholdings fostered environments conducive to the development of families that were cohesive and more stable. Plantations in Glynn County were larger and usually contained balanced sex ratios, creating an environment that increased bondpeoples' chances of finding a mate on the same plantation.[5] Spousal selection was almost always limited to one plantation. Planters rarely allowed their laborers to associate with those on other estates, and bondwomen and bondmen were pressured to find spouses on their respective plantations. This prac-

tice continued simply because bondpeople had no other options. Therefore, when an enslaved male found a prospective partner, he began the
courting process.

Courting Rituals

Enslaved family and community life began with courtship. Initially, "[t]he
man would go to the cabin of the woman whom he desired, would roast
some peanuts in the ashes, place them on a stool between her and himself,
and while eating, propose marriage. If the man was accepted, the couple
repaired to his cabin immediately, and they were regarded as man and
wife."[6] As enslaved men and women searched for companions on their
home plantation or on neighboring estates, they participated in a series
of flirtatious games in order to win the affections of a potential spouse.[7]
Former Wilkes County bondman Marshal Butler outlined the evolution
of this process in the following song:

> If you want to go a courtin', I sho' you where to go,
> Right down yonder in de house below,
> Clothes all dirty an' ain't got no broom,
> Ole dirty clothes all hangin' in de room.
> Ask'd me to table, thought I'd take a seat,
> First thing I saw was big chunk o' meat.
> Big as my head, hard as a maul;
> Ash-cake, corn bread, bran an' all.[8]

Although he received tough meat, cake, and corn bread, Butler seemed
overjoyed by the invitation to share a meal with his companion.

For young slaves, male and female alike, "courtship was both a diver-
sion and a delight" because love interests distracted some from the reality
of their oppression. It also represented an "intensely romantic" ritual that
often led to marriage.[9] From the female perspective, Mariah Callaway,
a Wilkes County bondwoman, noted that she enjoyed being courted by
bondmen from neighboring plantations. She testified that "often in the
evenings, boys from the other plantations would come over to see the
girls . . . they would stand in large groups around the trees, laughing and
talking."[10] Although men initiated the courting process by flirting with
females in the fields, at dances, during religious ceremonies, or in the
quarters, women controlled the pace through their responses to their
male suitors.[11]

While courting, bondmen had to receive permission to spend time
with potential mates; obtaining a pass represented one requirement for
regular visitation. This mandate held true for large social activities as

well; one ex-slave noted during an interview that "dances, corn-shuck-ings, picnics and all kinds of old time affairs . . . were attended by slaves for some distance around, *but they had to have passes.*"[12] Some bond-men, however, did not have the patience to wait for a pass, and they paid severe consequences for their disobedience. Marshal Butler's testimony serves as an example of the life-threatening risks enslaved males took to spend time with their female partners:

> I'se left home one Thursday to see a gal on the Palmer plantation—five miles away. Some gal! No, I didn't get a pass—de boss was so busy! Every-thing was fine until my return trip. I wuz two miles out an' three miles to go. There come de "Paddle-Rollers" I wuz not scared—only I couldn't move. They give me thirty licks—I ran the rest of the way home. There was belt buckles all over me. I ate my victuals off de porch railing. some gal! Um-m-h. was worth that paddlin' to see that gal—would do it over again to see [M]ary de next night . . . Um-m-mh—Some gal![13]

Slaveholders' attempts to control and monitor relationships were largely ignored by the enslaved because many, like Butler, did not feel obligated to wait for permission to visit loved ones.

In addition to clandestine and approved visits, courtship rituals involved the informal practice of giving gifts. Some bondpeople disliked the idea of giving presents to their prospective spouses. Butler critically noted, "Sometimes some fool nigger would bring a gal a present—like 'pulled-candy' . . . I had no time for sich foolishness."[14] His dissatisfaction with presents perhaps reflects that he had few, if any, material posses-sions to offer his female companion. One could assume, therefore, that those fortunate ones who had something to offer a partner probably had better chances of wooing their affections. Some women welcomed the addition of material items because hardly any bondpeople owned any-thing. Yet not all enslaved females sought partners with material posses-sions. Women like Adeline Willis of Wilkes County understood this and often preferred their mates' love instead of material items. "Lewis," she explained, "never bought me any presents 'cus he didn't have no money to buy them with, but he was good to me and that was what counted."[15] Clearly, love and affection took precedence over gifts for this enslaved woman. If the courtship was successful, marriage solidified the union.

Marriage Ceremonies

Marriage was one of the obvious outcomes and goals of courting. Although it was not legally sanctioned, enslaved partners viewed their unions with solemnity and pride and lived with the constant fear of being separated.

Despite the obstacles, some sealed their unions through formal ceremonies involving biblical scriptures and witnesses, while others became husband and wife during private, informal moments. The presence of a member of the planter class did not ensure formality; therefore, some marriages were not acknowledged by their slaveholders. However, in most cases, enslaved couples had to obtain consent from their owners and, if present, their parent(s) as well. On a small farm in Hancock County, Georgia, which was originally part of Wilkes County, Mary and Starobin were married during a ceremony that their owners witnessed. Farmer Benton Miller described this event in his journal. "Hill Reeves married them," he explained, and "there was a great many negroes here" to attend this ceremony.[16] It is likely that the presence of so many bondpeople reinforced the union and possibly added new members to this enslaved community.

Enslaved couples who had formal ceremonies were often the property of a judge, justice of the peace, or preacher, or their owners were friends and relatives of such persons. "My Marster wuz a Jedge so he married all his niggers whut got married," explained Manuel Johnson. "He married lots ov y 'uther couples too," he continued, "I 'members dat day use ter cum fer him ter marry dem."[17] Bondpeople who sought Johnson's owner had to obtain permission from their slaveholders as well. Clearly, some couples traveled to other parts of the county or across county lines to formalize their relationships. Most enslaved couples, however, recognized that their relationships had no legal sanction, and many legalized their unions after emancipation. "Dey ain marry den duh way dey do now," one slave explained. She stated that "attuh slabery dey hadduy remarry."[18]

Enslaved couples took marriage seriously because it was an important part of their culture. For some, it was the focus of their existence as well as a significant unifying moment when the entire community came together. When bondpeople found love, former slave Mariah Callaway explained, "a *real* marriage ceremony was performed from the Bible."[19] Interestingly, some associated "biblical" weddings with formality even though a large majority of enslaved persons were illiterate. Perhaps they recognized the importance of biblical instruction because they attended interracial prayer meetings and witnessed the sacred treatment of scriptures at these services. Benton Miller's enslaved workers left the plantation every Sunday to attend prayer meetings and wedding ceremonies all across the county.[20] Other enslaved individuals, such as Willis Cofer, had vivid recollections of the weddings on his plantation: "When slaves got married, de man had to ax de gal's ma and pa for her and den he had to ax

de white folkses to 'low 'em to git married. De white preacher married
'em. Dey hold right hands and de preacher ax de man: 'Do you take dis
gal to de bes' you kin for her?' and if he say yes, den day had to change
hands and jump over de broomstick and dey wuz married. Our white folkses wuz all church folkses and didn't 'low no dancin' at weddin's but dey
give 'em big suppers when deir slaves got married."[21] Although the "formality" of "biblical weddings" raises questions about slave religion and
the role of Christianity within the enslaved community, it appears that
slave nuptials included informal rituals such as "jumping the broom,"
receiving verbal permission, or simply recognition from other members
of the plantation community.

Less formal wedding ceremonies gave couples another avenue to
solidify their relationships. On Hampton Point Plantation, Frances Kemble questioned "old House Molly" about the marital bonds in the enslaved
quarters. Molly assured her that couples bound themselves "not much
formally" because their overseer ignored such relationships. Likewise,
in Wilkes County Adeline Willis claimed, "We didn't have no preacher
when we married. My Master and Mistress said they didn't care, and Lewis's Master and Mistress said they didn't care, so they all met up at my
white folks' house and had us come in and told us they didn't mind our
marryin'." Shortly after that her owner sanctioned the union by stating
that "there ain't no objections so go on and jump over the broom stick
together and you is married."[22] Upon receiving verbal permission, Adeline and Lewis became husband and wife and solidified their union by
"jumping the broom." This tradition was fairly common among slaves,
as indicated in several narratives. Emma Hurley recalled "being told to
'step over the broom stick,'" and those enslaved in other southern states
had similar recollections.[23]

Matrimony did not guarantee that enslaved couples could live with
their spouses, so there was a preponderance of abroad marriages. Enslaved
husbands with passes visited their wives once or twice per week on
Wednesdays and/or Saturdays.[24] Male geographic mobility for the purpose
of visitation shows that slaveholders supported a sharp gender division in
terms of off-plantation travel. Adeline Willis, for example, married Lewis,
who resided on an "adjoining plantation," but she proudly testified that
he "came to see me any time 'cause his Marster . . . give *him* a pass."[25]
Their relationship depended upon how often their respective owners
granted visitation passes. Adeline and Lewis continued to "court" after
their marriage. "I lived on with my white folks," she asserted, "and he
lived on with his and kept comin' to see me jest like he had done when
he was a courtin'."[26] Others experienced more flexible visitation patterns.

Jane Mickens and Wheeler Gresham both remembered that fathers could "come and go as [they] pleased."[27] Apparently, some owners supplied passes more readily than others, but enslaved partners often felt two weekly visits were not enough to maintain cohesive families. Reflecting on the relationship of his parents, Marshal Butler testified: "Mammy was a Frank Coller niggah and her man was of the tribe of Ben Butler, some miles down de road. Et was one of dem trial marriages—they'se tried so hard to see each other but old Ben Butler says two passes a week war enuff to see my mammy on de Collar plantation."[28] If it had been Butler's decision, he seemed to prefer that his parents see one another more than twice a week. In neighboring Oglethorpe County, originally part of Wilkes County, the pass system evolved in a fluid manner as bondmen "enjoyed [a] considerable freedom of movement." These visitation patterns marked regional trends that were customary to the Georgia upcountry.[29]

Abroad marriages were rare in the lowcountry. Only the narrative of Ryna Johnson of St. Simons Island noted that her "huzbun . . . [was] frum Sapelo," a neighboring island.[30] It is likely that work patterns and the policy of enforced isolation discouraged abroad relationships in this region or that records indicating otherwise did not survive.

Bondwomen and men had mixed opinions about abroad marriages because of the advantages and disadvantages of these unions. The husband/father had greater freedom of movement than men with partners on the same plantation. Geographic mobility provided these men with new experiences and exposed them to places unfamiliar to most slaves. They often shared travel adventures with their wives and children; these stories gave them the hope to one day travel together as a family during freedom. In addition, abroad marriages provided family members with "emotional" or "social distance," protecting them from witnessing their loved one's abuse, exploitation, or overwork. Most scholars agree that "emotional distance" was a survival mechanism for enslaved families, which created "choices" unknown to couples with partners on the same plantation.[31] Negative aspects of these unions included limited time for familial nurturing and greater vulnerability to their owners' punishment and whims. Men had to be on their best behavior because their owners could revoke their visitation privileges at any moment. Finally, because a couple and family in an abroad partnership lived apart from one another, they had higher risks of permanent separation than those residing on the same estate.[32] Despite such challenges, bondwomen and bondmen did everything in their power to maintain and preserve their familial and communal connections. Some found that working socials represented an opportune time for strengthening their bonds.

Working Socials

During periods of decreased labor, bondpeople socialized with one another at interplantation events such as corn shucking, log rolling, syrup making, roof mending, quilting, regional cotton-picking competitions, and harvest festivals, events that all involved work. Slaveowners sought to capitalize on their investment through group activities and communal labor.[33] Multiple-plantation working socials gave planters an additional way to increase their capital by exploiting slaves' social activities in which enslaved men and women socialized, courted, danced, and ultimately married. The enslaved men and women created a space to express themselves and used these gatherings to escape the monotony of their daily lives.

Wilkes County bondpeople lived in an open community where opportunities for working socials occurred frequently. The owners of some small slaveholdings, because of their low populations, were forced to grant their bondwomen and bondmen permission to attend and participate in these types of activities. Thus, bondpeople sustained familial relations and met the obligations of marriage and parenting not only from their own efforts, but also because of the opportunities of inter-plantation contact approved by their owners.[34] Slaveholders who permitted their laborers to attend multiple-plantation socials gave them an occasion to mingle with enslaved laborers on neighboring farms and plantations. Many of these joint social activities involved kin-connected planter households, which convinced owners that their human chattels were under trustworthy supervision. Such practices granted bondpeople geographic mobility and social interaction while at the same time furnishing them with additional options to select a spouse and, ultimately, create a family. For example, on Benton Miller's farm in Hancock County, just south of Wilkes County, an enslaved female named Mary found her husband on the farm of her owner's brother-in-law.[35]

Working socials usually occurred around harvest time. Ex-slaves across five upcountry counties including Oglethorpe, Clarke, Green, Lincoln, and Wilkes testified about cooperative labor ventures.[36] Corn shuckings seemed to be the most memorable of these activities. Historian Eugene D. Genovese found that most "ex-slaves remembered corn-shuckings as their only good time," and others said "they were the best."[37] Bondpeople regarded such festivities positively because they were social events that involved working for themselves. Some of their testimonies reflect the festive atmosphere as many recalled singing to the music of a fiddle and eating food such as fresh meat and pound cake.[38]

Since work was central to most of these events, the social activities occurred after the completion of a particular task. Harvest festivals, for example, represented one type of working social that slaves looked forward to because of their celebratory nature. These festivals existed to return "thanks to the gods for having protected the crop" throughout the year.[39] Former bondwoman Catherine Wing remembered that they "use tuh hab big times duh fus hahves, and duh fus ting wut growed we take tuh duh church so as ebrybody could hab a piece ub it. We pray obuh it an shout."[40] Social activities in the lowcountry involved events restricted to slaves' home plantation, but upcountry bondwomen and men interacted with people on estates throughout the region and often across county lines.

"Peoples use ter be so good 'bout helpin' one 'nother," explained former Wilkes County bondman Henry Rogers. "When a neighbor's house needed covering," he continued, "he got the shingles and called in his neighbors and friends, who came along with their wives. While the men worked atop the house the women were cooking a delicious dinner down in the kitchen."[41] Rogers implicitly identifies a sexual division of labor at this particular working social. Some enslaved women, once outside of their owners' supervision, functioned in traditional or stereotypical familial roles by completing tasks such cleaning, cooking, and sewing. Historian Deborah Gray White explains that such strictly defined roles appealed to female field hands after a long day of back-breaking labor because they created a designated time to spend with other women. These interactions served as a social space for bondwomen to talk to each other about pregnancy, birth, and childrearing.[42] Even though these occasions involved "long hours of extra work," bondpeople enjoyed working socials because of the "community life they called forth."[43] Despite the sorrow many bondpeople experienced, they found time for "happy hours" often focusing on religion and celebrations.[44]

Religion and Holidays

Group interaction among the enslaved did not always involve labor. Outside of work responsibilities, bondwomen and bondmen interacted with their families and larger communities at church, at mealtimes, and at plantation social events. Holidays such as Christmas, Easter, and the Fourth of July enabled communities of people to celebrate during leisure activities without the pressure of an overseer or driver monitoring their behavior. Such holiday festivities gave relief from work and the opportunity to socialize with extended family and friends from nearby and distant plantations. Emily Burke witnessed Sunday festivities and made the following remarks: "The slaves had finished the tasks that had been assigned them in the morning and were now enjoying holiday recreations. Some were trundling the hoop, some were playing ball, some dancing at the sound of the fiddle, some grinding their own corn at the mill, while others were just returning from fishing or hunting excursions."[45]

It is clear that bondpeople used Sundays for a variety of activities. However, some bondpeople expressed little understanding of the underlying religious or national significance of these holidays. "Us didn't know nuffin' 'bout what dey wuz celebratin' on Fourth of July, 'cept a big dinner and a good time," explained Willis Cofer.[46] Easter marked a special holiday for those residing on the Cofer plantation in Wilkes County because "dat was de onlies' day in de year a Nigger could do 'zactly what he pleased."[47] Only a few Glynn and Wilkes bondpeople testified that Santa Claus visited their cabins during Christmas, while some celebrated other holidays.[48] Emma Hurley noted, "I never heard of a Santa Claus when I wuz a child."[49] Christmas, for those who celebrated it, was a special holiday for enslaved people. It was a time for relaxation and jubilee because there was a respite from labor that on some plantations lasted as long as two weeks. The Christmas season served as the "climax of the year's work" and was celebrated by adults as well as children. Bondpeople enjoyed this holiday because they had a large feast; some couples even married during holiday social events. On St. Simons Island, laborers spent Christmas Eve at the "Praise House or little Church" anticipating the second coming of Christ.[50] On the Butler estate, a black preacher named London, the head cooper, delivered the sermon. Around the island, London was revered as "an excellent and pious man" who delivered sermons in his cabin on most Sundays to local bondpeople who did not attend worship services elsewhere.[51] Every year the Christmas Eve sermon revisited the story of Christ's birth, and the service ended with songs of praise and worship. Bondwomen and men enjoyed the following song at Christmastime:

> King Jesus he tell you
> Fur to fetch 'im a hoss an' a mule;
> He tek up Mary behine 'im,
> King Jesus he went marching' befo'.
>
> CHORUS.—
>
> Christ was bon on Chris'mus day;
> Mary was in pain.
> Christ was born on Chris'mus day,
> King Jesus was his name.[52]

The reference to a horse and a mule enabled bondwomen and bondmen to draw connections between their experience and that of "King Jesus."

Some members of the slaveholding class in Georgia, like those in other states, could not ignore religion among their bondpeople because, as one noted, there was "an immensely strong devotional feeling among these poor people."[53] This religious fervor was so apparent in Glynn County that those slaves belonging to Major Pierce Butler "petition[ed] very vehemently that he would build a church for them on the island" so that they could hold separate worship services and hear the word of God from slave preachers like London. But there was great concern over this request because "such a privilege might not be thought well of by the neighboring planters."[54]

When enslaved preachers and respected religious figures used their spiritual authority to influence their fellow laborers, planters feared the worst. On the Butler estate, a bondwoman named Sinda was revered as a prophetess with exceptional spiritual discernment, power, and authority over her peers. Bondwomen and men relied on her insight to help them cope with their lot, but in January 1839, Mr. King, the plantation overseer, felt that Sinda had taken her powers too far. When she predicted that the "world would come to an end at a certain time," all the enslaved laborers refused to work in the rice and cotton fields. This strike angered Mr. King, but he was even more furious with Sinda because of her influence over the other bondpeople. King threatened to punish her severely if her prediction proved false, and when the "day of judgment" came, he carried out his threat and quelled Sinda's "spirit of false prophesy" and returned the "faith of her people . . . from her to the omnipotent lash again."[55] The story of Sinda and her followers represents one reason that planters throughout the South feared the religious instruction of the enslaved. They knew that if an individual bondwoman or bondman gained influence or power over others, the results could be serious. One way to address this fear was to allow the enslaved to attend the religious services of the planter class.

Some Glynn County bondwomen and bondmen participated in Baptist and Methodist church services at their owners' congregations on the island and in Darien, a small town in neighboring McIntosh County. Low-country physician Dr. James Holmes, known in the area as "Dr. Bullie," remembered that "the colored people of the island were all Baptists, but our beloved Bishop always collected them together on the Sunday afternoons of his visitations and preached to them with understanding."[56] Those fortunate enough to have permission to travel to Darien could only attend services there once a month because slaveholders feared that frequent visits to other areas provided "opportunities for meeting between the Negroes of the different estates" that often led to "objectionable practices of various kinds."[57]

Members of the slaveholding class who were not so comfortable with slaves having separate worship services or accompanying their owners to service found ways to satisfy their religious conscience through private instruction. In March 1839, Frances Kemble found herself anxious about whether slaves on her husband's plantation would "come to prayers" in "the sitting room at eleven o'clock" one Sunday where she intended to "read prayers to them." She was pleasantly surprised when several came to this informal ceremony, especially since they came with "very decided efforts at cleanliness and decorum of attire." Boastfully, Kemble stated, "I was very much affected and impressed myself by what I was doing."[58] During this makeshift church service, Kemble struggled to contain her emotions when she read the scriptures to her enslaved "congregation." "It is an extremely solemn thing to me to read the Scriptures aloud to anyone," she expressed, "and there was something in my relation to the poor people by whom I was surrounded that touched me so deeply while thus attempting to share with them the best of my possessions, that I found it difficult to command my voice, and had to stop several times in order to do so." Clearly moved, Kemble dismissed the congregation of bondwomen and bondmen, feeling that they equally appreciated one another and respected one another's religious feelings.[59] Upcountry slaveholding women like Harriet Cumming of Wilkes County witnessed similar interactions with slaves on Sundays as her mother "taught them the Commandments, hymns, and a simple Catechism" in their family dining room.[60]

Despite religious instruction from members of the slaveholding class, some St. Simons Island bondpeople testified that they never participated in organized church activities. "Dey ain hab no church in doze days," explained former bondman Ben Sullivan, "an wen day wannuh pray, dey git behine duh house aw hide someweah an make a great prayuh. Dey ain suppose tuh call on duh Lawd; dey hadduh call on duh massuh an ef dey ain do dat, dey git nine an tutty."[61] Clearly, slaveholders tried to control the religious activities of their slaves, as this owner wanted slaves to pray to *him* rather than to "duh Lawd."

Religious activities represented a sacred time for family and community gatherings. Upcountry bondwomen like Arrie Binns of Wilkes County testified that her entire family worshipped together in a white church. She recalled being instructed to keep good manners during the sermon; there was "no lookin' to the right or the left." But this proved difficult the day a goat found its way into the church and disrupted the sermon so many times that Binns could hardly contain herself as she and her siblings struggled to suppress laughter. "We couldn't laugh a bit," Binns recalled, but ". . . I almost busted, I wanted ter laugh so bad."[62] She knew they would suffer from her parents' wrath if they did not mind their manners. Even though the Binns family interacted as a unit during services with whites, they also held their own private prayer meetings. "I 'members de meetin's us use ter have down in our cabin," she recollected, "an' how everybody would pray an' sing."[63] Obviously some enslaved families made it a point to hold their own services and prayer meetings outside their owners' supervision. They nurtured their spirituality by using the time away from their owners to worship with one another.

Religious activities on Jane Mickens Toombs's Wilkes County plantation represented communal activities in which *all* bondwomen and men participated. Toombs testified that "Everybody went to Church, de grown folks white and black, went to de preechin' an' den all de little niggers wuz called in an de Bible red an' 'splained ter dem."[64] Like Arrie Binns, Toombs recalled segregated services "down in de Quarters, but dat wuz at night an' wuz led by de colored preachers."[65] During the summer months, Toombs also remembered that her Uncle George Gullatt "use ter preach ter de slaves out under de trees."[66]

Whether held in the yard or at a "Praise House," religious services among the enslaved were sacred events. Some were so sacred that members of the slaveholding class commented on them in their journals. "I wish I was an artist so that I could draw a picture of the scene," exclaimed Eliza Andrews about the Praise House on her father's Wilkes County plantation. "The women, when they get excited with the singing, shut their eyes and rock themselves back and forth, clapping their hands" to songs such as this:

> Mary an' Marthy, feed my lambs,
> Feed my lambs, feed my lambs;
> Mary an' Marthy, feed my lambs,
> Settin' on de golden altar.
> I weep, I moan; what mek I moan so slow?
> I won'er ef a Zion traveler have gone along befo;
> Paul de' postle, feed my lambs,
> Feed my lambs, feed my lambs. . . .[67]

Witnessing such a scene was a privilege for whites. As Andrews noted, "they won't give way to their wildest gesticulations or engage in their sacred dances before white people, for fear of being laughed at." The day she visited the Praise House, several slaves had gone to the river bank and she "did not get a full choir," however "whenever the 'sperrit' of the song moved them very much, [they] would pat their feet and flap their arms and go through a number of motions."[68] Slave spirituals so impressed Frances Butler Leigh, daughter of Glynn County plantation owner Pierce Butler, that she marveled with envy at the skill and character of them.

> I often wish that I were a first-rate musician, that I might be able to collect, preserve, and harmonise some of their tunes. There is really nothing in the words, which if written down apart from the music, seem mere nonsense, but it is the way they sing the words, the natural seconds they take, and the antiphonal mode they unconsciously adopt. Also the remarkable minors that many of their songs are sung in, which it is almost impossible to imitate.[69]

Leigh not only noticed the rhythm, as bondpeople "always keep most exquisite time and tune," but she also found it remarkable that "no words seem too hard for them to adapt to their tunes, so that they could sing a long metre hymn to a short metre tune without any sensible difficulty." She also complimented those whose "voices have a peculiar quality that nothing can imitate; and their intonations and delicate variations cannot be reproduced on paper."[70]

Once the enslaved preacher stepped into the pulpit or makeshift pulpit under a tree, he greeted his "congregation" with joy in celebration of their gathering. Gender divisions were evident as the role of the preacher was reserved for males, even though enslaved women had active roles within the congregation. One woman testified that she was called to preach well after the abolition of slavery.[71] Attending church was an event, and women showed up in their best clothes.[72] Robert Shepard, an upcountry bondman, remembered that "[s]lave women had new calico dresses what they wore with hoop skirts they made out of grapevines." He also noted that they wore "poke bonnets with ruffles on 'em, and if the weather was sort of cool, they wore shawls."[73] As the preacher began his sermon, members of the audience responded by clapping, shouting, and singing praises.

Neal Upson, another former bondman, remembered his older sisters telling him stories about slave sermons. "There weren't many slaves what could read, so they jus' talked 'bout what they done heard the white preachers say on Sunday," he shared. "One of the favorite texts was the third chapter from John," he continued, "and most of 'em just 'membered a line or two from that." In addition to sermons and scripture readings, "there was sure a lot of good prayin' and testifyin'" at these meetings.[74] When the preacher moved his audience, bondwomen and men responded with call-and-response songs like the following:

What make the Preacher preach so hard,	O yes now.
The Prettiest thing I ever saw,	O yes now.
They study of religion while you're young,	O Yes now.
I lean in the Rock and never fall,	O yes now.
O march with the members,	Bound to go.
Aint you a member,	Bound to go.
Aint you a member,	Bound to go.
Believer fare you well.[75]	

This song represented the congregation opening the doors of the church, seeking those who had not officially joined the fellowship to answer the call. "When a nigger joined the church," former upcountry bondwoman Fannie Hughes recalled, "there so' was a lot of shoutin' and singin'. Wish you could heard it."[76] Once a person joined the church, "a colored preacher did the baptizing," usually in a local river; thus the slave was now part of a church family.[77] Ben Sullivan, a former bondman from St. Simons Island, noted, "Dey hab big baptizing in duh ribbah . . . an dey dip em on duh ebb tuh was duh sins away an dud preachuh he make a great prayuh tuh duh ribbuh."[78] Besides church services, baptisms, Sunday school, and other types of religious gatherings represented settings where courtship rituals, marriage ceremonies, and social interaction occurred. After prayer, worship, and the sermon, they concluded their religious celebrations with a dance.

Several bondwomen and bondmen had positive recollections about sacred and secular plantation dances. They testified about moving to the beat of a drum, swaying to the music of a fiddle, and other specially crafted instruments. Dr. Bullie commented on the fiddler at Raymond Demere's estate during one of his visits to St. Simons Island. "We met there a character by the name of Hickey," he explained, "who could play to perfection the country jigs popular in those days."[79] Apparently, "Hickey" was so skilled with the fiddle that Dr. Bullie could not resist taking a "turn on the grass plat before the door."[80] Similarly, ex-slave Ryna Johnson explained that "[w]en we is young, we use tuh hab big frolic an dance in a ring an shout tuh drum. Sometime we hab rattle made out uh dry goad [gourd] an we rattle em an make good music."[81] Several others remembered performing a dance called the "Buzzard Lope" that imitated the actions of different animals, particularly birds.[82]

As the participants hastened the pace, they also changed the rhythm of the dance.

Regardless of whether they worked or played, communal events such as working socials, religious ceremonies, and dances provided a designated time and place for the enslaved to interact with one another and to participate in courtship rituals. At dances, bondwomen and men expressed themselves spiritually, musically, and socially. Saturday nights "were always the time for dancing and frolicking," explained one Wilkes County enslaved male.[83] Another testified, "We sure frolicked Saturday nights. Dat wuz our day to howl and we howled."[84] Reflecting on one of these events, Jane Harmon boasted about her dancing skills: "I allus could dance, I cuts fancy steps now sometimes when I feels good. At one o' dem big ole country breakdowns (dances), one night when I wuz young, I danced down seben [7] mens, dey thought dey wuz sumpin'! Huh, I danced eb'ry one down!"[85] Enslaved males readily admitted that their women partners had impressive dancing skills. "Our gals sure could dance," stated Butler, "and when we wuz thirsty[,] we had lemonade and whiskey . . . de gals all liked it."[86] It appears that planters sanctioned these dances, which is not surprising considering the open nature of the upcountry enslaved community; however, it is difficult to determine how often these events occurred. Some slaveholders participated in or witnessed the festivities. In fact, planters had such vivid recollections of enslaved dances that they wrote about them in their journals, diaries, and letters. One Wilkes County planter even recalled the lyrics to a song titled "The Negro Caller," and kept the lyrics in his personal scrapbook:

> Get yo' pardners, first Kioatilliou!
> Stomp yo' feet, an' raise 'Em high;
> Sure is, "Oh, dat water—milliou!
> Gwine to git a houre lively."

> S' lute yo' pardners! scrape politely;
> Don't be bumpim' give the res'
> Balance all! now step out rightly
> Alluz dance yo' level bes.

> Fo' ward, foak! Whoop up niggers!
> Back agin! Don't be so slow;
> Swing Comahs! Min' de figgers;
> When I hollers, den yo' go

> Hands around! hol' up yo' faces;
> Don't be lookin' at yo' feet;
> Swing yo' pardners to yo' places!
> Dats de way—dat's hard to beat

Sides forward! where you's ready
Make a bow as low's yo' kin;
Swing against wid opsit lady!
Now we'll let yo' swap agin

Ladies Change! Shet up dat talkin';
Do yo' talkn' after while;
Right and lef'! don't want no walkn';
Make yo' steps, an' show yo' style.[87]

Given the title, it appears that this song is reflective of a dance (cotillion) orchestrated by a "Negro Caller" who used an authoritative tone to shout directives that controlled the pace and movement of the dance. Considering that this record appeared loose in a planter's scrapbook, it is likely that someone in the slaveholding family witnessed this ritual and documented what they saw. Even though the author and origin remain lost to history, it is clear that someone witnessed bondpeople dancing to the commands of a person referred to as the "Negro Caller," and they deemed it interesting enough to keep in their family scrapbook.

Although dances were fairly common in Wilkes County, some enslaved parents did not permit their children to participate in such events. Emma Hurley testified that she "ain't never danced a step nor sung a reel in my life. My Ma allus said we shouldn't do them things an' we didn't, she said if we went to the devil it wouldn't be 'cause she give us her 'mission!"[88] Enslaved mothers and fathers had their own sets of rules and regulations for the rearing of their children despite owners' desire to control the physical and social activities of their "property." Resisting their slaveholders' authority gave enslaved parents like the Hurleys space to enforce *their* own ideals and morals. For others, dances became sites for courting and for the maintenance and development of functional families regardless of demographic constraints.

Family Structure

Creating a family was important to the enslaved because relatives served as outlets necessary for their survival. Whether in abroad marriages or in home plantation relationships, extended familial connections were extremely important even after the abolition of slavery in 1865. Former Wilkes County bondwomen and men reunited with their relatives after Emancipation because they were accustomed to geographic mobility and the multiplantation interaction they had had during slavery. Abroad spouses and family members often lived in neighboring counties, yet searching for them was not as challenging as it was for those who had to look out of state. For example, forty-one families from Wilkes County appear in the records of the Freedman's Savings and Trust Company from 1870 to 1872.[89] These former bondwomen and bondmen applied for bank accounts in Augusta, the primary urban center of the Georgia upcountry. Their applications included biographical sketches of their extended families, marital status, children, occupation, age, and complexion.

Many of these individuals had substantial kin networks and complex families. The family of Julie Ann Truett serves as a good example. Truett was fifty-nine years old when she filed for an application in 1871. She and her deceased husband Alligan had only one child, named John, but she had seven siblings, of whom two were listed as "dead." Her brother Toby was "carried off to Alabama," and the whereabouts of her father Sandy were unknown. Truett said he "was carried off many years ago when I was small."[90] Her mother Molly appears in the record as "dead." Truett lived in Wilkes County, "7 miles from Washington" all of her life and she worked as a cook, which is probably the same work she did during slavery.

The former bondwomen and men in these records had large kin networks and a variety of occupations; several were "taken to Texas" while others were "carried off to Alabama," and a significant proportion of their siblings had died. The females of childbearing age had at least one child, while one woman, "Mat Basket," was expecting because her file listed her second child as "Baby not born."[91] Thirty-five knew both parents' names (sometime surnames), two knew of only one parent, three had white fathers, and one had no knowledge of his parental ties.[92] More than one-half of those that filed for bank accounts (twenty-one) listed a spouse. Louisa Kane, for example, was forty-nine years old when she submitted her application in 1872. She worked as an agricultural laborer ("farmer") in Washington during bondage and was in a relationship with a white man named "Robert," whom she "never married." It is difficult to determine whether "Robert" was Louisa's former owner or a man she met after slavery, but the fact that she listed him in the column marked "Husband" signifies evidence of miscegenation and suggests that Louisa believed she and Robert were husband and wife even though they "never married."[93]

Extended families were crucial to Glynn County slave family stability as well; relatives in this region often lived together for many years. Enslaved Africans on St. Simons Island made references to aunts, uncles, cousins, and grandparents. Charles, for example, recalled "Muh gran, she name Louise an come frum Bahama Ilun."[94] Likewise Charles's wife Emma had some memories of her grandmother: "gran Betty she wuz

African."[95] In addition to matrifocal and extended family patterns, Glynn County bondpeople established conjugal relationships with or without their owners' permission. Nuclear family structures represented one outcome of such relationships. Enslaved families in this region expanded across two and sometimes three generations.

When J. D. Legare visited Glynn County in 1832, he said that Hopeton Plantation, operated by James Hamilton Couper (J. H. Couper), "is decidedly the best regulated plantation we have ever visited, and we doubt whether it can be equaled (certainly not surpassed) in the Southern States."[96] Hopeton contained 4,500 acres of land and was the home of as many as 600 enslaved laborers during the antebellum period.[97] Situated on the south side of the Altamaha River "about five miles from [the town of] Darien, [and] fourteen miles from the sea," Hopeton produced, rice, cotton, sugar, Irish potatoes, cow-peas, turnips, and rye.[98] On 14 March 1830, 390 slaves lived in 110 family groupings at Hopeton. This population had 199 females, 159 males, and 32 illegible names.[99]

The family structures at Hopeton included nuclear, single-parent, couples without children, and extended connections. Nearly half the families represented (fifty) belonged to nuclear households, and thirty-two families included extended kin connections. Eighteen couples appear without children, like "Old Dick" and "Camba" who were sixty and sixty-one years old, respectively. Of the other family structures, thirteen included mothers and their offspring, and three fathers appear with offspring. Several couples had six children living with them on this estate— much different than the family structure in the Georgia upcountry, where it is difficult to trace paternal ties. Other estates in Glynn County contained significant family connections.[100]

Families at Retreat Plantation had few disruptions to their connections because the King family rarely sold their Retreat slaves. Thirty bondwomen and men appeared on both the 1827 and 1859 lists and by the latter date contributed to seventeen nuclear families, which indicates some stability on this plantation. The enslaved population exceeded 100 slaves during the antebellum period, consisting of 140 in 1827, 112 in 1850, 129 in 1859, and 142 in 1860.[101] Between the years 1827 and 1860, the population did not change much. In 1827, for example, females represented 47 percent of the population while males made up 53 percent of the workforce.[102] Thirty-two years later, the population decreased by 8 percent from 140 to 129. Of this later population, women totaled 55 percent while men represented 45 percent of the labor force. These statistics suggest a relatively balanced slave population; however, age distributions allow additional conclusions to surface.

The age distribution among enslaved men and women at Retreat was conducive to the formation of families except in 1859. The number of available males between the ages of ten and nineteen was significantly lower than the number of females. Women in this age group (ten through nineteen) made up 17 percent of the total enslaved population while men represented only 6 percent. Thus, by 1859, teenage women may have had trouble finding a mate at Retreat because they outnumbered men nearly three to one. For those men and women in their twenties, the age distribution was even, with ten men and ten women, which probably created a good chance for finding a mate at that age. Single men in their thirties outnumbered women 1.4 to 1.

Anna Page King identified seventeen nuclear families among the 142 enslaved men and women listed at the time of her death, which included 68 percent of the slave population.[103] Such high percentages indicate that the majority of Retreat slaves lived on a plantation with relatives present. Thus, individuals such as Alfred and Liddy grew up, married, had children, and lived together at Retreat for more than thirty years. This couple, like several others, appeared on the 1827 list as infants, but by 1860 they had given birth to two children, Frederick and Adalette. When considering these statistics, particularly in settings where demographic conditions provide a climate conducive for monogamy and nuclear families, enslaved couples often selected their spouse "based on a complex combination of reasons."[104] Some slaves preferred not to marry to avoid becoming attached to a partner only to witness their abuse or sale, while others did all they could to find a partner for support. Many of the reasons enslaved couples chose one another are still unknown to contemporary scholars.

Family and Community Interaction

Despite physical distance between family members, enslaved parents nurtured and disciplined their offspring, creating family interaction that was intimate and personal. Wives socialized with their husbands in small log cabins approximately sixteen by twenty feet, containing one or two rooms depending on the size of the family.[105]

Enslaved families utilized all possible avenues to maintain cohesive family units. As a child, Henry Rogers testified that "the fust thing I 'members is follerin' my Mother er 'round . . . everywhere she went I wuz at her heels."[106] Others also expressed deep love and affection for their mothers. "The first thing I recollect is my love for my mother," explained Adeline Willis. "I loved her so," she continued, "and would cry when I couldn't be with her." Even after Adeline married and had children of her own, she continued to love her mother "jest that-away."[107] Maternal bonds marked the strength of family unity and were reinforced through legal codes. The connection between mother and child became legally sanctioned through the Georgia Slave Code of 1755, which read in part that "slaves shall follow the condition of the mother and shall be deemed in law to be chattels personal in the hands of their owners and possessors."[108] In addition to this mandatory legislation, slaveholders reinforced female-headed families by assigning cabins, food rations, clothing, and land (i.e., garden plots) to enslaved mothers.[109] These practices and the Georgia Slave Code explain why some slaveholders preferred more women over men—a woman's capacity to bear children represented a constant source of additional labors. Birth lists rarely denoted the "father" of a particular child because of this practice of identifying slaves through maternal lineage. For example, when Hugh Fraser Grant of Elizafield Plantation noted the enslaved births and the distribution of supplies such as blankets and tools, he only listed the mother's name.[110]

By ignoring the father-child association through this legal stipulation, enslaved families developed matrifocally, leaving many of the parental obligations solely to enslaved mothers. The challenge to maintain stable families increased; such laws hardly considered the father after the birth of new slave progeny. Although owners encouraged women to give birth, they made few promises regarding the maintenance of paternal bonds. In spite of the legal recognition of the mother-child connection, enslaved fathers found ways to raise their children. Jane Mickens's father, for example, lived on a different plantation but she recognized his authority despite his absence. "My Pa didn't 'low his chillun ter go 'roun'" she explained. "No'm, he kep' us home keerful lak."[111] Clearly, her father was able to keep his fifteen children from visiting other slaves, even though he did not live at the same "home." Thus, distance and time did not stop fathers from parenting.[112] Despite parentage, many understood that in reality, "all de chilluns b'longed to de gal's white folkes."[113]

Mealtimes provided periodic contact among enslaved families and the larger community because they created a space that was sometimes outside their owner's presence. On estates with large workforces, a plantation cook, usually an older woman, prepared all the meals.[114] Marshal Butler of Wilkes County recollected that they ate breakfast at dark, lunch in the fields, and dinner in the slave cabins; the first two meals were for the entire plantation community, the last was shared with individual family members.[115] Butler's memory of breakfast "at dark" suggests that this first meal was served before dawn, prior to entering the fields. Bondwomen and bondmen started their day with a 4:00 A.M. wake-up horn and they had to be in the fields forty-five minutes later, so this meal had to be a quick one. Likewise, lunch was probably rushed as well since it took place in the fields and overseers kept their workers on a rigid schedule during daylight hours. Dinner in the cabins was most likely the best meal for family socialization; one can speculate about the types of conversations that they participated in during this "family time"—seeing how each member made it through another monotonous day of agricultural or nonagricultural labor, or they might have talked about recent runaways, upcoming religious or working social events, or the marriage of a new couple. It is also feasible that they discussed plans to put an end to their enslaved status.

Willis Cofer of Wilkes County described communal mealtimes on his master's plantation: "Dere wuz so many chilluns dey fed us in a trough. Dey jes poured de peas on de chuncks of cornbread what de had crumbled in de trough, and us had to mussel 'em out. . . . De only spoons us had wuz mussel shells what us got out of de branches [creeks]. A little Nigger could put peas and cornbread away mighty fast wid a mussel shell. . . . When a boy got to be a man enough to wear pants, he drawed rations and quit eatin' out of de trough."[116] Mealtimes for Cofer functioned more like a survival-of-the-fittest competition. There was little time for socialization (i.e., conversation) during his meals; instead, Cofer and the other adolescents struggled to eat with much haste because they did not have the appropriate utensils. Clearly, eating was a communal event. Although Wilkes County bondwoman Jane Harmon's mealtimes differed in location from Cofer's, she also ate from a trough. Harmon explained that the bondpeople on her plantation, "et in de white folks' kitchen out' n er big tray whut wuz lak a trough."[117] Regardless of where enslaved women, men, and children ate their meals, the demands of labor forced them to eat according to their owner's preference.

Summary

Bondwomen and men created, maintained, and interacted with their families and communities despite spending most of their time working for their slaveholders. Bondpeople nurtured familial and communal connections during working socials and during periods of rest (i.e., holidays, religious services, weddings, and dances). They had fond recollections of these interactions because relatives helped them deal with the hardships of their condition. They used this space to express love for one another, to hope for a better day, and to dream of freedom. On small holdings in

Wilkes County, the opportunities to create families differed from those on large plantations because bondpeople had to select a mate from another farm or estate. Enslaved men and women on small holdings were often involved in abroad relationships and were at the mercy of their owners for visitation. Large holdings were conducive to stable family formation on the home estate. Once slaves found partners, either on or off their home plantation, they married and usually had children. Families enjoyed participation in communal activities, but the reality of their enslaved status was always present.

4 "O, I Never Has Forgot Dat Last Dinner wit My Folks": Enslaved Family and Community Realities

> Though one may be overpowered, two can defend them-
> selves. A cord of three strands is not quickly broken.
> —Ecclesiastes 4:12 NIV

In the early 1840s, the late owner of Kelvin Grove, Benjamin F. Cater, "choosed out" sixty-one slaves and gave them to Hugh Fraser Grant of Elizafield Plantation. Next to this transaction his ledger showed "Cash from H. F. Grant on a/c [account] first payment on Purchase of 61 Negroes."[1] Grant's initial payment was for $586.66. Although it is unclear how many transactions followed, we know that sixty-one slaves and many families were uprooted by this sale.

The Kelvin Grove debts still affected slave families even fifteen years later. On 20 January 1855, an enslaved male named Smart, who was owned by the King family at nearby Retreat Plantation, lost his wife and six children when their owner (James Postell of Kelvin Grove) sold them along with seven others. Prior to their separation, Smart and his wife represented one of the few abroad marriages in Glynn County. It is likely that because their owners were connected through guardianship, Smart and his wife saw one another on a fairly regular basis. That changed in January 1855. When Anna Page King got news of her bondman's family's sale, she wanted to purchase the family. "I wanted your council sadly today," she wrote to her husband. "Smarts wife who you recollect came to us begging us to buy her and her six children," was mortgaged with her children to an agent for $3,100. Lamenting over the sale, Anna King said, "I have not the money. I am sorry as the woman is prime and the children very promising."[2]

Anna King was upset because she missed the opportunity to purchase a "prime" woman and her "promising" children, but Smart endured an even greater deprivation. He could no longer enjoy the company of his wife and children and was left brokenhearted at Retreat. Two years later, on 27 April 1857, "poor Smart died for want of proper attention—first on Floras part & then on Pussys."[3] Apparently, no woman could replace the loss he suffered when his wife and children were mortgaged to cover a debt.

This chapter examines the realities of enslaved families through an exploration of their inner lives. Bondpeople experienced several challenges to their family stability: forced breeding, domestic conflict, interference, separation, and sale. No matter how well-liked they were in the eyes of their slaveholders, their lives were altered when their owner's situation or circumstances changed as a result of illness, death, financial hardship, marriage, divorce, or legal action. Enslaved couples fortunate enough to marry and lead relatively autonomous lives in the quarters still had to contend with domestic disruptions from their slaveholders, overseers, and drivers. The only alternative to submission was resistance; as a result, some ran away to find relatives or to establish new family ties elsewhere.

Bondpeople relied on rituals, ceremonies, and routines to help maintain familial stability, but even so, bondpeople had trouble maintaining their relationships. Jane Mickens of Wilkes County recalled that there was "a heap of us slaves" and that she "wuz one of fifteen chillum." However, "all de slaves whut belonged to de McMekins" she explained were "choosed out . . . [because] dat's de way dey use ter do back in slavery time." "De young Mistresses an' Marsters choosed out de little niggers dey wanted fer their'n," and slaves were left with no recourse but to adapt and concede.[4] Clearly, the preservation of families took adaptation, creativity, and flexibility. However, these survival strategies and mechanisms were often not enough when confronted with the difficult situation of sexual exploitation.

Forced Breeding

Enslaved men and women experienced several forms of sexual exploitation that affected their familial connections. Breeding was one method of sexual coercion that some members of the slaveholding class relied upon to control and increase their slave populations. Slaveholders had strong feelings about which slaves should become "partners"; therefore, they used breeding to influence, force, and sanction sexual activity among the enslaved.

Southern planters held public discussions on "Raising Negroes." One slaveholder described the practice of breeding to his colleagues in an agricultural journal. "Some make a business of raising horses, beeves [sic], hogs, and sheep," he began, "but few devote particular attention to raising negroes." Continuing, he explained that "[s]uccess in negro raising is not only a matter of great concern to their owners, but to be insured, it must be conducted as a *business* separate from and unconnected with the market crop." According to the author, participating in the business of slave breeding helped those interested in this practice to reduce the "number of stillborn, and death, among" their enslaved populations. Likewise, this business venture afforded slaveholders the opportunity to "give more attention to pregnant women" and mothers. Lobbying for others to participate in this practice, he encouraged those managing large plantations to establish a place for pregnant women to live during the last month of their pregnancies. This "spot," he explained, consisted of "tight and convenient houses" near small fields and a nursery where women could continue working "as long as they could." He also suggested that enslaved females stay fit, "by way of exercise [that] was required of them." Apparently, this owner realized the value of "a good breeding woman"—as he closed the article, he encouraged his readers to "compel our negroes to take care of themselves, and their young," simply because "they will be the happier, and we the richer for it."[5]

Southern planters also used similar practices of animal husbandry to raise healthy livestock. Dependent on cattle, sheep, pigs, and horses, some slaveholders prioritized the reproduction of healthy animals that they used in conjunction with enslaved labor to work the land. The similarities between human and animal propagation are apparent. "Rules for Breeding," according to one southerner, required that animals be well-fed and "that the power of the female to supply her offspring with nourishment is in proportion to her size, and to the power of nourishment herself from the excellence of her own constitution." Animal domestication, as with humans, required breeders to focus on the health and potential productivity of females as well as the quality of the male "stock." The subjects must be well cared for, as "one good animal well attended is worth more than two inferior ones neglected."[6] Notice the economic undertones in both descriptions. It is clear that the connection to profitability was important to planter and animal breeders.

Scholar Richard Sutch argued in the 1970s that slaveholders found human breeding profitable "for the same economic reasons that led some nineteenth-century Southern farmers to practice mule breeding."[7] Building on this argument, it is important to recognize the impact of breeding on the children conceived, the enslaved parents, and the slaveholders who sanctioned the act. First we must begin with a clear set of definitions.

Broadly defining *breeding* as any method employed to produce offspring for the slaveholding class (including evidence of the use of force to accomplish it) links slave breeding to larger discussions of rape and power. One cannot ignore the connection between power and sexual violence because most incidents of rape (and forced breeding) involved an aggressor exerting his or her power over another person (or persons).[8] The institution of slavery, particularly the master-slave relationship, involved a significant amount of coercion, control, dominance, negotiation, resistance, and, in some cases, compliance. Forced sexual intercourse remains a constant part of the broad interpretation of these sexual violations despite changes in the legal definition over time. Sometimes these acts occurred as a result of threats from a slaveholder, overseer, or driver.

Clearly, definitions of rape vary. One scholar recently reminded us that the legal definition of rape "is a narrow one . . . that leaves out many [other] forms of sexual abuse."[9] In this regard, it encompasses any unwanted sexual act perpetrated by an acquaintance or a stranger through the use of force, coercion, or manipulation. For the most part, however, rape represents "a conscious process of intimidation."[10] Defined in this way, *rape* includes all acts of sexual violence that took place during slavery. Thus, it appears that there is a connection between these two sexual transgressions.[11]

Rape and breeding are unified by the use of force—both physical and mental. The word "force" is used here both as a noun and a verb. As a noun, *force* represents "physical strength or energy accompanying action or movement" and *forced* as a verb involves making someone "do something against their will."[12] Slave breeding represented one form of sexual abuse that adopted the machinations and mannerisms of rape because it forced people to engage in unsolicited sexual activity. These definitions are not restricted to gender; both males and females are victims. Nor do they consider the roles of third-party offenders such as slaveholders, overseers, and slave drivers in nonconsensual sexual intercourse. In an effort to revise these definitions, this study suggests that forced breeding in the slave quarters manifested itself as an indirect form of rape where *powerless* enslaved males and females became the victims of reproductive abuse to which they did not *willingly* give their consent.

Until the mid-1980s, discussions of rape assumed that men were the perpetrators and women the victims. But how does one account for unsolicited sexual acts that bondmen experienced *along with* bondwomen? Enslaved men without leadership positions were also powerless victims of breeding who suffered in ways similar to their female counterparts. Even though enslaved women became victims of white male power, it is clear through their testimony that enslaved males in positions of authority (i.e., drivers) violated bondwomen as well, and this complicates the discourse.[13] Black drivers used their power and elevated status over women to inflict physical and sexual abuse. Many drivers raped enslaved women like their owners did, indicating that their actions were still dictated by gender bonds with white men.[14] It was a way for them to enforce their power in a society dominated by a strict social hierarchy.

In the late 1830s, on a Georgia cotton plantation, Morris, a black slave driver, raped Sophy, an enslaved female. Following this violation, Sophy explained to her mistress that she did not resist Morris because "he have strength to make me" and her "poor flesh [needed] some rest from the whip."[15] Sophy experienced the mental manipulation of Morris's power as well as the physical and psychological violation of her body. Bondwomen were not only forced to have intercourse with enslaved male drivers, but they also had to ward off the sexual advances of *all* men in antebellum society. Judy, another bondwoman on the same estate, was forced to have sex with her white overseer. When she objected to his advances, he "flogged her severely for having resisted him, and then sent her off" to a remote swamp as punishment for *her* "offense."[16] Later, Judy gave birth to his son.

Why was Judy punished when she objected to her overseers' advances? Slaveholders reprimanded women like Judy because they assumed that black women (and men) were naturally promiscuous.[17] With one exception,[18] enslaved women rape victims had no protection under nineteenth-century legislation.[19] However, it is doubtful that antebellum legislation would have precluded the victimization and sexual abuse of black women. The testimonies of Sophy, Judy, Maria, and Auber of Georgia, along with several others like Harriet Jacobs (North Carolina), Rose Williams (Texas), and Celia (Missouri), suggest there were numerous documented and undocumented examples of rape that occurred during slavery.[20]

Looking at the experiences of individual men and women brings evidence of sexual exploitation to the fore. John Brown, an enslaved male from Virginia taken to Georgia, recalled the story of a woman victimized by slave traders. The "poor girl was stolen from her mistress and *forced* to get up in the wagon with Finney [the slave speculator], who brutally *ill-used her*, and permitted his companions to treat her in the same manner." Brown added that "this continued for several days" and that "women talked about this very much, and many of them cried, and said it was a great shame."[21] Clearly, sexual exploitation affected all members of slave society, even those who had simply heard about an offense. Perhaps these women cried because they too had experienced a similar violation or because they empathized with the enslaved girl who was gang-raped by a slave trader and his companions. The fact that John Brown relayed this story in his narrative suggests that witnessing episodes of sexual abuse had a profound impact on him, and likely on other enslaved males as well.

Evidence of gang rape was common in other slave states as well. Mary Peters, an enslaved woman from Missouri, believed that she entered the world as a result of her mother being gang-raped. She testified that her mistress's boys "threw her [mother] down on the floor and tied her down so she couldn't struggle, and one after the other used her as long as they wanted . . . and that's the way I came to be here."[22] The recollections of Brown and Peters indicate that sexual violence affected bondmen and bondwomen equally.

Bondmen felt victimized because in many cases they could neither freely choose their partners nor protect the women they loved. The testimony of a Louisiana bondman illustrates this. Stephen Jordon explained that "I myself had my wife on another plantation," and "the woman my master gave me had a husband on another plantation." "Everything was mixed up," he explained. "My other wife had two children for me, but the woman master gave me had no children. We were put in the same cabin, both of us cried, me for my old wife and she for her old husband."[23] Although Jordon noted that he never slept with this unnamed woman, he still felt victimized and the two of them went to great lengths to help one another see their loved ones. The assignment of "spouses" suggests that forced relationships had emotional effects on enslaved females *and* males, even though many scholars assume that men were the perpetrators and women were the victims of such acts.

Bondmen were keenly aware of the many forms of unsolicited sexual activity that occurred on southern plantations. Many of them commented on breeding in their narratives. Fred Brown, for example, noted that the slave driver on his plantation was "used fo to father de chilluns." "Him picks de po'tly, prolific, an' healthy womens dat am to rear de po'tly chilluns," he continued. "Dem dat him picks, he overlooks, an' will not 'low dem to mai'y or to fuss 'round wid de udder niggers. If dey do, 'tis de whuppin sho."[24] Lewis Jones, on the other hand, testified about his father who served as a male breeder. "My pappy had twelve chillun by my mammy an' twelve by anudder nigger, name' Mary. You keep de count. Den, dere am Lisa. Him have ten by her. And dere am Mandy. Him have eight by her. And dere am Betty. Him have five or six by her. Now, let me 'lect some more. I can't bring de names to mind, but dere am two or three others what have jus' one or two chillum by my pappy . . . close to 50 chillun . . . my pappy am de breedin' nigger."[25] Testimonies from Brown and Jones indicate the complexities of enslaved families and reinforce the importance of extended kin networks.

Most of the enslaved women in Glynn County, for example, were fortunate to have a family network to rely on and gain support from. Bondwomen on these estates were "married" and had several children; for example, Frances Kemble of the Butler plantations viewed them as "wives," assuming that they had one "husband." She was surprised, however, when she encountered two mothers with "illegitimate children." During a conversation with seventeen-year-old Maria of Hampton Point Plantation, Kemble noted that she was one of the few single mothers on the estate. Kemble learned this after she asked Maria to name her husband; Maria informed her "that she did not possess any such appendage."[26] What did Maria mean by this statement and why did she refer to husbands as appendages? Perhaps she was aware of the ambiguity of slave "marriage" and that she understood that couples could be torn apart at a moment's notice. It is also likely that she did not want a husband and she could have been trying to claim some measure of control over her sexuality. Equally probable was that Maria preferred being single to decrease the chances of witnessing or experiencing the abuse of *or from* her partner. Having only one child by a man she chose not to recognize could have been Maria's way of coping with her lot.

The bondwoman Auber made similar decisions. She complained of back pain caused by "constant childbearing" and a literal and figurative "life of labor." According to Kemble, Auber had five children and "she [too] had never been married."[27] Like Maria, Auber had a number of children by a man or men that she chose not to identify. The paternity of Maria and Auber's children remains a mystery. It is possible that these women were the victims of forced breeding. It is also likely that they chose not to share the paternal identity in an effort to keep their lives private or to protect themselves from the painful memories of sexual abuse.

In addition to the internal relationships connected to the use of force and consent, third parties such as slaveholders, traders, and overseers were also perpetrators of sexual violence because they required certain slaves to become partners. With this in mind, one must assess the slave-holder's role in breeding. Although they may not have been present when the acts of intercourse occurred, they were responsible for setting up the "union" and for coercing the enslaved "couples" to comply. Focusing on such interactions makes those in power responsible for systematically destroying or severely altering the familial connections of the enslaved. Their actions were often for economic reasons and, like livestock breed-ers, sometimes sought to reproduce specific qualities in (i.e., hearty, strong, and able) enslaved workers. Planters required certain slaves to impregnate or become pregnant for the purpose of adding additional labor-ers to the workforce. Breeding also confirmed slaveholders' beliefs about slaves' licentious behavior because many assumed falsely that bondmen and bondwomen were accustomed to multiple partners.[28]

Planters, overseers, and drivers used extreme, calculated efforts to maintain their workforce through the manipulation of enslaved male and female sexual activity. By requiring slaves to breed with one another, owners sanctioned the practice of "forced promiscuity," which was some-times misconstrued as polygamy.[29] Therefore, when slave owners forced their slaves to breed, they subjected both males and females to partici-pate in nonconsensual sexual activities with several partners. Again, it is useful here to draw upon the testimonies of enslaved males from all over the South. William Matthews testified, "If a man a big, stout man, good breed, dey gives him four, five women."[30] Because it is not clear whether bondmen consented to these recurring acts of intercourse, one could argue that bondmen who were forced to participate in sexual rela-tionships with women who did not give their consent were by definition victims of rape.[31] Forced breeding was endemic to the antebellum slave experience in many communities.[32]

Several enslaved males and females throughout the South testified that they did not want to become intimate with the person assigned to them as their breeding partner, yet in most cases they were left power-less and had to concede.[33] The story of Molly, a slave at Hampton Point Plantation in Georgia, provides evidence of forced breeding and the level of powerlessness apparent in slave relationships. Appealing to her mis-tress, Molly inquired about the recent sale of her "*real* husband," but her mistress was under the impression that a slave named Tony was Molly's husband. Molly assured the mistress, however, that Tony was just the man the overseer "provided" for her. Controlling the sexual practices of the workforce, this overseer forced Molly and Tony to have inter-course and the pair conceived nine children together.[34] Former slave Ryer Emmanuel also recalled slave breeding on her plantation: "White folks would make you take dat man when' if you want him or no."[35] These testimonies, among many others throughout the antebellum South, confirm that sexual exploitation occurred frequently on slave plantations and, as a result, enslaved women gave birth to several children from these unions. The only alternative was to receive a severe whipping or endure another form of punishment.

Domestic Conflict

Domestic abuse and violence[36] occurred not only between enslaved husbands and wives, but also as a result of direct and indirect actions on individual slaves or couples. Slaveholders, overseers, and drivers constantly exercised their authority over enslaved relationships and expressed their power by establishing strict rules of conduct. It is not surprising, of course, that many of these interactions contained forms of abuse and violence simply because the origins of these connections often involved force.

Enslaved couples or breeding partners constantly faced interference by a third party. Couples who were part of forced or unforced unions residing on West Point Plantation, for example, suffered severe consequences when domestic abuse and violence occurred. The owner of this estate, W. W. Hazzard, made the following remarks regarding domestic conflict:

> I never permit a husband to abuse, strike or whip his wife, and tell them it is disgraceful for a man to raise his hand in violence against a feeble woman, and that woman too, the wife of his bosom, the mother of his children, and the companion of his leisure, his midnight hours. If the wife teases and provokes him by her nightly clatter, or crabbed deportment, and he complains and established the fact; she is punished, but it sometimes happens that the husband petitions for her pardon, which I make it a rule not to refuse, as it imposes a strong obligation on the wife to use her tongue with less bitterness, and be more conciliating in her behavior.[37]

In this article rich with nineteenth-century gender conventions, Hazzard addresses the complexities of enslaved relationships. He includes subtle references to female weakness and submission and makes the assumption that women are at fault for any domestic altercations between "husbands and wives." Yet despite his efforts to control the interactions between couples, Hazzard neglects to explain *how* he prevents such abuse from taking place, which suggests that at least in some cases the slaves sorted out disputes among themselves.

In addition to the strict rules of conduct like those at West Point Plantation, slaveholders also discussed methods of control, including physical correction, in agricultural journals. In 1855, one planter noted multiple relationships among slaves and offered this advice: "Men should be taught that it is disgraceful to abuse or impose on the weaker sex, and if a man should so far forget and disgrace himself to strike a wom*an*, the wom*en* should be made to give him the hickory and ride him on a rail. The wife; however should never be required to strike her husband, for fear of its unhappy influences over their future respect for and kindness to each other."[38] Note the different responses this planter expected of wives and "wom*en*/wom*an*." These other women could very well have been the breeding partners or other bondwomen on the estate. Clearly, women had little authority to protect themselves from male violence and abuse and they were expected to show deference to enslaved and free men.

An enslaved woman's life in most slave communities included cycles of physical and reproductive labor along with domestic and sexual abuse. Frances Kemble described slave motherhood as "mere breeding, bearing, suckling, and there an end." As for fatherhood, she explained that male slaves had "neither authority, power, responsibility, or charge" over their children.[39] As discussed in chapter 3, marriage did not represent a formal union on her husband's plantations. For example, these unions were "utterly ignored" by the overseer Mr. King. "If he heard of any disagreement between a [slave] man and woman calling themselves married," King immediately bestowed "them in 'marriage' on other parties, *whether they chose it or not.*"[40] Such acts of interference indicate that King essentially had the authority to "divorce" and "remarry" bondmen and bondwomen as he wished.

How did slaves respond to sexual and physical violence? Contemporary studies indicate that emotional responses to rape include depression, anxiety, anger, guilt, self-blame, sexual dysfunction, nervousness, flashbacks, suicidal feelings, and posttraumatic stress disorder (PTSD). Physical responses to rape include loss of appetite, nausea, stomachache, headache, memory loss, withdrawal, and change in sleep patterns. Researchers recently found that men had slightly different reactions to rape including an increased sense of vulnerability, damaged self-image, and emotional dysfunction.[41] Now imagine how these psychological and physical reactions to violence manifested among enslaved men and women. Also consider that an individual's response probably had an effect on slave family formation and the relationships between slaveholders and slaves. Making these connections allows scholars to cure their "historical blindness" and, as scholar Nell Irvin Painter discusses, move closer "toward a fully loaded cost accounting" of the impact of violence on black families.[42]

The well-known narrative of Harriet Jacobs of North Carolina addresses the impact of physical and sexual violations between slaveholders and the enslaved. In a narrative full of psychological abuse, Jacobs recounts the experiences of a bondman named Luke. Like Jacobs, Luke was a victim of abuse that appears to involve evidence of excessive power, physical, mental, and sexual violence.[43] Luke's owner suffered from a condition that required him to remain bedridden for the final years of his life. During this time, Luke received lashings at his owner's bedside. The slaveholder "would order his attendant to bare his back, and kneel beside the couch, while he whipped him till his strength was exhausted." Because these whippings were so frequent, Jacobs explained, "Some days he [Luke] was not allowed to wear any thing but his shirt, in order to be in readiness to be flogged." Knowing that on some occasions Luke's shirt was the only garment he wore suggests that the remainder of his body was left uncovered, exposing his genitals to whoever was in the house or in his owner's room. Jacobs added that his owner was "entirely dependent on Luke's care, and was obliged to be tended like an infant." Moreover, "[a]s he lay there on his bed, a mere disgraced wreck of manhood, he took into his head the strangest freaks of despotism; and if Luke hesitated to submit to his orders, the constable was immediately sent for [to administer a whipping]." Jacobs was so bothered by the interactions between Luke and his owner that she could not relay all the cruelties he suffered: "Some of these freaks were of a nature too filthy to be repeated." Harriet Jacobs lived with the memory of Luke "chained to the bedside of this cruel and disgusting wretch" until years later when she ran into him as a fugitive slave.[44] Even though Luke was not used as a breeder and we know nothing about his family, it is clear that this slaveholder exploited Luke for his own sadistic pleasure.

Being pregnant or giving birth gave some bondpeople value and/or protection from continued acts of abuse. A former slave on the Butler plantation noted that "tho' we no able to work, we make little niggers for massa." Old Sackey, another Butler slave, warned Kemble that the women's health on the rice plantation failed because of overwork, before, during, and after pregnancy. "[S]o many of the women have falling of the womb and weakness in the back," Kemble explained, "and if he [the overseer] continued on the estate, he would have utterly destroyed all the breeding women."[45] Other slaves understood the value of childbearing mothers, as one recollected that her aunt "was er breeder 'oman en brought in chillun ev'y twelve month' jes' lak a cow bringin' in a calf."[46]

Slaveholders, although for different reasons than bondpeople, also understood the importance of breeding, and they developed strategies to encourage procreation. As a result, an informal system of rewards and punishments evolved on plantations where breeding occurred. Slaveholders and other men of power manipulated slaves into participating in sexual intercourse by offering slaves various incentives.[47] Large slave families in Wilkes County, for example, were offered the luxury of a two-room cabin instead of the standard one-room holding. Glynn County slaveholders, however, offered more extensive rewards. For example, William W. Hazzard of West Point Plantation gave one cow to families who had six children. "When the family increases to ten *living* children," he explained, "I require no other labour from the mother than to attend to her children."[48] Notice that he made no mention of the father, further emphasizing the challenge and the pressures slaves faced when attempting to maintain a cohesive family unit.

Commenting in her personal journal on the breeding of slaves on her husband's estate, Frances Kemble noted that the bondpeople's "lives for the most part [are] those of mere animals, their increase is literally mere animal breeding, to which every encouragement is given, for it adds to the master's livestock and the value of his estate."[49] More important, she was aware that enslaved women in particular had "distinct and perfect knowledge of their value to their owners as property" and, from an enslaved female's perspective, "the more frequently she add[ed] to the number of her master's *livestock* by bringing new slaves into the world, the more claims she [had] upon his consideration and good will."[50]

Overseers such as Roswell King Jr. discussed incentives to prevent bondwomen and bondmen from absconding and to control the behavior of enslaved males in positions of power. He found that the key was to "impress on their minds the advantage of holding property." Part of that property no doubt included having a spouse on the same plantation. King also remarked that "no Negro [male], with a well stocked poultry house, a small crop advancing, a canoe partly finished, or a few tubs unsold, all of which he calculates soon to enjoy, will ever run away."[51] Thus, by satisfying bondmen's desire to attain property and authority, King suggested that his workers (drivers) remained on the plantation and become involved with bondwomen at the same residence. Yet on other occasions, King expressed his dissatisfaction with privileged men's promiscuous behavior. Justifying the discipline of bondmen on his plantation, he stated that "the grand point was to suppress the brutality and licentiousness practiced by the principal men . . . (say the drivers and tradesmen)." Furthermore, he explained that "when an equitable distribution of rewards and punishments is observed, in a short time they will conform to almost every rule that is laid down."[52] Curiously, he was displeased by the "licentiousness" of male drivers and tradesmen even though these men could create additional offspring and thus future laborers with their behavior. Perhaps King's reasoning behind controlling the sexual activity of drivers and tradesmen stemmed from his need to differentiate between *his* *power* and theirs. Regardless of his rationale, slaveholders and overseers interfered with slave relationships frequently.

Even though some members of the slaveholding class disapproved, licentious behavior occurred, and these interactions added to the tension between the enslaved and free. Anna King and several other residents on St. Simons Island, for example, expressed their concern over the behavior of "Young McIntosh [Alexander McIntosh]," the island lighthouse keeper. His conduct was so bad that "he was becoming a confirmed drunkard," and he developed a reputation for hosting wild parties. Anna King learned from her sons that McIntosh "gets negros men & women at his house, drinks & carousing—terrible proceedings (as described by a respectable white man who witnessed it)." These parties, perhaps orgies, were causing the white gentry, including the Kings, "great injury" because some of their slaves attended.[53]

Although some slaveholders enticed slaves into sexual relations with one another, some bondmen and bondwomen openly rejected various acts of sexual coercion. The story of Judy, a slave at Hampton Point Plantation, reflects one woman's dissatisfaction with multiple spouses. According to Kemble, Judy sadly reported that her husband Temba found "another wife" after she went "mad." Judy explained that she once absconded while married to Temba and lived in isolation "for some time," but upon her return discovered that Temba had found himself another companion.[54] A different Judy on the same plantation had a similar testimony. This enslaved female—the wife of Joe and mother of two of his children— discovered that her spouse had another wife named Mary who resided on the rice island. Because it was not uncommon for slaves to work on both rice and Sea Island cotton plantations owned by the same planter, Joe and Judy's story shows how slaveholders used multiple dwellings to encourage multiple spouses.[55]

Separation and Sale

Family separation among enslaved couples and their children occurred regularly. Some of the first writers of the peculiar institution noted that breaking up enslaved families was common during all periods of enslavement in the United States, and this pattern was no different for families in antebellum Georgia's upcountry and lowcountry. Patterns of separation and sale in Wilkes and Glynn Counties reflected the open and closed nature of the communities. Because lowcountry bondpeople tended to live with several generations on the same plantation, they experienced sales and auctions in groups. In upcountry counties, however, slaves were often sold individually, through advertisements in local newspapers, through probate records, or through county clerks to cover debts. Upcountry sales occurred on a regular basis.

The high incidence of family separation in the upcountry was directly related to plantation demographics and the open nature of the enslaved community. Wilkes County residents fostered the development of families between plantations and across farm boundaries and county lines. Because the majority of slaveholders in this piedmont county owned fewer than fifteen slaves, large planters and small farmers alike made regular adjustments to their enslaved labor force, often in response to crop demands. Although the small slaveholding left little room for generations of families to reside on the same property, some were fortunate enough to live with other relatives.

Emma Hurly remembered the day her owner separated her family. "I recollects good when Mr. Seaborn Callaway come over to the place an' bought my Grandma an' some other slaves an' took 'em away," she painfully recalled. "We jest cried an' cried an' Grandma did too," she continued, "Them white folks bought an' sold slaves that way all the time."[56] Hurly was one of few enslaved people in Wilkes County who lived on the same plantation as her grandparents. Mary Ferguson was only thirteen years old when a slaveholder separated her family. She claimed it was "a day I'll never forget." After dinner with her relatives, Ferguson remembered that she felt "lak sumpin was gwineter hapin." "O, I never has forgot dat last dinner wit my folks," she recalled, and when the speculators came to take her away, she "c'menced [to] cryin' an' beggin'," but that did not prevent the separation. Sadly, she stated, "I ain't never seed nor heared tell o' my Ma an' Paw, an' bruthers, an' susters from dat day to dis."[57] Ferguson may have found adopted relatives at a new plantation, but her testimony shows that it was difficult, if not impossible, to fully regain the connections shared among blood relatives after being sold. Esther Brown had vivid memories of the day she and her six siblings went to the auction block. "All of us wuz sold," she explained, and she too remembered that "dey wuz all sold off to diffunt parts of de country, and us never heared from 'em no more." Separation at any age had to be traumatic for children, but what is most heartbreaking about

Brown's testimony is that she was quite young at the time of her sale. Even though her specific age was not mentioned, Brown said, "I wuz so little dat when dey bid me off, dey had to hold me up so folkses could see me."[58]

Not all upcountry slaveholders chose the auction block as the place to separate families. Upon his death, Enoch Callaway allowed the trustees of his estate to transfer thirty-one slaves to his widow Martha. Rather than sending them to the auction block, Callaway's trustees used a different method to divide the estate. They drew names out of a hat and distributed the remaining slaves to local relatives and friends. According to his last will and testament, "[t]he slaves were numbered 1 . . . 10 . . ." on a piece of paper and placed in a hat. The names of all the potential owners "were written on another piece of paper & put in another hat." The trustees then made sure that "the hats were both well shaken, [and] a name was then drawn from the hat capturing the names, then a number was drawn from the hat capturing the numbers: & in that manner continued till all were drawn."[59] Clearly, a method such as this would not ensure that families would remain intact.

The state government played a role in family unity (or lack thereof) in its attempt to control the number of enslaved females and males imported to Georgia. In 1817, Governor William Rabun established a restriction on importing slaves. To control the influx of slaves being brought into Georgia, primarily by planters from South Carolina and Virginia and by travelers migrating through Wilkes County as part of the westward expansion of slavery, Governor Rabun placed an injunction on all imports. He established regulations that required owners to register their enslaved property through local county courts. All registrants had to adhere to the Georgia Penal Code, which stated that "he or she is the lawful owner of the said slave(s), that the said slave(s) are introduced into this state for the sole purpose of being held to service and labor." In addition, each petitioner had to agree not to "sell, transfer, barter, lend, hire, [or] mortgage" the said slave without permission from the court. Thus, all transactions relating to newly purchased slaves required verification from the court. Petitions also defined bondpeople, stating that their "sole purpose" was "being held to service and labor."[60]

The familial status, physical characteristics, occupation, and occasionally the age of bondpeople are revealed in these petitions. The majority (70 percent) of the slaves accounted for during 1818 consisted of children between the ages of ten and seventeen.[61] Such patterns coincide with local newspaper advertisements, confirming the disruption of slave families. Enslaved youth or mothers with young children appeared in county records without other family members, indicating owners' disregard for the physical stability of slave families. On 13 October 1818, for example, Edward Callaway petitioned to bring Phillis, a twenty-one-year-old female, "dark complexion, field hand"; Ned, a boy "age two"; and a "small suckling girl child about seven weeks old" into Wilkes County.[62] According to the petitioner, the infant had to be recorded as a "small suckling child" because the mother refused to provide a name.[63] It is plausible that Phillis resented the fact that she and her children were uprooted and taken to Georgia, away from other relatives, seven weeks after giving birth. Even more likely, this mother probably chose not to provide the name of her newborn to avoid having a written record of her child's enslaved status. For whatever reason, Phillis clearly did not want her youngest child's name listed in the Wilkes County court records, which was probably a way for her to resist and defy slavery.

Nevertheless, it was not the desire of all members of the planter class to separate families. Owners such as Phillepe Thurman sought to maintain the integrity of the slave family by purchasing couples. On 29 June 1820, for example, Thurman submitted a petition for the importation of "Moody, a boy about nineteen years old of yellowish complexion, Polete, his wife sixteen years old of black complexion" along with three other "boys" about the same age, "all field slaves."[64] The recognition of Moody and Polete as husband and wife indicates that Thurman sought to preserve their union. Assuming that the young couple had no children, Thurman also became the legal owner of any progeny procured from this couple, allowing him to increase his labor force without incurring the cost of purchasing additional slaves.[65] John Dodson's petition to bring a woman named Charity, "about 18 years old of Black complexion, and her child Peter, 8 or 9 months old, a Mulatto," into Wilkes County provides evidence of miscegenation. As a "house woman," Charity interacted with the white gentry more than her agricultural counterparts, which suggests the reason she had a "Mulatto" child; it is likely that either Dodson or another former owner raped Charity or she was forced to serve as a concubine. Some enslaved females believed that giving birth to mixed-race children resulted in material privileges not available to others. Regardless of the paternal lineage of her child, Charity entered Wilkes County on 20 April 1821 without any choice about where she could raise her son. Questions about the familial lives of these slaves prior to being uprooted to Wilkes County, as well as their fate after relocation, remain hidden in the historical record, yet it is clear that importation disrupted family unity in a way similar to the disruptions caused by sales.

In an unusual departure from the norm, an entire family of multiple generations was advertised for sale. Looking specifically at this rare family provides further insight. On 27 March 1828, an advertisement appeared in a Wilkes County newspaper for the sale of twenty-eight slaves in three different families. The ad in part read: "Twenty-eight negroes . . . Frank and Sarah, and *their* children, Cinthia, Charlotte, Memory, Mariah, Milsey, and Primus, also Isaac and his wife Polly, and *their* children Garrision, Simeon and January, Bob and Delpha and *their* children, Martha and her young child not named, West, Patsey and her young child not named, Chloe and her children, Caroline, Betsey, Pompy, Sam, Peggy and Clary together with all the stock. . . ."[66] Husbands and wives are clearly noted, as are grandparents. Take, for example, the family of Bob and Delpha. This couple had four children: Martha, West, Patsey, and Chloe. Also, three of *their* children had children of their own: Martha and Patsey each had a "young child not named," while Chloe had six offspring: Caroline, Betsey, Pompy, Sam, Peggy, and Clary. These eight children were the grandchildren of Bob and Delpha. Despite the obvious recognition of enslaved families found in this advertisement, family stability after the sale was not guaranteed.

A sample survey of advertisements in six antebellum Wilkes County newspapers indicates the vulnerability of enslaved families in this region. Of the seventy-three notices of slave sales that contained female slaves, 42 percent (thirty-one) appeared as mother/child listings, 30 percent (twenty-two) contained families or group sales, while the remaining 27 percent (twenty) represented children sold alone.[67] A typical ad with a mother and her offspring stated, "One negro woman by the name of Roxana and two infant children George and Jim."[68] Another mother, Phillis, appeared with "Cezar and Ned her children."[69] Group sales were similar to the following ad placed by Matthew Talbot: "Thirty-seven Likely Negroes sold . . ." or "Eighteen negroes . . . all levied on as the property of Matthew Talbot, deceased," followed by a list naming each slave.[70] Ads with slave children listed alone read as follows: "ONE NEGRO GIRL named Fan, eight or nine years old . . ." or "One negro girl named Rachel nine or ten years of age . . ." or "A negro Girl named Matilda, levied on as the property of Thomas Bolter . . . Fan, Rachel, and Matilda." These ads could have originated from families like Bob and Delpha's family; however, they were not listed with their parents, underscoring that they were indeed sold alone.

Slaveholders in the Georgia lowcountry faced regulations as well. On 6 July 1837, for example, the editors of the *Brunswick Advocate* published the following announcement: "Sales of NEGROES must be at public auction, on the first Tuesday of the month between the usual hours of sale, at the place of public sales in the county where the letters testamentary of Administration or Guardianship, may have been granted, first giving SIXTY DAYS notice thereof, in one of the public gazettes of this State, and at the door of the Court-House, where such sales are to be held."[71] According to these instructions, county residents had to give prior notice of sales and they had to advertise each sale in at least one public newspaper within the state.

Glynn County planters placed ads to *purchase* slaves more frequently than they announced public auctions to *sell* them. Slaveholder Francis M. Scarlett, for example, placed an ad on 15 June 1837 looking to purchase "A GANG of ONE HUNDRED NEGROES, for which the *Cash* will be paid."[72] Exploring sale ads further, it appears that in some cases planters sold small groups of slaves, and in others mothers and their children. B. B. Gowen of Glynn County placed an ad for an "Executor's Sale" to settle the estate of Elizabeth Harrison by selling "THREE NEGROES, Jim, Tamer, and Albert."[73] Likewise, John Couper Jr. advertised the sale of "three Negroes" on 30 November 1837.[74] Similar to Wilkes County, Glynn County planters sold mothers and children. In a "Sheriff's Sale," advertised from 9 February 1839 through 4 May 1839, Camden County Sheriff William Baker advertised "LUCY and her four children."[75] Camden County bordered Glynn County, and it was common practice for planters to advertise in other state and local newspapers.[76] In fact, James Piles placed an ad in the *Darien Gazette* on 13 February 1821 for the sale of eleven Glynn County slaves and eighty acres of land.[77]

The story of Oney exemplifies the effect that separation had on husbands and wives in Glynn County. According to Frances Kemble, Oney's husband "had gone away from her for four years" because the former overseer decided to switch occupations by going into "slave driving."[78] "He [Mr. King] carried her better half . . . away with him," lamented Kemble, "and she never expects to see him again."[79] When enslaved couples were separated, they assumed the worst—that they would never see each other again. Although Kemble explained that Oney's husband was gone for four years, Oney probably told herself he was gone forever.

Familial patterns at Kelvin Grove Plantation were not as stable as those at Retreat Plantation because sales uprooted several enslaved families.[80] Kelvin Grove's slave population gradually declined from ninety bondpeople in 1841 to eighty-one in 1853 and to sixty-two in 1860.[81] On 5 June 1840, owner Benjamin F. Cater sold twenty-six slaves to four different planters (of which only two resided in Glynn County) to pay $6,830 of debts. Thus, on this date alone, the owner uprooted a portion of the population, and almost certainly several families, and sent them to live with new owners. Although the inventory contains the names of all twenty-six bondpeople, the total enslaved population on the date of the sale (5 June 1840) is unknown. A sale of this magnitude underscores the instability of slave families on this estate.

The 1859 Butler plantation sale is probably the best description of a slave auction. One reporter from the *New York Tribune* who attended the auction wrote about the event in great detail, and even though some historians question the accuracy of his report, it serves as a good portrait of slave sales.[82] The auction was referred to as the "Great Auction Sale of Slaves" and was held in Savannah, Georgia, on 2 and 3 March 1859; it marked the largest single slave auction in U.S. history.[83] What is especially interesting about this auction of 436 enslaved women and men is that they all belonged to a single family—the Butler family of Glynn County, Georgia. Apparently, Butler lost his money during the "great crash of 1857–58" and was left with no other recourse but to sell all his chattel property.[84] Joseph Bryan, the manager of the sale, had special instructions to maintain slave family units because "the breaking up of an old family estate is so uncommon an occurrence that the affair was regarded with unusual interest."[85] However, one must consider how the auctioneer defined "family." One witness of the sale noted that "a man and his wife were called a 'family,' their parents and kindred were not taken into account; the man and wife might be sold to the pine woods of North Carolina, their brothers and sisters be scattered throughout the cotton fields of Alabama and the rice swamps of Louisiana, while the parents might be left on the old plantation to wear out their weary lives in heavy grief, and lay their fields in far-off graves over which their children never weep."[86] Thus, "family" as defined by the auctioneer did not equal the same "family" for the enslaved.

It took days to transport the 436 slaves to Savannah from McIntosh and Glynn Counties, and when they arrived, the auctioneer placed them in horse stables at the Ten Broeck racecourse. Prospective buyers had the opportunity to view the slaves in the days leading up to the sale. The *Tribune* writer described the scene: "The Negroes were examined with as little consideration as if they had been brutes indeed; the buyers pulling their mouths open to see their teeth, pinching their limbs to find how muscular they were, walking them up and down to detect any signs of lameness, making them stoop and bend in different ways that they might be certain there was no concealed rupture or wound; and in addition to all this treatment, asking them scores of questions relative to their qualifications and accomplishments."[87] One woman named Sally caught the attention of a few bystanders. A man interested in her noted that she was the wife of "shoemaker Bill." As he examined her, he noticed that she was a "big strapping gal, and can do a heap o' work." Even so, he decided to pass and move on to the next slave because, Major Butler said, "it's been five years since she had any children."[88] This suggests that planters and buyers alike valued female slaves for their reproductive ability. Of course, the capacity to bear children, although a valuable "asset" in the marketplace, added to the burdens borne by enslaved females in ways unknown to males.

The story of Daphney and Primus exemplifies one of the many challenges faced by enslaved parents. Daphney, Primus, and their three-year-old daughter Dido stepped up to the auction block and caused a small controversy. Apparently, Daphney had wrapped herself in a blanket, which prevented potential buyers from thoroughly examining her limbs. "What's the matter with that gal? Has she got a headache?" one person asked. "Who is going to bid on that nigger, if you keep her covered up," another added. But when they finally took the blanket off, the bidders were surprised to find a three-week-old infant nestled against her chest. Writing about this incident, the *Tribune* reporter made an appeal to female readers. "Since her confinement," he noted, she had done an extensive amount of traveling:

> Daphney had traveled from the plantation to Savannah, where she had been kept in a shed for six days. On the sixth or seventh day after her sickness, she had left her bed, taken a railroad journey across the country to the shambles, was there exposed for six days to the questionings and insults of the Negro speculators, and then on the fifteenth day after her confinement was put up on the block, with her husband and her other child, and with her new-born baby in her arms, sold to the highest bidder.[89]

One cannot assume that Daphney's "sickness" was the birth of her child, but because she left her home plantation when the baby was less than one week old, it is plausible that she was still recovering from childbirth. Of course, the travels she endured and the conditions in which she stayed during her trip to the auction block, not to mention the stress of being separated from her extended family, would likely make Daphney more susceptible to illness.

Some enslaved women had health issues unrelated to pregnancy. Molly caused quite a stir among potential buyers. When it was her turn to step up on the auction block, the auctioneer announced that "Molly insisted that she was lame in her left foot," but he was not convinced of it, so he brought a physician to examine her. "Molly was put through her paces, and compelled to trot up and down along the stage," the reporter stated, but her "left foot *would* be lame." The reporter does not indicate why Molly was "complaining" about her left foot or why she resisted her sale. But one can only imagine the myriad of reasons she might have feigned an injury. Perhaps Molly had a loved one that was already sold to another owner and she sought to discourage all other potential masters from purchasing her. Or maybe Molly knew she could remain with the Butler family if the sale was unsuccessful. She may have feared moving to an unfamiliar plantation community and tried to do all she could to stay in a physical environment to which she had grown accustomed. Many bystanders must have thought she was "shamming" her injury because Molly was indeed sold on that day.[90]

Despite the ample evidence of family separation, there were slave-holders in upcountry and lowcountry Georgia who, like Butler and Thurman, did all they could to maintain the familial ties of bondwomen and bondmen, especially in their wills.

On 13 June 1856, Stephen G. Pettus of Wilkes County willed "George my carriage driver & his wife Charlotte & *their* five children, Betsy, George, Matilda, Jack, & Susan" to his daughter along with $20,000.[91] Interestingly, Pettus mentioned George's occupation but did not provide information regarding Charlotte's work responsibilities. It is possible that he deliberately chose not to list Charlotte with an occupation because she had recently given birth to one of her five children, or because Pettus felt that her occupation was not worth noting. Pettus also willed Alek the "brick mason" and his wife Nancy "& *her* child Alek [Jr.]" to his daughter. Even though it was customary to define slave offspring based on the status of their mothers, Pettus chose to acknowledge George and Charlotte's children as "their children," but Alek [Sr.] and Nancy's son as "her child." It is likely that there was a paternal connection between the two Aleks; however, it is also likely that Pettus felt some sense of obligation based on something other than paternity.[92]

Similarly, Margaret Wylly of Glynn County tried to maintain enslaved family ties in her last will and testament. On 23 December 1846, she bequeathed "the following family" to Alexander William Wylly: "Harry [father], Hannah [mother], and *her* children James and MaryAnn."[93] She also gave "Martha and her children [not named]" to her son, sons-in-law, and daughters "should they marry." She made no indication as to how Martha and her children would function under multiple ownership, but it was clear that her daughters were to receive their services if they married. Wylly willed other enslaved individuals to her relatives and friends, but she did not mention them by name. Instead, she gave these beneficiaries "one fifth part of the Negro slaves" or "two fifths of the Negro slaves."[94] Although there is no extant documentation indicating the total number of slaves Wylly owned besides Harry, Hannah, Martha, and their children, the 1850 census lists fifty-three slaves in her possession.[95] By recognizing slave families in their wills, planters allowed certain families to be sold as a unit, but they could not always guarantee that they would remain together.

A significant number of slaveholders made their decisions about family unity using a narrowed definition of "family" that was based on the age of the slave children. Because they were primarily concerned with young children, slaveholders' decisions about which relatives should remain together created partial "families" that disrupted the bondperson's complete family (as defined by the bondperson). Wylie Hill of Wilkes County, for example, stipulated in his will that "Edward and his wife Sarah and *their* two youngest children" and "Jacob and his wife Grace and *their* youngest children" remain in possession of his wife.[96] Such instructions suggest that these couples had other older offspring; because those willed were the "youngest children," Hill and Pettus made an effort to keep at least them with their parents, yet likely disrupted the parents' relationship with their other children. Older children had no guarantee of remaining with their parents.

Anna Page King tormented herself over the division of her estate and did all she could to make sure her children would be satisfied with her decisions, only to find that it was difficult to please all of them. Apparently, her daughter Hannah (whom she referred to as "Tootee") was so unhappy with her mother's arrangements that she sent back one of the slaves because the division separated some of the enslaved families. In a letter to her daughter Hannah, Anna King made the following remarks: "I am very sorry you sent back little Bell. I am certain you must miss her services small as they were. I am sorry you sent her back—As regards the rest of that family my dear Tootee I am sorry to perceive that you consider the matter in the light you do . . . . I did not at the time consider that the little I have should be held together."[97] Anna King explained her rationale:

> I gave you Middleton from the time he was a child—but did not think it necessary I should give you a deed of him—I will do so now if you prefer it. I would prefer consulting with your Father before giving up all right to Christiann[,] her child & future children. I now tell you in good earnest. That I considered her as yours & Nora as Annas [Anna Rebecca Couper, Hannah's daughter,]—her future children as yours [.] Clementine must remain with me as long as your Father & I live—Bell I want for Georgia

[Georgia Page King]. . . . You recollect I made Georgia a promise of giving her Rhina—Florence [Florence Barclay King] Maria—& Appy [Virginia Lord King] Ellen. They have nothing to show for them—neither will they have. They must [be] content if I can give them each a maid Georgia has long since relinquished R[hina] & Annie—Flora claims only Tilla—& Appy claims no one of Ellens family. Christiann is yours as soon as you say so. As long as she stays here she is virtually yours—for she is put aside to sew for you alone. Whilst you were with me I required only that she should wait at table on Sundays. I do not wish to give you the papers for C[hristiann] until I speak to your father. Especially as I gave you Middleton without his knowing any thing about it. The only thing you can object to in this may be the short delay. As there is no doubt he will approve still the compliment is due him—and now Tootee let this subject be dropt—you are to understand distinctly that M[iddleton] is yours & C[hristiann] & her child as soon as you "say send her to me."[98]

The manner in which King and her daughter discussed the fate of their enslaved property emphasized the proper documentation that was needed and clarified the type of work bondpeople would be expected to perform and the nature of enslaved family ties. Clearly, Anna King thought her decisions were sound, but her daughter felt otherwise and wanted to settle this prior to her mother's death.

Often when a planter died, the estate was divided between the living beneficiaries. However, if a slaveholder had several residences, as was the case with many large planters, slaves would still be considered the property of the planter yet might be reassigned to another of the owner's plantations.[99] Alexander Pope Sr., one of the wealthiest slave owners in Wilkes County, tried to avoid this by ordering in his will that "Gus and his wife are to remain on the river place but to be accounted for as part of my estate."[100] Pope had more than one plantation, and he wanted this slave couple to remain on a specifically designated property. Although Pope made careful instructions for this couple, his brother John H. Pope provided a female slave named Sarah with an unusual privilege. His will reads: "Sarah be allowed to choose either my son John or William Henry for her master and the one she does not choose is to take old man Juba and take care of them respectively." A few items later, he clearly changes his mind, but allows her to make another choice: "It is my will that my brother William H. Pope take my old woman Sarah if she does not wish to go to Florida." Perhaps John Pope knew that his son John Jr. had plans to move to Florida; therefore, it was his desire to let Sarah stay with his brother William in Wilkes County if that was her "choice."[101]

Some owners preferred to keep families intact. In her will dated 17 April 1857, Anna Page King requested that all her children "who may be living at the time of my death" receive "equal rights to be divided between them." She continued stating that her children should "share and share alike as tenants in common and not as joint tenants."[102] According to property law, "tenants in common are co-owners of real property that are regarded by the law as each owning separate and distinct shares which may differ in size. Upon death the share of a tenant in common does not pass directly to the survivor or survivors but is instead passed through inheritance as directed in the deceased's will. Each tenant in common has unrestricted rights of access to the property. Each tenant in common can petition for and secure a partition of the property at any time. This form of ownership is common where the co-owners are not married or have contributed different amounts in the acquisition of the property."[103] In this case, joint tenancy meant that if one of the King children died, then that child's assets (slaves) would be given to his or her surviving siblings. Those who owned property as "tenants in common" had the ability to pass the ownership of their property (slaves) to his or her heirs. It is clear that King wanted her children to have their ownership of the slave property and be able to pass it on to their heirs. Preceding these instructions, King itemized and divided 133 enslaved workers among her eight living children. Within the list of property, King made special instructions to keep slaves in family units.[104] Therefore, to guarantee family unity, she listed each slave, their respective value, and the names of their relatives. Eight of her children received slaves; the other two were deceased at the time of her death.[105] She also tried to maintain family ties with the exception of the thirty-three individual slaves who appear on the list not attached to a family unit.

Wilkes County slaveholder Middleton Pope went one step further than King in attempting to give his bondpeople choices in their placement after his death. In addition to distributing slaves among his children, Pope enabled a young boy named "Reuben to select to *which* of children he will belong to" upon Pope's death.[106] Perhaps the open nature of slavery in this region encouraged Wilkes County slaveholders to grant their slaves choices in their probate records. After dividing his enslaved property among his wife and children, another upcountry slave owner, Garland Wingfield, stated in his will that "[i]f any of my negroes are dissatisfied with the division I make of them, it is my will and desire that such negro or negroes be appraised by their desired men & such negro or negroes be sold by my Executrix to such persons."[107] Wingfield's human property benefited from the opportunity to select new owners, granting them certain privileges and choices, possibly even allowing families or couples to remain together. Giving such choices to enslaved women and men was highly unusual because they rarely had the opportunity to make decisions about their fate, treatment, or place of residence.

In addition to affording slaves a modicum of choice in their lives, some slaveholders like Hill left specific instructions regarding the maintenance of slave families:

> Now my dear wife I have left old man Edward to you during your natural life. I want him treated well and never to be put out under an overseer. I wish for him to do any thing he can for you, but not to be treated ill by anybody, and let him have time to make him a little crop, and land convenient for him to tend, he has been a faithful slave to me, and I want him favored in his old age. I should have left him to have served nobody but I have seen the evil of it they have come to suffer, and when it is the will of God to take you, I wish for him and his wife to go and live with any one of my children that they wish to, that will treat them well, let them have their choice, he has helped me to get what I have got.[108]

This passage exemplifies Hill's affection and concern for a loyal member of his enslaved property.[109] Not only does he stipulate that Edward should be "treated well" by his wife, but Hill also requested that he be equally well treated by his new owner, one of Hill's children. Hill implies that by eliminating the authority of an overseer, Edward and his wife could escape mistreatment and have some governing power over their lives. In fact, willing them to one of his children probably ensured that these elderly slaves would receive adequate treatment for the remainder of their lives. In addition, by giving Edward and his wife some choice about which of Hill's children to live with, Hill may have given them a chance to reunite with other family members who might be living there already. Despite these provisions, Hill expressed some remorse because he did not free the pair. However, he immediately justified this decision, stating that he spared this couple of "the evil of it [manumission] they [slaves] have come to suffer [when freed]."[110] In other words, Edward and his wife would receive better care if they remained with one of Hill's children as opposed to being free in a slave society. Still, one wonders about Edward's wife; was she a "faithful servant" as well, or did she simply receive privileges because she was Edward's mate?

Resistance

Enslaved women and men in Glynn and Wilkes Counties were not simply victims of their oppression; they often did all they could to defy the power of those who kept them in bondage, and it helped if their owners expressed concern for their familial ties. However, many resisted their enslavement by openly defying their slaveholders. Gendered evidence of resistance surfaces in the historical record and is apparent in their daily lives. Recall the spiritual resistance of Sinda on St. Simons Island. Her religious influence over fellow bondwomen and men motivated them to go on strike—"they refused to work" for a period long enough to threaten the success of the rice and cotton crops in 1839. Sinda was so influential that the lash even lost "its prevailing authority" and the overseer "acquiesced in their determination not to work."[111] Other bondwomen acted alone. Judy, also from St. Simons Island, did her best to refuse the sexual advances of her overseer, but to no avail; she was banished to a remote swamp for her offense. Although Sinda's and Judy's acts of resistance involved considerably different strategies, the two had similar goals: to circumvent their oppression. The most common form of resistance, however, was running away.

In a recent publication on slave resistance in the United States from 1790 to 1860, John Hope Franklin and Loren Schweninger found gender differences among runaways. They noted that "the great majority of runaways were young men in their teens and twenties."[112] Their findings concur with other studies of gendered patterns of resistance; therefore it is not surprising that similar patterns occurred in the Georgia upcountry and lowcountry. Like other parts of the South, runaway slave advertisements in Wilkes and Glynn predominantly involved males.

William, Nace, Jeffrey, Joe, Peter, Hampton, Allen, Jacob, Guy, and Osborne all absconded from their Wilkes County farms or plantations during the antebellum period. Some owners did not believe that these men developed the idea of absconding on their own; instead they believed that a white male "scoundrel" stole them or enticed them to flee. When the enslaved man William left James Whatley's plantation in February of 1828, for example, Whatley stated that although "[h]e may be in the Eastern part of Wilkes County, where he is well acquainted," it is more likely that William was "carried away by some white man."[113] Similarly, B. B. Moore advertised to "Stop the Scoundrel" who stole two enslaved boys from him in 1842. Certain of the thief's identity, Moore added that the two boys might "have been taken by a man named JOSEPH DAVIS." He then added a description of the alleged thief: a "stout built, about thirty years of age, dark hair, blue eyes, and fair skin—a Carpenter by trade."[114] It appears that any "suspicious white male" who interacted frequently with the enslaved became a suspect. Casey, a white man accused of stealing Jacob from his owner, received the same amount of print as the runaway Jacob. Described as someone who lived in the area "for some time past," Casey "was seen in town some short time ago, mixing and associating with negroes . . . about forty five years of age, has but one eye . . . a blacksmith by trade."[115] Evidently, some slaveholders made connections with enslaved tradesmen and incidences of running away.[116]

In Glynn County, R. Towson Jr. searched for his runaway blacksmith named Thomas. On 24 March 1839, Towson made the following statement in his advertisement: "[Thomas] is a blacksmith by trade, and has doubtless procured free papers from some person, and has gone to work at that business in either in South Carolina or Georgia." More likely, he added, Thomas was probably "lurking about Savannah, as I understand he engaged in the steamboat 'Thorn.'"[117] Whether they sought work on a steamboat or on a canal, the primary objectives of runaways were clear: they wanted their freedom and they wanted to locate relatives. Skilled slaves working on the Brunswick Canal may have been visited by their fugitive relatives, as was the case with Dick and Ned. Francis Scarlett placed an ad in the *Brunswick Advocate* for this pair, noting that "both have relatives on the Brunswick Canal [and] it is very likely they may be in the vicinity."[118]

Absconding to locate loved ones represented a primary factor in the decision to run away. Nace and Jeffrey left Wilkes County in 1826 in hopes of reaching Alabama. According to their owner, Abner Wellborn, the pair left during the Christmas holidays, a time when many of the geographic restrictions were waived due to end-of-year harvest festivals and religious ceremonies. However, Nace "has runaway heretofore" Wellborn noted, and he lived in Alabama as a "freeman." Along with his cohort's earlier success in reaching Alabama, Jeffrey also had plenty of reason to escape to that locale because his mother lived there and it is likely that this twenty-one or twenty-two-year-old wanted to reunite with her. Wellborn emphasized that "it is probable that both He and Nace are gone to that state."[119] Several other fugitives absconded in search of lost relatives or to a previous place of residence.

A ten-dollar reward was issued for Guy, who left his owner's plantation in Wilkes County hoping to reach Charleston, South Carolina. The owner believed Charleston was Guy's destination because "he was brought from that place years ago."[120] Enslaved females also ran away to reunite with their relatives. Recall the notice for Mariah and Beck, a mother-and-daughter duo known for their skilled seamstress work in Wilkes County, who fled to search for relatives in Augusta, Georgia, and Columbia, South Carolina.[121]

Rather than travel in pairs like Mariah and Beck, Bob, a fugitive from Glynn County, fled with Cato, Ona, and July in search of his wife who lived "at Dr. West's place on Cat-head Creek near Darien." Apparently Bob and his wife had been apart for two years. However, James G. Pepper, the owner of these fugitives, could not understand any other reason why they would abscond because all "had [not] received an angry word or stroke for the last ten months . . . had performed their work faithfully and appeared perfectly satisfied to the night of their departure."[122] Other lowcounty fugitives chose Savannah as their final destination, perhaps because they believed an urban environment would be an ideal place to hide and find work. Some like "Jacob, commonly called Gold," went to this urban locale because "[h]e was purchased near Savannah, and is probably making [his way to] that place."[123] Three other men, Larkin, Dick, and Cato, the latter two described as "African by birth," left Waverly Plantation and all were "well acquainted in and about Savannah."[124] Will, a twenty-five-year-old enslaved male who "was raised in Glynn county" by a man referred to as "Grant" (possibly Hugh Fraser Grant) and had a previous owner in Savannah, probably made "his way back to one of those places."[125]

Summary

Although the pressures of forced breeding/rape marked part of their everyday lives, bondpeople were hardly ever free from their owner's interference in their relationships. Slaveholders constantly exercised their authority over these interactions and expressed their patriarchy by establishing strict rules of conduct and separating families through sales, auctions, and estate divisions. But slaves challenged these boundaries when they ran away or otherwise attempted to reunite with other family members; even if they were not always successful, enslaved males and females sought to resist their situations and break free from slavery's yoke.

5 "For the Current Year": The Informal Economy and Slave Hiring

The hired hand is not the shepherd who owns the sheep. So when he sees the wolf coming, he abandons the sheep and runs away.

—John 10:12 NIV

At a provisions store in the coastal town of Darien, Georgia, a bondman named Quash and a shopkeeper named Mr. Harmon argued about the price of various goods. Quash had traveled to Darien from one of the Butler plantations to sell his chickens and purchase a calico dress for his wife. When he measured ten yards of cloth and gave Mr. Harmon a "ten-cent piece for each yard," an argument quickly ensued. "There's your money, boss," Quash said. "Oh, no," replied Harmon after counting the money. "That dress comes to a dollar and a quarter." Quash replied, "Well dere it is, cordin' to the way you count de ten-cent pieces when you pay us for our chicken and our eggs." Determined to purchase a dress for his wife at a fair price, Quash tried to negotiate the cost. In the end, Mr. Harmon allowed him to take the material, but Quash was instructed "to come back with some more chickens and eggs."[1]

Bondmen and bondwomen throughout Georgia and elsewhere sought to make their lives more comfortable, and some, like Quash, were fortunate to buy, sell, and trade goods in exchange for food and clothing to share with their families. Bondpeople in counties such as Wilkes and Glynn participated directly and indirectly in market-related economic activities from the colonial period through Emancipation in 1865. Such undertakings involved exchanging, bartering, and trading money, goods, and various services. Direct market activities are transactions that benefited slaves. Indirect market activities, such as the hiring out of slaves, involved exchanges in which slaves served as the central component of a transaction but remained on the periphery in terms of payments and/or benefits. Examples of the informal slave economy and incidences of hiring offer two opportunities to study the direct and indirect market-related undertakings of the enslaved because both show them as producer and consumer in environments beyond their slaveholders' direct supervision.

Enslaved men and women with provision grounds or small gardens often sold the goods they produced at local markets and received financial compensation or traded items of equivalent value for these goods. Those involved in hiring contracts were also paid for their services; however, they rarely received direct financial compensation for their labor. By comparing these two types of economies, this chapter explores the conditions, patterns, and circumstances involving labor through the "secondary institutions" of the informal economy and hiring. Examining labor in these settings allows for a deeper understanding of how the situations bondpeople endured and the restrictions placed on their economic activities affected not only bondpeople but also their families.

"Paid" Labor

Both the informal economy and slave hiring functioned as secondary institutions within the institution of slavery, and both had a significant impact on the development of enslaved families. The informal economy is probably the most useful example of an economic activity that directly benefited enslaved families; these activities also taught slaves how to place values on items and provided a means to understand the monetary value of certain goods. By definition, the informal economy represented any transaction that involved selling, trading, or bartering goods produced *by* the enslaved on their own time for *their* use and consumption. In return, producers exchanged their goods for money and/or items such as food, clothing, blankets, and other giftware. Historians refer to such interactions as the "informal," "clandestine," or "illicit" economy; these terms are often used interchangeably.[2]

The informal economy enabled slaves to purchase and trade material possessions for the benefit of their families. By traveling to the marketplace or receiving money from their owners, bondwomen and bondmen used these transactions to create a more comfortable environment for themselves. But access to the informal economy was by no means equally available to all bondpeople. Participation in the informal economy in Glynn County, for example, was reserved for those bondpeople with mobility or special skills. Once given permission to sell their wares, these privileged bondpeople shared their proceeds with their families, giving them benefits unknown to those without permission to visit local markets. Wilkes County bondwomen and bondmen, on the other hand, had greater access to an informal economy because of their ability to travel across plantation boundaries. Despite the benefits to enslaved families from this, it was nevertheless difficult to create cohesive families because of the frequency of hiring and the high incidence of abroad relationships.

Gender played a prominent role in the accessibility to these markets. Typically, men had more avenues to participate in informal economies because of their monopoly of artisan work and greater access to geographic mobility. Planters provided passes to men for conjugal visits, for trips to the market, and for running errands. Several enslaved men on St. Simons Island operated as boatmen as they ferried their owners around the regional estuaries. Travel of this nature was so common in Glynn County that many enslaved men lost their lives on the waterways. For example, five "Negro" boatmen drowned on 14 September 1824 along with their owner Raymond Demere of St. Simons Island during a return trip from Darien; it is likely that these men had been at the market.[3] When Emily Burke visited the South, she witnessed boatmen throughout Georgia "engaged in the transportation of goods and produce of all kinds" that they transported "up and down the rivers."[4]

Enslaved women, on the other hand, spent most of their time in the fields and homes of their owners and found it difficult to acquire a pass, let alone receive permission to travel—unless, as noted in chapter 3, they were accompanying the planter family on vacations, running errands, or temporarily hired out to work for another slaveholder. Bondwomen discovered ways to further utilize their skills and access the informal economy from within the property's boundaries by raising chickens, cultivating corn, churning butter, and producing honey and other items. Some sold their produce for small fees to fellow bondpeople or their owners, even when they did not have permission to trade these goods at local markets; others used them for personal consumption, thus improving their family's diet.[5] "Mom Betty," a nonagricultural laborer owned by the Troup family of Glynn County, made butter and even though "the quality of the butter was not equal" to that of the neighboring planters, she "found ready purchasers in Darien."[6] That the Troups allowed Mom Betty to travel to Darien shows that this enslaved woman had special privileges.

Although hiring required bondpeople to travel and work away from their home plantations, allowing access to the informal economy rarely benefited them directly. Hiring is defined as a written agreement between two parties—the slave owner and the person who hired the enslaved worker for a contracted period of time (usually one year, but sometimes as short as one day, week, or month). This definition does not include the practice of self-hire, from which enslaved men and women benefited from the fruits of their labor by hiring *themselves* out for wages during their "spare time." The practice of self-hire is deliberately omitted from this discussion because this practice was not common in either region until the Civil War, after which it became the basis of post-Reconstruction work relations.[7]

Through hiring contracts, a slave owner charged the renter a fee (or rate) for the use of his or her enslaved workers, while the renter was responsible for their food, clothing, and shelter. In some cases, as with the informal economy, hiring involved price negotiation brokered through a middle person or agent, and even though prices sometimes reflected larger market patterns, there were significant differences between the two economic institutions. The informal slave economy was *planter-influenced* in that some bondpeople received payment from their owners and/or could travel to the marketplace on a regular basis. Hiring, on the other hand, represented a *planter-controlled* activity in which the enslaved had no role in the decision-making process.[8] The informal economy did not abide by a written contract; instead, it was supported by planters who provided provision grounds to their laborers, allowing them to work under their own discretion. Hired-out bondwomen and bondmen in Wilkes and Glynn Counties entered a system that transferred their supervision to a temporary employer or a nominal owner for a specified duration. The informal economy had the opposite effect in that it enabled bondpeople a measure of independence because they worked for themselves. Those that could access it gained some control over their material lives, and possibly the strength, hope, faith, and pride to endure the hardships of slavery. From the slaveholder's perspective, the informal economy helped some become economically efficient. For the enslaved, the informal economy provided mobility through their travel to marketplaces, where they purchased, sold, or traded goods and money. At the market, bondwomen and bondmen escaped the rigors of agricultural and nonagricultural labor.

Wilkes and Glynn bondpeople participated in an informal economy and in hiring, but the nature of each economic community influenced the frequency and likelihood of these undertakings. Enslaved men and women residing in Glynn County generally had several opportunities to participate in an informal economy because their owners allowed them to use their own time and provided them with gardens (i.e., provision grounds). Because coastal plantations operated under the task system and the bondpeople already cultivated secondary crops for personal consumption, slaveholders found that the informal economy encouraged enslaved laborers to complete their tasks with haste so they could work for themselves. Wilkes County enslaved laborers lived in a community that frequently denied such independence. Their labor system was open; therefore, upcountry bondpeople often participated in communal work activities (working socials), which explains the widespread evidence of hiring and relatively infrequent documentation of an informal economy in this region. Despite such trends, Emily Burke was impressed with the way bondpeople on one Georgia plantation "took . . . charge . . . and carried to the market the cotton and the other products." They also "attended to the sale of them, and made all the purchases for the whole plantation, and all the slaves looked so happy and contented";[9] in contrast to other enslaved workers in the area, these bondpeople clearly left their plantation and were able to travel, entrusted with money, to the local market.

Legislation was another obstacle to independent, informal economic activities. The Georgia slave codes contained legislation that attempted to restrict or curtail the economic activities of the enslaved as early as 1765. Laws relating to independent economic activities among slaves appeared in general state legislation, patrol regulations, and city ordinances with clauses that aimed to limit slave geographic mobility. On 18 November 1765, for example, members of the General Assembly passed "[a]n Act for the establishing and regulating patrols, and from preventing any person from purchasing provisions or any other commodities from selling such to any slave, unless such slaves shall produce a ticket from his or her owner, manager, or employer."[10] Even if a bondwoman or bondman produced provisions on their own time, this act stipulated that "masters, managers, or employers" had to provide consent for the sale of these goods by signing a ticket or license. From this perspective, the independent enslaved economy might be more appropriately termed a dependent economy, but such conclusions imply that bondpeople actually, and always, sought the permission of their "masters, managers, or employers." Secondary literature from the West Indies and other U.S.

regions suggests that it was common for slaves to participate in an under-ground market where they traded goods outside of their supervisors' realm of control and without their permission, as well as in an informal economy with their supervisors' permission.[11]

Bondmen and bondwomen, along with free persons of color, *tried* to involve themselves in an independent economy in this region despite local legislation. The town ordinances for Washington, the commercial center of Wilkes County, addressed market-related activities among slaves and free blacks. In 1822, under legislative act 8, the board of commissioners mandated that slaves and free persons of color "within the corporate limits" obtain permission to sell their wares. Specifically, this legislation required that retailers obtain a license for liquor sales (free people of color only) at a "rate not exceeding five dollars for one year" and they were also subject to taxes. The tax could not exceed "five dollars for each day, on pedlars [sic] and itinerant traders."[12] The board also placed restrictions on the items sold. "Licenses at the rate of four dollars per year" appeared in section XLIII for the sale of "any cake, bread, cheese, beer, cider, oysters, or [?] victuals" in "any place within the corporate limits except in a house occupied by a white person."[13] Restrictions and fees appeared on items such as jewelry, dry goods, leather, groceries, tobacco, iron, hardware, and clothing, but most of this legislation addressed activities of free blacks. Ordinances pertaining to the enslaved focused on hiring contracts.

The Georgia slave codes of the colonial period offer no indication that planters hired out their slaves, but one cannot assume that this practice did not occur. By the antebellum period, hiring was quite common in Georgia. In fact, it was so common that county officials enacted statutes preventing slaves from hiring out *themselves*. Self-hire was not permissible in Wilkes County; the city ordinance for nearby Washington stated, "No slave within the Corporate limits shall hire his own time from his master, or have the use of his own time therein by virtue of any contract made with his master out of these limits."[14] This legislation prevented slaves from initiating or administrating their own contracts. In addition to limiting slaves' roles in these transactions, the ordinance had similar terms for people of color. "No colored person shall be considered as a hired or house servant within the meaning of this ordinance, when the person to whom he is such *pretended* servant exacts only a partial or casual or nominal service from him."[15] In other words, these individuals must be employed full-time and, more important, under direct supervision. In addition to these terms, "[a]ny slave residing within the corporate limits and not under the control of some white person therein, or any free person of color residing therein who shall not have a Guardian in the county may *respectively* be treated as runaways."[16] Based on this legislation, it is clear that whites controlled hiring practices for the enslaved and the free.

Lowcountry Informal Economy

Despite the legislative attempts to curtail economic activities between various groups, some lowcountry bondwomen and bondmen found support from planters and their overseers. W. W. Hazzard, owner of West Point Plantation on St. Simons Island, noted that he "encouraged industry" among his slaves by allowing everyone "a task of ground, and a half task for each child capable of working." In addition, he gave them "one Saturday to prepare, and another to plant their ground," and provided a mule and plow when they could be spared. He stressed their independence in these activities, allowing them to "manage it their own way, and the entire produce is appropriated to their own purposes." They also had the opportunity to raise "as many poultry as they pleas[ed]."[17]

Similarly, Roswell King Jr., the manager of the Butler plantations, allowed slaves at Hampton Plantation geographic mobility. In a letter written on 13 September 1828, King stated that "[a] certain number [of slaves] are allowed to go to town on Sundays, to dispose of eggs, poultry, coppers' ware, canoes, &c." Although he granted travel privileges to "a certain number," they had to return "home by 12 o'clock" unless a special permit was issued. Anyone who exceeded this deadline or returned "intoxicated"—which he noted in parentheses was "a rare instance"—was sent "into stocks, and not allowed to leave home for twelve months."[18] The town King referred to was most likely Darien or Brunswick, both less than fifteen miles from the plantation. The identity of the bondpeople to whom he granted permission to travel on Sundays is a mystery and so is his selection process. However, it is likely that both enslaved males and females sold their food and wares at these local markets.

Employing a similar management strategy as Hazzard, King tried to impress upon the enslaved minds "the advantage of holding property, and the disgrace attached to idleness."[19] Ironically, the slaves themselves were also property. Although other slaveholders may have criticized his philosophy and "think that they lose time, when Negroes can work for themselves," he explained that "the reverse on all plantations under good regulations—[happened because] time is absolutely gained to the master."[20] Glynn County planters understood King's logic because provision grounds were common on the island. Visitors on trips to this region noted that the majority of the fourteen large estates provided gardens for their enslaved laborers.[21] But what goods did bondpeople produce and how much money did they yield from their gardens? Moreover, did gender affect the payments and prices of these items and were there any patterns in terms of cost? The records of the interactions between the enslaved laborers and residents at Retreat Plantation provide a window through which to examine the goods they traded and the profits they accrued.

Between 1844 and 1869, Anna Page King and her children paid enslaved workers for various goods produced on their own time. Some received cash payments for the goods they produced while others had a revolving account. Approximately 194 (enslaved) names appear in the records for this twenty-two-year period, along with the names of nearly forty planters and their relatives.[22] Although Anna Page King maintained the accounts spanning more than two decades, she only listed payments for the years 1844–1846, 1854, and 1856–1858, and it appears that former bondpeople received payment after her death and during the post-slavery era from 1868–1869. She did not separate the enslaved from the planters and it is clear that she had no standard for costs or payment. Other patterns depict cash loans, credits, and debts owed to and paid for by Anna Page King. She gave enslaved laborers and other slaveholding families money for items such as corn, chickens, eggs, grain, fodder, honey, turkeys, oranges, baskets, tobacco, bread, butter, fans, fish, cloth, and molasses.[23] She also paid other planters' slaves—those belonging to the Armstrongs, Butlers, Caters, Coupers, Demeres, Goulds, Grants, and Hamiltons—money for their goods.

At first glance it appears that these planters hired out their enslaved laborers to Anna Page King, but there are no extant contracts to confirm such conclusions. Instead, Anna Page King had transactions with other planters' slaves and she certainly paid them for goods as well. For example, Marcia, an enslaved woman belonging to Benjamin F. Cater of Kelvin Grove Plantation, received $1.25 for ten chickens. Others, not identified by their gender, appear as "Hamilton's Negro" or "Butler's Negro."

A careful examination of the informal economy of the King laborers reveals interesting gender patterns. The four highest-paid enslaved laborers represent a gender imbalance; one female, Pussy [*sic*], and three males, Quamina, Peter, and Neptune, received the most compensation. Pussy received a total of $45.48 for the period, Peter received $39.69, Quamina received $37.86, and Neptune received $21.89½.[24] Anna Page King supported the participation of both sexes in the slave economy. Looking at the items these individuals produced, however, uncovers a much different story in terms of gender equity. According to the account,

Pussy raised and sold at least 131 chickens and Peter received money for 67, yet their total payments differed by only $5.69. They both received money for their accounts, and in 1844 Anna Page King gave Pussy $17.05 for an "old debt." In addition to chickens, Pussy and Peter also sold eggs and corn to their mistress. One year later, Peter sold 145 oranges and received $4.00 for "a present." It is plausible that Peter used this present to court a female suitor on the plantation, which would explain his need to borrow $4.00 for "a present."[25]

Neptune raised chickens, but he also received money for honey and on one occasion $2.50 "for work," indicating that some bondpeople received small wages or a modicum of compensation for their labor. Quamina produced the same goods and received $1.43 for his account during one year. Other noteworthy laborers such as Clementine, the seamstress, sold cloth and molasses, while men such as Alic, Butler, Ned, and Frank received payments for hats, baskets, and shoes. This suggests that they acquired the skills necessary to complete these crafts, or perhaps that their wives and other family members did. One woman named Florence received $1.50 "for work," while others were given "cash to purchase" items, perhaps from other enslaved laborers or from free persons who frequented the local market.

Evidently, bondpeople at Retreat Plantation participated in informal economies in overt ways. They received payments for their services even if the price was inconsistent, low, or delayed. Other slaves on the island practiced clandestine economic activities at night. On 8 March 1821, James G. Pepper placed an ad in the *Darien Gazette* regarding four slaves who absconded from his plantation on the Turtle River. He noted that these men all "work[ed] faithfully" but it was "very customary" for them to leave their houses at bedtime "with their nets to go a casting on a small creek. . . ."[26] Bondmen could sell their fish or use them to supplement their family's diet. Fishing represented a gender-specific male contribution to the family's material well-being and economy.

Upcountry Informal Economy

It was not common for Wilkes County bondpeople to participate in an informal economy, although some extant evidence suggests that they nevertheless found ways to participate in clandestine economic activities. For example, bondpeople belonging to the Alexander, Gilbert, Hillhouse, and Cumming families had garden "patches" provided for them to work for their own benefit. In a letter written to her niece about "plantation life," Harriet Cumming recalled that slaves "raised potatoes, peas, cabbages, or corn and cotton as they chose." She also remembered that "[t]hey all had some money from selling poultry, cotton, etc., or taking in a little washing," indicating that some Wilkes County bondwomen and bondmen participated in an informal economy.[27] Another resident, S. G. Burnley, placed a notice in the local newspaper on 23 July 1840, claiming, "All Persons are cautioned from trading, or having any dealings in any way whatever with my Negroes, as I will enforce the law against them for so doing, without my leave."[28] It is unclear whether these bondpeople traded their produce in the market town of Washington or to neighbors, but the fact that at least some enslaved workers had gardens and "some money" suggests some participation in informal economies.

In addition to the small slaveholding pattern that failed to fully support independent, informal economic activities among Wilkes County bondwomen and bondmen, their distance from large-scale urban markets acted as a deterrent to economic activities. Coastal bondpeople resided in close proximity to three local markets; some owners like the Butlers, Kings, and Troups allowed them to travel to nearby cities like Brunswick, Darien, and Savannah. However, those in Wilkes County, located nearly 180 miles from Savannah, relied on the urban center of Augusta, approximately fifty miles away.[29] Usually, only members of the planter family traveled to Augusta from Wilkes County. Although the connection to Augusta is significant in terms of slave trading, purchases, and sales, Wilkes County slaveholders rarely allowed their laborers the opportunity to travel such long distances. Dr. Hill, the largest slaveholder in the county, sent his son instead of his enslaved laborers to Augusta. On 4 May 1843, Dr. Hill wrote, "My son, L. M. Hill gone to Augusta to sell his cotton."[30] It is plausible that either Hill sent his son to the market because he did not trust his bondpeople to travel such distances, or that he was fed up with their behavior and sent his son to reinforce the boundaries between the enslaved and the free. Neither of these scenarios is surprising considering that in the past, Hill expressed his frustration with his slaves, stating, "had a nuff with some of my slaves for stealing I am tired with my property. . . ."[31]

Hiring Patterns, Industrialization, and Slave Labor

Despite the many deterrents to a thriving informal economy, larger forces such as industrialization bolstered the country's economy, creating markets, trading centers, and additional sites for economic interaction. As industrialization swept the nation, U.S. residents found new ways to reach one another and had access to urban centers that in the past had been too far away to frequent. The market as a *place* played an important role in informal economies and was less significant in hiring contracts.[32]

The transportation revolution, which led to the burgeoning development of canals, railroads, bridges, and roads in the 1820s, affected the economic activities of slaveholders and slaves throughout Georgia. By the 1830s, the state government began improving roads, building canals, and establishing railroads that led to town centers, cities, and markets. The Georgia Railroad & Banking Company, founded in 1833, was the primary firm that established transportation routes throughout the state.[33] As railroad expansion occurred, a group of Boston investors teamed up with several wealthy slaveholders to establish trade routes that linked these new and improved transportation routes to one another. They did so by creating the Brunswick and Florida Rail Road Survey in 1836 and sending a team of engineers, geologists, and investors to examine the land.[34] Their goal was to connect the Brunswick Canal with the rail that linked Savannah and Darien to central, northern, and western Georgia, and ultimately to Alabama. Most slaveholders in Wilkes and Glynn Counties responded favorably to the growth in this industry because they knew it would provide additional economic opportunities. They expressed their enthusiasm in local newspapers, diaries, letters, and reports.

As early as the 1820s, before major construction took place, Wilkes County residents noted the impact that a proposed canal would have on trade relations. Locals supported improvements in transportation because they believed that new routes encouraged trade with residents in other parts of the state; however, some Augusta residents feared that these routes would suppress trade in their city. "It is rumoured that a Canal is to be constructed," one newspaper article began, "from the Ogechee to the Savannah River, near the city of Savannah." The writer noted that "if this project be effected, it will turn the trade of a great portion of the eastern section of the state to that city, which now goes to Augusta which was the largest market near Wilkes County."[35] Residents in Augusta feared that the proposed route would prevent their city from becoming a leading marketplace that offered stiff competition to the cotton trade in Savannah and Charleston. More than two decades later, journalists promoted the Augusta market. "Augusta was about one dollar per bale better than either [Charleston or Savannah]," a writer claimed. In addition, a trader who comes to Augusta "has three markets before him . . . and loses none of his chances by the Augusta route."[36]

Ten years earlier, Loammi Baldwin, the chief engineer of the Brunswick Canal and Rail Road, submitted a report outlining the advantages of an improved transportation and trade system in Glynn County.[37] Baldwin had local interests in the trade and focused on the coastal Georgia region. By connecting the Little Satilla, the Great Satilla, the St. Mary's, and the St. John's Rivers with a port in Brunswick, he explained, "the market for cotton, rice, and lumber" would link Charleston, Savannah, Darien, and Brunswick with the rest of the state.[38] Not all residents shared this positive vision. Fanny Kemble was one who had some reservations. Well aware of the potential benefits of new trade routes, she stated that "the Brunswick Canal" could improve "the prosperity of the town of Brunswick, by bringing it into immediate communication with the Atlantic," if land and labor did not present so many challenges.[39] "The speculation . . . from all I hear of the difficulties of the undertaking," she explained, "from the nature of the soil, and the impossibility almost of obtaining efficient labor, is not very likely to arrive at any very satisfactory result." Kemble found it "hard to conceive how this part of Georgia can possibly produce a town which can be worth the digging of a canal."[40]

Contractors encouraged local planters to hire out their enslaved laborers to assist in the building of the Brunswick/Altamaha Canal. On 18 January 1837, the following ad appeared in the *Brunswick Advocate:*

WANTED TO HIRE

THE undersigned wishes to hire ONE THOUSAND NEGROES, to work on the BRUNSWICK CANAL, of whom one third may be women. $15 per month will be paid for steady prime men and $13 for able women. Payments will be made quarterly and ample security will be given. Those who are disposed to hire may rely upon a most careful superintendence and they are desired to make immediate application. The Negroes will be abundantly provided for, well lodged, and the sick will be placed in an accommodations Hospital where they will receive the daily attendance of a well educated physician. For further particulars references is respectfully made to J. Hamilton Couper, Esq. And Lieut. J. L. Loske, the Resident Engineer.[41]

Consider the difference in the way the potential employers addressed bondmen and bondwomen. They sought reliable men and capable women for rates that gave men two dollars more per month. Additionally, of the 1,000 laborers they requested, "one third *may be* women," which indicates a strong preference for male workers.[42] It is also a clear recognition of bondwomen as manual laborers, despite gender disparity. The ad incorporates details that might be appealing to planters interested in hiring out their slaves, male and female alike. Slaveholders not accustomed to hiring may have been fearful that their slaves would run away or become ill under different supervision; thus, Couper and Loske assured interested parties that their human property would be closely managed and properly cared for during the duration of the contract.[43]

Joseph Lyman, another agent working on the Brunswick Canal, placed a different notice in the newspaper on 14 June 1838. His advertisement requested the services of "A NUMBER of Prime Negro MEN" to work any length of time between two and eighteen months at a rate of $16 per month.[44] Lyman did not seek female laborers. Perhaps the reason behind his omission had something to do with the first wave of laborers. Assuming that planters responded to the request to hire out male *and* female hands, there may have been problems during the first year. Being mindful of the closed plantation system in this region, canal work likely allowed enslaved males and females to form relationships that would not have been permitted otherwise. Moreover, canal work probably utilized a different form of supervision than that found on local plantations, allowing more time and space for courtship. If an enslaved female became pregnant, her condition would disrupt the contract, which was also a primary reason why so few slave women occupied artisan positions.

Despite the risks inherent in hiring out their enslaved workers, Ophelia B. Troup of Glynn County noted that her father "hired his people for three years, at $10,000 a year" to the contractors involved with the canal project. The Troup hiring contracts included a clause that enabled the overseer the opportunity to visit "when required." Allowing their slaves to serve in this capacity "saved" Troup from suffering financial losses, "for the three canal years (from 1837–1840) were not good rice years, and this money reduced his debts."[45]

From September to December 1838, the local contractors claimed that they were "desirous to hire a number of PRIME NEGRO MEN" to work on the canal for a minimum of twelve months.[46] Assuring potential clients that adequate services were provided, "[t]hese negroes will be employed in the excavation of the Canal" and "[t]hey will be provided with three and a half pounds of pork or bacon and ten quarts of goard [sic] seed corn per week." Their lodgings, described as "comfortable shanties," included the constant attendance of a "skillful physician."[47] Once again, the contractors were not looking for female laborers. This might have something to do with slave owners recognizing the reproductive value of enslaved women at a time when the only way to acquire additional workers besides purchase was through natural reproduction and/or forced breeding.[48]

Allowing their enslaved workers to work on canals and railroads was a significant risk for slaveholders seeking to protect their property. Several bondmen and a handful of bondwomen were stolen, lost, killed, or injured during the railroad work. By contrast, others hired out to railroad companies looked to the railroad tracks as an avenue for escape. Clearly, the railroad left many slaveholders vulnerable: more than a dozen took their cases to the Georgia Supreme Court hoping to receive compensation for their losses due to the "negligent running of their cars."[49] Whatever their rationale, after 1837 contractors did not seek the services of enslaved females to work on the canals or railroads in Brunswick.

Fanny Kemble expressed strong opinions about the use of slave labor to build the Brunswick Canal. She had some concerns about hiring in general, and the working relationships between Irish and slave laborers in particular. "This hiring out of Negroes is a horrid aggravation of the miseries of their condition," she claimed. Focusing on the manner in which slaves were treated under such contracts, she continued, "For if, on the plantations, and under the masters to whom they belong, their labor is severe and their food inadequate, think what it must be when they are hired out for a stipulated sum to a temporary employer, who has not even the interest which it is pretended an owner may feel in the welfare of his slaves, but whose chief aim it must necessarily be to get as much out of them, and expend as little on them, as possible. Ponder this new form of iniquity. . . ."[50] Kemble recognized that the lessee (in this case, the Brunswick Canal Company) did not have the same vested interest in the physical welfare of rented slaves. She also challenged the way in which slaveholders cared for their human chattels, noting that they too did not provide an adequate diet for their property. Even though she recognized that slaves received "nothing at all for their work," she questioned planters who hired their slaves to individuals (or companies) that sought "to get as much as possible out of them" and expressed concern for slaves' protection against "ill-usage."[51]

The use of Irish laborers represented Kemble's second concern with the hiring practices of the Brunswick Canal Company. She made several comparative references to the low social position of slaves and "Irishmen" and pondered how the two groups would work with each other, asserting that they had to have separate work and living arrangements.[52] According to her interpretation, the Irish workers were to receive $20 per month for wages, "abundant food, and the best accommodations," while slaves received no wages and "nothing more than the miserable Negro fare of rice and corn grits."[53] Kemble's references to the canal and its workers indicate that there was indeed public discussion and debate regarding the practice of hiring in this region.

Despite the mixed opinions regarding the effects of the improvements in transportation systems, it is clear that enslaved laborers played an important role in these projects. Some were hired to help build the canals, improve the roads, and work on the railroad. Others utilized the new markets that were created to participate in the informal economy that flourished in the semiurban metropolises that the railroad, canals, and roads used as their anchors. Of course, despite whatever benefits may have been gained, slave hiring represented another dimension of slavery that challenged the stability of enslaved families.

Hiring allowed a significant number of people other than wealthy slaveholders the opportunity to have slaves, even if for a short period of time.[54] For some renters, hiring offered an "honorable and profitable compromise" to slavery.[55] People who hired slaves in Kentucky, for example, used the extra hands to assist white women with domestic chores so that their homes adhered to nineteenth-century expectations.[56] Slaveholders who hired out their enslaved workers often sent laborers who they believed drained plantation expenses, such as pregnant women, small children, and new mothers. Some slaveholders maintained that these slaves were financial liabilities, and it was in their best interest to hire them out so that someone else would clothe, house, and feed them. By contrast, wealthy planters with large workforces often hired out prime male slaves at high prices when they had an excess number of workers. Thus, slave owners greatly benefited from hiring out their enslaved workers because they capitalized on laborers who represented both assets and liabilities. By establishing short contracts, they had access to their slaves in the event that their economic or agricultural situations changed.

Hiring was an obstacle to family cohesion. Bondmen and bondwomen who were hired out had multiple owners, gave birth to offspring, and experienced losses through death and sale, yet still had to work through their yearly contracts. Switching homes year after year caused stress, trauma, and confusion for many enslaved families. Despite this, slave hiring benefited some families, particularly when their owners insisted on keeping relatives together. Some slaveholders went to great lengths to place restrictions on those that hired slaves because they wanted assurances that their property would return in the same "condition." One way to guarantee the proper treatment of their enslaved workers was to lend them to relatives or neighbors.

Bondpeople worked as domestics and artisans, and they used their unique skills for contracted labor in urban settings. Some bondpeople desired these arrangements because it gave them time away from their owner's direct supervision and provided geographic mobility and a modicum of freedom. Others felt assured that the bonds of slavery were becoming less rigid.

Local, national, and international markets often served as catalysts to slave hiring, particularly after the invention of the cotton gin in 1793. This invention marked a crucial economic development in Wilkes County because it enabled residents to switch from tobacco cultivation to cotton. Planters throughout the South began cultivating short-staple cotton, especially in the fertile soil of the Georgia upcountry. Many slaveholders from the Carolinas, Virginia, and the Georgia coast moved to the Georgia upcountry to capitalize on this new crop. Thus, by the early nineteenth century, the Georgia cotton belt was in full operation. Industrialization and improvements in transporting goods through canals, railroads, and by wagon trains fueled local markets. Commercial centers in Augusta and Savannah became important markets as planters and traders alike filled the streets in hopes of receiving high prices for their cotton. Of course, planters needed a workforce to produce this new crop, and some whites who could not afford to purchase slaves turned to hiring as an alternative.

Upcountry Hiring Patterns

Although slave hiring was common throughout the antebellum South, it played a significant role in the lives of Wilkes County residents. The majority of those who hired slaves in this community were slaveholders themselves. Comparing 1850 slave census records to estate inventories and wills indicates that there were a number of slaveholding/hiring families in Wilkes County. Families like the Snelsons, Normans, Wellborns, Measwells, Fraisers, Williamsons, Greens, and Murphys owned *and* hired slaves.[57]

Significant patterns relating to the nature of slavery in upcountry Georgia emerge when one examines hiring records. First, enslaved families changed households year after year. Second, planters separated enslaved families according to their own needs. Third, slaves received different yearly rates, which changed based on a variety of factors including gender, age, skill, and health. Finally, slave hiring represented an important institution that was not as permanent as a sale, yet long enough that it had an impact on the daily lives of those in bondage.

It appears that planters were not concerned with family ties when it came to hiring, *unless* those hired out were mothers and their children. None of the hiring contracts recognize paternity, although some extant slave bills of sale list spouses and their offspring in family units. Slaveholders typically did not use children under the age of ten for heavy labor; thus it was in their best interest to hire them out to avoid paying any excess expenses to care for them. Some slaveholders preferred someone else to support enslaved mothers and their offspring until they reached an age that benefited the plantation needs. Phrases such as "for keeping," "for support," or to the "lowest bid" appear throughout the records, replacing a monetary rate for these women and children. Such language suggests that the owners did not want the added expense of "keeping" these slaves because they viewed them as liabilities.

Hiring rates represented a percentage of the slave's appraised worth. Annual hire rates reflected the market's appraisal of the productive value of a slave based on a one-year contract. Planters took into consideration the age, health, skill, family constraints, and value of slaves when establishing hiring rates. Although estate inventories represent a great source for hiring data, not all owners provided such detailed information. Out of nearly four hundred records between the years 1825 and 1845, only two planters included the ages of their slaves. The others listed slaves in categories labeled "boy," "girl," "man," and "woman," which makes it difficult to discern how age affected hiring rates and whether it played a *more important* role than gender and skill.[58] Curiously, for the two plantations that contain age statistics, there is absolutely no data for hiring.

Planters determined rates by the slave's gender, health, skill, and projected value. In some instances, slave hiring rates represented anywhere from 12 to 15 percent of the total value of the slave or as low as 5 to 8 percent of their value.[59] Slave purchase prices, on the other hand, reflect the market's appraisal of the slave's productive value for the "balance of their lives," not just for the year.[60] Archibald L. Hays of Wilkes County listed twenty slaves with price and hiring rates that reflect similar patterns (table 5.1). The price ranges for these slaves ranged from $300 to $1,100. Hiring rates ranged from $0 to $110. One slave, a "boy" named Allen, was hired out for 60 percent of his price, while Bryan, "a man" worth $1,100, was hired out for $140 per year, or 13 percent of his price. The majority of the women listed received rates between 0 and 11 percent of their total cost. Hays also provided brief comments about slave families and health concerns. "Old" Peter, for example, and his "wife Aggy" were priced and hired out as a unit. Nancy, described as "an Old woman," is listed with her three children, Lucinda, Louisa, and Palatia. The executors of the estate noted that Nancy was a "sick" woman "in hope[s] of a speedy recovery" and suggested a $20 deduction from her fee because of her illness.[61]

On 2 January 1829, Robert, Charles, and other members of the Wheeler family submitted a document to the inferior court in Wilkes County, Georgia, for the hire of their slaves. This, however, was not the

Table 5.1. Value and Hiring Rates of Slaves Belonging to Archibald Hays, Wilkes County, 1831

Name(s)	Value	Hire Rate	Percent	Comments
Old Peter & Aggy his wife	$400	$60	15%	
Ceresa a girl about 7 yrs.	$325	$—	N/A	
Young Peter	$1,100	$140	13%	
Ismir a boy	$550	$42.50	8%	
America a boy	$550	$32.50	6%	
Blancha a girl	$450	$35	8%	
Bryan a man	$1,000	$110	11%	
Jourdon a man	$900	$100	11%	
Patsy a girl	$600	$65	11%	
George a boy	$600	$50	8%	
Allen a boy	$50	$30	60%	
Sam	$500	$50	10%	
Winter	$500	$25	5%	
Phil	$500	$25	5%	
Carolin & Jane	$800	$25	3%	
Aggy & child	$800	$35	4%	
Mary & child	$800	$35	4%	
Julia a woman Harriet	$700	$65	9%	
Sophia & child	$300	$—	N/A	
Nancy an Old Woman and her 3 children (Lucinda, Louisa, and Palatia)	$300	$—	N/A	Woman sick & hopes of speedy recovery deduct from hire for Old Nancy & kids $20

Note: Compiled by the author from the Estate of Archibald L. Hays, Wilkes County Court of Ordinary, Inventories, Appraisements, and Wills, 31 December 1839, Georgia Archives, Morrow, Georgia.

first time the Wheeler family hired out their enslaved workers. In 1824, John Dyson, the administrator of their estate, placed the following ad in a local paper: "Notice. Will be hired at the house of Simeon McLendon's, on Wednesday the 10th of January next, a number of Negroes: Men, Women, Boys and Girls belonging to the minors of Rachel Wheeler, dec'd for the ensuing year."[62] The 1829 advertisement began with the phrase, "For the current year," which indicated the duration that most planters hired out their slaves to other residents. The Wheelers stipulated that their bond-people entered hiring contracts "with interest [in case payments did not arrive in a timely manner] . . . in two suits of clothing suitable for the winter and summer, a hat, blanket, and pair of shoes. . . ."[63] Although this seems like a simple contract with few clauses, slave hiring was much more complex, particularly if viewed from the perspective of the enslaved.

The Wheelers, like other slaveholding families, hired out their slaves annually and placed advertisements in local newspapers from 1827 to 1832. Among the list of bondwomen and bondmen advertised were individuals and families. One woman, Betsy, and "her children" appeared in 1827, 1828, and 1829. Each year, they were hired out to a different "owner," which meant that each year they had to adjust to a new environment with its own set of rules and regulations. Whether intentionally or because of poor record keeping, someone in the Wheeler family presented conflicting information on the number of children Betsy had. The record keeper failed to list their names, ages, and sexes. In 1827 Betsy is listed with "two children." A man named John Dyson rented them for $5 that year.[64] One year later, Betsy and her two children have an increased rental rate of $9 and they left Dyson's home to work for Silas Pullen (their second temporary owner). Finally, in 1829, Betsy and "her children" (no number listed) lived with the Danforth family (their third temporary owners), and their hire rate decreased to $8.06¼. It is unclear whether Betsy had more than two children or where they were located after 1829 because they disappear from the records. Perhaps they died, were sold, or "the children" were hired out to other owners under their respective names, which are not listed. Regardless of the outcome, it is clear that for three years Betsy's children remained with her and worked in the homes of three different Wilkes County families. Changing residences forced this family to make yearly adjustments to their daily routine. Their father's identity, residence, and relationship with his offspring remain a mystery.

Men were not hired out to different people as frequently as enslaved women were. Hiring trends for males reflect different patterns because they had higher rates than their female counterparts. Yearly rates for men in the Georgia upcountry ranged from $15 to $75 per year, whereas women did not receive rates above $60 per year (most women cost less than $20 per year). For example, over a five-year period, Prior, an enslaved male owned by Charles Wheeler, changed residences three times, yet each year he remained with a member of the Wheeler family.

Gender created distinctly different hiring patterns. For example, bondwoman Esther, who was also owned by Charles Wheeler, changed residences four times over a five-year period and even moved twice in the same year. Other patterns suggest that male rates increased annually whereas females had significant price fluctuations. In 1827, Prior had a yearly rate of $36, but by 1832 it increased to $75.45½. By contrast, Esther's rate started at $38.25 in 1827 and during the second half of that *same* year she was hired out to another individual for $60, which is exceptionally high in comparison to other females. In 1828 her rate decreased to $40.25, and in 1829 it increased to $44. In 1831 and 1832 her rate was $13 and $25, respectively.[65] Rather than a steady increase, Esther's rate fluctuated.

Like the Wheelers, the Wellborns of Wilkes County hired out several slaves annually. Upon the death of the patriarch, Lat. Wellborn, on 11 June 1827, the executors of the estate divided his property between his two children, John and Caroline. Each child received fifteen slaves, and they hired them out to other Wilkes County residents. Nearly half of the bondwomen they hired out had children. In 1827, a different bondwoman named Esther, with four children, was hired out to C. R. Green, the Wellborn family guardian, for $45.93¼. Over a six-year period, they changed residences five times and their rate decreased every year to $16.50 at the end of the period. A closer look at Esther and her children reveals that sometime during 1830 she conceived or acquired another child, because in 1831 she appeared on the inventory with *five* children. The identity of the father(s) of any of her children remains uncertain, and considering that she switched residences annually, the father(s) could have been any number of people, from another slave to a white renter.[66]

Bondwoman Judy had a different experience than Esther. In 1827, Judy and her three children were hired out to G. Francis for a rental fee of $13.75. One year later, she was transferred from Francis to C. R. Green, the same man who hired the Wheelers' slaves. In 1828, Judy and her progeny received a rate of 6¾ cents for the year. This sharp decrease makes sense considering that in 1829 she only had *two* children and their rate increased to $2 for the year. Judy probably spent the majority of 1828 caring for a sick child and was not useful for heavy labor. It is likely that the child was born in 1827 and died before his or her first birthday. The loss of a child could have been devastating for Judy and the other siblings; therefore, the Wellborns did not charge Green more than six cents that year.[67] It is also possible that the Wellborns sold one of Judy's children, but because the 6¾-cent rate is given to other pregnant women on this list, it may have been the going rate. By hiring Judy and her children to another Wilkes County resident, the Wellborns relieved themselves of the responsibility of caring for bondpeople that were likely considered to be a financial burden.[68]

C. R. Green hired several of the bondwomen owned by the Wellborns and Wheelers. It may be that Green was a compassionate person or that he was a physician who could easily care for these women and children. It is also plausible that he was simply exercising his guardianship over the Wellborn children, their property, and their friends' property. Hannah, for example, was another female owned by the Wellborns who was hired out to Green with her two children. In 1827, their rate was 6 cents per year, and in 1829, she appeared with *three* children. Although Green's interest in Hannah, Judy, Esther, and their children is not indicated, it is clear that the Wellborns and Wheelers trusted them in his care.[69]

Slaves in poor health always represented a financial burden to planters because it was difficult to sell them, and providing medical care for them was not always a high priority. Ellen, for example, worked in the homes of three different families between 1827 and 1829. Her rate dramatically decreased from $17 in 1827 to $10 in 1828 and finally to $1 in 1829, where the record keeper noted "sickly" in the column next to her name. Health considerations clearly played a role in decisions about this woman's rates.

Some Wilkes County slaveholders hired out individual laborers based on their skills, whereas others sought to hire them out in large groups. On 4 December 1824, Laurence C. Toombs placed a notice in the local newspaper for the hire of "60 Negroes . . . among whom is a good seamstress."[70] Another notice placed on 5 January 1830 requested the hire of "ten valuable negroes, consisting of men, large boys and a first rate woman as a cook or a house Servant."[71] The need to hire enslaved females for their skills is evident in these notices. Some people even requested that the hireling have good hygiene: "WANTED TO HIRE A GIRL accustomed to household services who can come recommended as industrious and cleanly in her habits."[72] One planter placed a notice in the *Augusta Chronicle* stipulating that the terms of the hire include that the hirers clothe, pay taxes, and pay the doctor bills of his slaves.[73] They even requested that the person who previously hired the slaves return them to their owners in "good condition." Such ads stated, "Those persons who have hired the Negroes for the past year, will have them well clothed according to the terms of the hiring."[74] Each of these notices confirm the annual nature of slave hiring in this region.

Hiring created difficulties for enslaved couples by preventing loved ones from spending time with each other. In all likelihood, some renters may not have allowed bondmen to visit their spouses on neighboring plantations or on their home estates because of the amount of work they needed them to complete during the contract period. In addition to disrupting contracted labor, visitation probably made enslaved hirelings long to see their relatives more often.

Expectant enslaved females, particularly those residing in Wilkes County, experienced hiring at a crucial time in their life cycles and were possibly inconvenienced by the multiple residences they were forced to serve. It is likely that Hannah, Esther, and Judy had arrangements for the birth of their children, only to have them interrupted by new hiring contracts. Did these women have help during childbirth at any place of "employment"? Likewise, did relocation put them at a greater distance from their offspring's father, or were their children fathered by one of their white male employers? Frances Kemble reminds us that "[the] case of a master hiring out his slaves to another employer, from whom he receives their rightful wages, is a form of slavery which, though extremely common, is very seldom adverted to in those arguments for the system which are chiefly founded upon the master's presumed regard for his human property."[75]

Lowcountry Hiring Patterns

Regional demographics in Glynn County supported an informal economy, so it is not surprising that hiring rarely occurred in tidewater Georgia. Most coastal planters believed that they maximized their enslaved workers' labor by permitting informal economic activities as opposed to lending them to others through hiring contracts. The task system, in their opinion, enabled them to make good use of their slaves' time. Another reason to support the informal slave economy rather than hiring was directly connected to the production of two crops (Sea Island cotton and rice) as opposed to one. In short, Glynn County planters could not afford to hire their laborers out as frequently as their Wilkes County counterparts because of their year-round cultivation demands. "The practice of hiring slaves to work for persons other than their owner was not common in Glynn County," explained the late local historian Margaret Davis Cate, "but when this was done, the contract usually ran from January 1 to Christmas."[76]

Extant evidence of hiring in Glynn County appears in newspaper advertisements from the *Brunswick Advocate*. On 23 November 1837, J. Davis submitted an ad for "A FIRST RATE COOK and two Waiters, for a Hotel."[77] It is difficult to determine whether Davis preferred to hire slaves, free blacks, or white indentured servants because he neglected to distinguish which group he desired. Additionally, since there is no indication of hiring rates, the duration of the labor, or any other terms, it is difficult to determine whether Davis intended to hire slaves only.

Unlike most planters in the upcountry, some slaveholders in coastal Georgia had strong reservations about hiring out their slaves to other residents. Hugh Fraser Grant, however, had no problem placing his enslaved men and women under hiring contracts. Even though he wanted certain guarantees, his philosophy regarding their labor was quite generous. For example, on 14 October 1848, he "sent all Hands to assist Mr. Forman save his crop." In addition, he sent letters of inquiries to government officials seeking to hire out some of his excess hands. In one letter addressed to a Mr. Miller, he noted that he had "15 or 16 Men" he could "furnish" to "work on the fortifications about Savh [Savannah]" for $45 per month for each man. Grant assured Miller that he presently hired out two or three men monthly and that he was accustomed to these practices. However, he was concerned about their diets because the last time his hirelings went on contract, "they were badly fed." This time, Grant continued, "if my Negroes go on now I wish them to be fed agreeable to the contract." He even volunteered his female laborers, asking Miller to let him know whether "they require women" because he could also "send a few of them" as long as he knew their price. "I should suppose" he stated, "they will require one woman at least to Cook & wash your mess." Clearly, Grant understood that women could perform similar work as their male counterparts; however, he also recognized women for their cooking and washing skills. Grant was willing to send nearly twenty of his enslaved workers, men and one female, to Savannah to work, but he wanted assurance that they would receive proper care during their absence.[78]

The only other extant evidence of slave hiring practiced in the low-county relates to brickyard labor. On 8 October 1838, the "Howard & Gage" company sought to hire "TWELVE prime Negro hands" and "six half hands" to work in their brickyard. Although they provided "Liberal wages," they allowed "no deduction for medical attendance or loss of time" for those "if taken sick in the yard."[79] Perhaps Howard & Gage did not have as urgent a need for a workforce as did the builders of the Brunswick Canal because the former neglected to offer incentives like "adequate" medical care. Note also that there are no indicators of gender in this advertisement. In early January 1839, the same company changed its policy, this time specifically requesting the services of female laborers. "Wanted, To hire two prime Negro hands, eight women and eight boys, to work in a Brick Yard."[80] From the language in both ads, it is clear Howard & Gage considered "prime Negro hands" to be male. However, it is noteworthy that they requested the use of bondwomen to work in the brickyard. Generally, mason work was reserved for artisans, and enslaved females rarely left their owners' homes to work in brickyards.

That Howard & Gage opened their yard to women (and boys) suggests that they did not assume prime male slaves were the only ones capable of completing this work.[81]

The process of making bricks was labor-intensive and harsh work. It began in the fall when workers harvested clay from the earth and shaped it into ten-and-a-half-inch rectangles. The next step was to place the samples into square pits approximately 14" × 4" (or 14" × 2") where they stood during the winter months. During this stage, brickmakers removed lumps, trash, or excess pebbles from the bricks, a process called "malming." After soaking the bricks and allowing for the proper consistency, laborers added "street sweepings" to prepare for the firing process. An upstriker (usually a young boy) then molded the clay while the off breaker (also a young boy) took the bricks out of the mold to allow for a twenty-four-hour drying period. An upranger would then place the bricks into a shed for three additional weeks. After this step, the bricks were ready for the firing process in the kiln, subsequent cooling, and finally sale.[82] Some found brickyard work so labor-intensive that petitioners in Maryland, for example, did their best to "lessen the harshness of labor" by altering the size and shape requirement.[83]

The fact that the Brunswick Canal contractors and the Howard & Gage brickyard company sought female employment requires further discussion. Allowing women to work in the city of Brunswick meant that their owners granted them some degree of geographic mobility. It also separated these women from their familial obligations, assuming they resided on an estate with their children and/or spouse. Perhaps the women who went to work on the canal and in the brickyard were "done breeding" and it was in their owner's best financial interest to hire them out. Glynn County planters who sent bondwomen to work on these two projects may have employed the same strategies as planters in Wilkes County who were more likely to hire women out than men. These planters did not have to worry about women's offspring because many assigned mature slaves the task of caring for infants and children in the absence of their mothers. With the exception of these few examples, hiring was not common in this region.

Summary

Examining the secondary institutions of slave hiring and the informal economy provides rich evidence to explore gender distinctions in enslaved work and family settings. Determining male and female access to these activities and the impact on family relations shows how these economic endeavors affected family development. If informal economic activities gave enslaved families the opportunity to provide a modicum of material comfort to their meager conditions, then it was likely an institution in which bondwomen and bondmen preferred to participate, whether given permission or not. Certainly there were benefits to these activities including travel privileges, the chance to interact with other groups of people (free blacks, Native Americans, whites, and other bondmen and bondwomen), and additional dietary supplements, all of which created certain luxuries that otherwise might not have been available to them. Likewise, informal economic activities reinforced interactions with their owners as they bartered, sold, and exchanged money and miscellaneous goods for their services. Bondpeople in Wilkes and Glynn Counties received wages for some of their labor during slavery, and they demanded payment after abolition.

Looking at the market endeavors of bondwomen and bondmen in both regions confirms that each county developed its own set of patterns. For the most part, coastal slaves actively participated in an informal economy because regional demographics such as a dual-crop economy, the task system, and positive planter philosophies supported these endeavors. Enslaved women and men in Wilkes County, on the other hand, rarely received payment for their labor because their owners controlled hiring contracts. Upcountry laborers remained on the periphery of financial transactions and had little control over their time because the gang labor system kept them busy from dawn to dusk. When they entered hiring contracts, it was usually with another Wilkes County resident, and it required the hireling to change environments on an annual basis.

Whereas the informal economy benefited the enslaved families that were able to participate, the practice of hiring tore families apart. Upcountry bondwomen and bondmen found themselves traded each year to work in the homes and farms of planters throughout the county. This constant removal and replacement took its toll on the development of cohesive families in an environment that depended on abroad relationships. Lowcountry hiring practices, by contrast, involved intense labor in the urban areas of Brunswick and Darien, but the closed system prevented those on large plantations from extensive travel to work under yearlong hiring contracts. By the early 1840s, however, much of this work was reserved for men.

Considering the stories of bondwomen and bondmen under hiring contracts and those who participated in informal economies enables us to answer old questions and present new ones; in doing so, we complicate the history of slavery and provide another view into the inner lives of the enslaved.

Epilogue: The Aftermath of Slavery

"Yes," says the Spirit, "and blessed rest from their hard, hard work. None of what they've done is wasted; God blesses them for it all in the end."
—Revelations 14:13 NIV

On 21 July 1865, a warm summer afternoon in Wilkes County, former slaves Charity and Hamp met near the Andrews Plantation to exchange vows in holy matrimony. They were not alone; thirty-three other couples participated in this large wedding. The ceremony was officiated by a Freedman's Bureau missionary from New England commonly known as "Dr. French" or "the Frenchman." The newly freed couples wanted lawful unions even if they had been "married" while enslaved. Some used freedom to formalize unions with their true loves—not the person their former owners selected for them.

As news of this ceremony reached the ex-slaveholders, they did all they could to prevent the event from taking place on their grounds. Dr. French and his eager couples then settled for a 3:00 P.M. service at the "negro cemetery." One witness noted that "the candidates for double matrimonial honors went trooping out to their cemetery on the Tan Yard Branch to be married over again." Unfortunately, "the ceremonies were interrupted by a thunder storm that drenched the composite bridal party and all the spectators."[1] Despite the rain, Charity and Hamp and the other couples completed the ceremony and became husband and wife.

Members of the former slaveholding class were shocked by this event because, at least from their viewpoint, many of these couples had been married to other individuals during slavery. Eliza Andrews spoke about Charity, who was once owned by her family in Wilkes County. Andrews recalled that Charity was married six years ago to a "Mr. Waddy's Peter." She "remember[ed] how father joked Peter, when he came to ask for Charity, about having him for a 'nigger-in-law,' but now, Charity has taken to herself Hamp, one of father's plantation hands—a big, thick-lipped fellow, not half as respectable looking as Peter."[2] Referring to these unions as "double" marriages, Andrews did not realize that the relationship Charity had during bondage was not with the person she chose for herself. When the two exchanged words after the ceremony, Andrews was amused by Charity's pride in her new name; "I'se Mrs. Tatom now," boasted Charity. For the first time, Andrews realized that "they have their own notions of family pride."[3]

Bondmen and women married, remarried, and exchanged vows once they became free. They used their independence to participate in unions of their choice regardless of their marital status during slavery. Forced partnerships in bondage often prevented couples from being with the spouses of their choice, and the couples who stood with Charity and Hamp corrected this once they were freed.

Upon Emancipation, ex-slaves solidified their unions, searched for work, and established lives for themselves. They enjoyed their newly found freedom even if the transition was a challenging one. Former bondmen such as Bram of St. Simons Island had a difficult time during freedom. "After the war he had bought a patch of ground (about twenty acres)" and started off well. He had livestock and a few chickens, but his crops did not yield any profits. "His son had left him to set up for himself," and his wife, "for whom he had a great deal of affection had died." Bram was left "alone in his old age" without any means of support.[4] The chaos of the postslavery era presented challenges for former bondwomen and bondmen seeking new ways of survival in a world still dominated by their former slaveholders and by conceptions of them as slaves.

Similar to Bram, Arch of Wilkes County fled his former plantation when he learned of freedom. He left without saying "a word to anybody" but his owner. Considering "the real cause of his departure," Eliza Andrews noted that Arch feared that "his wife will come after him from the plantation" because he was "about to marry Mrs. Pettus's Betsy." Similarly, Isaac departed from his plantation "because he has a new wife here and an old one there that he don't want."[5] Such behaviors confirm that some bondmen selected their own spouses during freedom and left relationships they had during slavery. Freedom for bondwomen was much different.

Not all formerly enslaved women were as fortunate as Charity during freedom. It appears that sexual exploitation of women continued after slavery. In the small urban town of Washington, Georgia, a group of Union soldiers "established a negro brothel" or "a colony of them [brothels]" where they paraded arm in arm with their "negro mistresses" nightly. Eliza Andrews recalled that they could "hear them singing and laughing at their detestable orgies." In her opinion, it was "the greatest insult to public decency . . . right up under our noses, in the most respectable part of the village . . . where our citizens have always been accustomed to walk and ride in the evenings." On a footnote to this discussion, Andrews made the following remarks: "It is possible that these associations may not have been, in all cases, open to the worst interpretation, since Northern sentiment is, theoretically, at least, so different from ours in regard to social intercourse between whites and negroes; but, from our point of view, any other interpretation was simply inconceivable."[6] Were these interactions between white men and black women continued forms of exploitation or were they the development of loving relationships? If the former is true, then how does one interpret the irony of Union soldiers exploiting African American women when Andrews notes that these interactions may not have been exploitative? Regardless of the nature of such relationships, it is evident that black women's sexuality remained at the center of controversies even during freedom.

Looking at life during and after the Civil War, two former planters' daughters shared their experiences in Wilkes and Glynn Counties in the 1860s and 1870s. Frances Butler Leigh, daughter of Frances Kemble and Pierce Mease Butler, lived on St. Simons Island from 1866 to 1876. When she visited the plantations that were once the home of hundreds of bondpeople, she noted that "[t]he fine houses have fallen to decay or been burnt down; the grounds neglected and grown over with weeds; the plantations . . . [are] choked up with undergrowth."[7] Likewise, Eliza Andrews, daughter of Wilkes County planter Judge Garnett Andrews and Annulet Hall Andrews, shared her experiences in the upcountry during 1864 and 1865. Reflecting on plantation life during the war years, she stated, "This dreadful war is bringing ruin upon so many happy homes."[8] The "happy homes" destroyed by the Civil War were once the workplaces for thousands of bondpeople who labored, lived, loved, birthed, and died.

Andrews and Leigh had something in common. Both women adopted different political allegiances from their slaveholding parents. Andrews, a staunch Confederate, despised the Union and was thoroughly disgusted with the behavior of "Yankee soldiers." Her father, Judge Andrews, on the other hand, supported the Union and boasted about the way he treated his "servants." Leigh agreed with her father Pierce Butler's slaveholding sentiments and supported the Confederates, but her mother, Frances Kemble, was an abolitionist, at least to some. When the two young

women moved to their parents' former plantations during and immediately following the war, they witnessed drastic changes among their
former enslaved workforce.

Former slaves in both communities had different conceptions of labor
during the 1860s and 1870s. Leigh and her father were frustrated by their
former bondpeople's apathy. "The negroes talked a great deal about their
desire and intention to work for us" after the war, she explained, "but
their idea of work, unaided by the stern law of necessity, is very vague,
some of them working only half a day and some even less." Leigh found
that "no Negro will work if he can help it."[9]

In Wilkes County, Andrews witnessed similar patterns. On 15 January 1864, she maintained that "we can't take control over them [former
enslaved laborers], and they won't do anything except just what they
please."[10] Judge Andrews had such strong feelings about guaranteeing his
bondpeople work that he went out of his way to negotiate labor contracts
with them. He even tried to convince them to move to his plantation
in Mississippi and work for $7 per month, plus food and clothing for the
rest of the year; but, as Eliza noted, former slaves "have such extravagant
ideas as to the value of their services that they are sadly discontented
with the wages they are able to get."[11] As the Andrews family struggled
financially, they turned to a practice common during slavery—hiring.
The war years enabled bondmen and bondwomen to practice self-hire
for the first time; this provided them with a modicum of control over
their work lives, despite the low wages.[12]

Former slaves used their skills during freedom as they had done during slavery. "Uncle Lewis," once enslaved by the Andrews family, had
the gift of preaching, but it was his sons' "excellent trades" that enabled
this family to survive during freedom. Osborne, one of Lewis's sons, was
"as fine a carpenter as there is in the county" and one of the Andrews'
most valuable servants.[13] With these skills, the Andrews family did not
worry about their transition to freedom.

As former bondmen and bondwomen put down their sickles, hoes,
and axes to claim their freedom, they refashioned their lives to their lik-
ing. In some cases, little changed; for others, life was drastically different. Newly freed men and women first tried to reconstruct their families,
then searched for employment and housing. During this transition, gender roles changed, often emulating patterns found in white slaveholding society.

In 1874, reflecting on the lives of former bondpeople once enslaved
on his family's plantations in coastal Georgia, James Leigh made the following observation:

But most travelers see nothing of the inner life and character of these poor people. To know and understand the negro in his present position, you must see and hear him on the floor of the State Legislature, and transact business with him on a plantation, as well as chat familiarly with him on a pleasure excursion, or be waited on by him in a hotel. I have done all this, and therefore have some authority in speaking, and yet I can scarcely say that I know the emancipated African thoroughly yet.[14]

Even though slaveholders and their children interacted with enslaved men and women on a daily basis for generations and boasted about their "good and faithful servants," it was not until after emancipation that planters realized they did not truly know their enslaved laborers.

Swing the Sickle defines and outlines the complex nature of gender among the enslaved, focusing specifically on agricultural and nonagricultural labor skills, the creation and maintenance of families, and opportunities for economic activities. Although slaveholders made decisions about the workloads, marriages, and mobility of their enslaved laborers, they made these decisions "without regard to sex."[15] Georgia slaveholders were more concerned with productivity and skill than with a person's sex. Occasionally, some women were singled out because of their skill or set aside because of their physical confinement. Some bondpeople with special talents had the opportunity to travel well beyond plantation boundaries, and others who were able to travel, such as Rhina of St. Simons, longed to be back on the plantation with their children, other relatives, and friends.

Enslaved people craved the stability of family and attempted to use all the skills at their disposal to create the best possible life for themselves and their relatives. By detailing the various aspects of bondpeople's skills and showing how these skills in turn affected family and slaveholder relationships, *Swing the Sickle* illustrates how gender, labor skill, and economy dictated every bondperson's way of life and influenced all familial relationships.

APPENDIX A

Enslaved Male Occupations on the Butler Plantations, 1849[*]

Occupation:	Name	Age
Driver		
1.	Frank	57
2.	Angus	36
3.	Harry	50
4.	Cudjo	39
5.	Henry	37
6.	Morris	39
7.	Bram	37
8.	Morris	63

Occupation:	Name	Age
Carpenter		
1.	George	47
2.	Abram	37
3.	George	58
4.	London	32
5.	Primus	22
6.	George	29
7.	Isaac	18
8.	Primus	55
9.	Alex	28
10.	Andrew	35
11.	Sandy	56
12.	Jacob	74
13.	John	50
14.	Sambo	37

[*]This table was created by the author based on information in the estate inventory. Question marks were added to illegible names and words. 1849 "Inventory and Appraisement of the Estate of Capt. John Butler, dec'd," Butler Collection, Historical Society of Pennsylvania (HSP).

15.	Bram	50
16.	Joe	40
17.	Jeffrey	59
18.	Rintee	30

Occupation:	Name	Age
Cooper		
1.	Cato	37
2.	Quacco	37
3.	Jeffrey	41
4.	London	59
5.	London	56
6.	John	28
7.	Dary or Davy	29
8.	Wallace	25
9.	Aaron	29
10.	Israel	32
11.	Nero	58
12.	Phillip	28
13.	Charles	39

Occupation:	Name	Age
Smith		
1.	Dandy	37
2.	John	30
3.	Sawney	55
4.	Jack	70

Occupation:	Name	Age
Engineer		
1.	Ned	58
2.	Ned	36

Occupation:	Name	Age
Miller		
1.	Pompe	38
2.	Sam	45
3.	Pompe	53

Occupation:	Name	Age
Mason		
1.	Gorham	25
2.	Sancho	55

Occupation:	Name	Age
Shoemaker		
1.	Bill	48
2.	Rintee	49

Occupation:	Name	Age
Sawyer		
1.	Peter	67

Occupation:	Name	Age
Boatman		
1.	Quash	51

Occupation:	Name	Age
Gardener		
1.	Wallace	58

APPENDIX B

Wilkes County Slave Hiring Patterns *

Wheeler Family (Robert, Charles, & Rachel) 1827, 1828 & 1829—first hires appear under the estate of Garland W. Darracott

A) ROBERT B. WHEELER'S NEGROES 11 AUGUST 1829

Thirteen slaves total, only the five women are listed below

Slave Name	Hire Rate (year)	Person hired to
BETSY and children	$8.06 ¼	Samuel Danforth
MILLY	$22.50	Jordan Norman
RACHEL	$22.06 ¼	William Andrews
POLLY and children	$10.81 ¼	Silas Pullen
NELLY	$10	Wylie B. Jones

B) CHARLES A. WHEELER'S NEGROES 11 AUGUST 1829

Twelve slaves total, only the six women are listed below:

Slave Name	Hire Rate (year)	Person hired to
MOLLY and children	$25	George Wolf
ESTHER	$44	Merdick Pullen
EVALINE	$43	John Benson
NANCY	$31.43 ¾	Samuel Cole
EMILY	$41.37 ½	Samuel Danforth
ELIZA	$21.75	Sandford Pullen

---

*This table was created by the author based on information in the Wheeler estate inventories. Female names are in all capitals to distinguish them from male names and do not appear like that in the original documents. Wheeler family estate inventories, Wilkes County Court of Ordinary, Inventories, Appraisements, and Wills, 1821–1831, GDAH.

"For the current year, notes with approval and security with Interest from their dates if not periodically hired payable on or before the 2nd day of January 1829 to hire the Negroes in two suits of clothing suitable for the winter and summer, a hat, blanket, and pair of shoes, the usual Holiday allowed them."

ROBERT B. WHEELER (2 JANUARY 1828–2 JANUARY 1829)

Slave Name	Hire Rate (year)	Person hired to
Dick	$46	William Pool
BETSEY and children	$9	Silas Pullen
MILLY	$30.31 ¾	David Waller
RACHEL	$20	D. Buckner
Dave	$16.25	Johnson W. D----[?]
Joe Alick	$13.50	Polly Cooper
William	$19.31 ½	Clif Woodcut
Benedict	$49	George Oglesby
POLLY and children	$1	John S. Wheeler
NELLY	$10	Wylie B. Jones

CHARLES A. WHEELER (2 JANUARY 1828–2 JANUARY 1829)

Slave Name	Hire Rate (year)	Person hired to
MARY	$44.73	Jacob Wolf
MOLLY and children	$5	George Oglesby
ESTHER	$40.25	Major Pullen
Prior	$50.75	John S. Wheeler
EMILY	$15	S. Danforth
ELIZA	$12.75	Pullen [?] Dyson
JENNY and children	$2.12 ¼	Eldon Sedove
Isac	$10.10	Elizabeth Pope
NANCY	$20	Thomas S. Wheeler
Ned	$6.25	John S. Deet
ADELINE	$40.06 ½ —	John Bunson

THOMAS J. WHEELER 3 JANUARY 1827

Slave Name	Hire Rate (year)	Person hired to
RUTH Beamake [?]	$26	Lewis R. Bimeau [?]
George Beamake [?]	$69	Lewis R. Bimeau [?]
Robert Beamake [?]	$50	Lewis R. Bimeau [?]

HARRIET Beamake [?]	$50	Lewis R. Bimeau [?]
Thomas Beamake [?]	$41	Lewis R. Bimeau [?]
LOUISA Beamake [?]	$40	Lewis R. Bimeau [?]
MARY Beamake [?]	$10	Lewis R. Bimeau [?]
LIZZY and 4 children	$28	Wyclife Jackson

"Loans of Hire of the Negroes belonging to the heirs of Rachel Wheeler deceased for the present year notes with approval and security with interest from their dates if not have truly hired, payable on the 1st day of January next, to feed the Negroes. Hired with sufficient Winter and Summer clothes, a pair of shoes, hat and blanket to return said Negroes the same as above required by the 1st January next and the usual Holidays allowed their hire . . . May 3, 1827."

JOHN SEYBERT WHEELER'S NEGROES (NO DATE, PROBABLY SOMETIME IN 1827)

Slave Name	Hire Rate (year)	Person hired to
JOY	$67	John H. Dermount
Harry	$85	Ruben Scot
DICEY and 4 children	$195	San Flannery (lowest bid)
LAVINA	$55	Asher Layn
ANNA	$30.50	Taliafero [?] Jones Tolliver
Jacob	$50.25	Jerimiah Walker
Alvis	$80.50	Enoch Dodson
Selby	$10	Enoch Dodson
Anchor (died in a month)	$17.10	Gibson Walker

JOHN SEYBERT WHEELER'S NEGROES (NO DATE, PROBABLY SOMETIME IN 1827)

Slave Name	Hire Rate (year)	Person hired to
JOY	$55	Andrew Wolf [?]
Harry	$61	Taliafer Jones or Tolliver [?] Jones
DICEY and 4 children	$5	John Dyson
LAVINA	$38	James Pullen

ANNA & child	$23	Taliafer [?]
		Tolliver [?]
Jacob	$36.50	Jeremiah Walker
Alvis	$55	Alasoa [?] Jones
Selby (Sibby)	$N/A	For support
Archer (died in a month)	$ "for support"?	For support

ROBERT B. WHEELER [NO DATE, PROBABLY SOMETIME IN 1827]

Slave Name	Hire Rate (year)	Person hired to
Dick	$84	William Pool
BETSY and 3 children	$8.00	[?]
ASHLEY	$35.50	Adolphus Sale
RACHAL	$18.64	Daniel Braceburnar
Dave	$22.50	James Cansby
Jack Alic	$30.00	Wyclife Jackson
William	$20.12 ½	Daniel Shumate
Benedict	$45.00	William Pool
DOLLY and children	$15 (lowest bid)	Lewis R. Beamake [?]

A) ROBERT B. WHEELER [NO DATE, PROBABLY SOMETIME IN 1827]

Slave Name	Hire Rate (year)	Person hired to
Dick	$44	William Pool
BETSY and 2 children	$5	John Dyson
MILLY	$25	John Laber or Saber [?]
RACHAL	$11	Meredith H. Pullen
Dave	$7	John Dyson
JacAlick	$10	Mrs. Polly Cooper
William	$43	G. M. Maher
DOLLY and 5 children	$3 (lowest bidder)	Jefferson Wheeler
AMY	$6.25	Wylie Jones

B) CHARLES A. WHEELER (NO DATE, PROBABLY SOMETIME IN 1827)

Slave Name	Hire Rate (year)	Person hired to
Harry	$57.50	John Psalmdeer [?]
MOLLY and children	$0	John Psalmdeer [?]
ESTHER	$60	Arther Hayton
EMILY	$22.25	Garnett Biskley

ELIZA	$7.50	John Coals [Coats] [?]
Isac	$36	Thomas Psalmas
NANCY	$34	Sam Walker
H LUCY	$17	Edward A. Lewis

B) CHARLES A. WHEELER (NO DATE, PROBABLY SOMETIME IN 1827)

Slave Name	Hire Rate (per year)	Person hired to
Harry	$52	G. W. Wheeler
MARY	$1	Garnett Oglesby
ESTHER	$38.25	Elison Grave
Prior	$36	Thomas J. Wheeler
EMILY	$11	Samuel Danforth
ELIZA	$11	John Coats [Coals] [?]
DICEY	$0	Eldred Lydon
Bender	$4	Eldred Lydon
Isac	$25	James Pullen
NANCY	$20.75	John Saler
Ned	$6.50	John Dent [?]

ANDREW WHEELER (MINOR, SILVESTER B. CRATON = GUARDIAN) 1831

Slave Name	Hire Rate (1831)
Harry	$57
Prior	$55
Ned	$36
James	$21
MOLLY	$40
EMILY	$27
EVELINE	$9.31 ¼
Ritter	$9.12 ¼
LUCRETIA	$3.16 ¼
ESTHER	$13
ELIZA	$36
Isac	$6
Bradley	$50
Henry (HENNY)	$10.50
Jackson	$8
Capy	$13.18 ¾

ANDREW WHEELER (MINOR, SILVESTER B. CRATON =
GUARDIAN) 1832

Slave Name	Hire Rate (1832)
Harry	$67.06 ¼
Prior	$75.45 ²/₄
Ned	$42
James	$32.25
MOLLY	$40.12 ½
EMILY	$42
EVELINE	$5.56 ¼
Ritter	$15.25
LUCRETIA	$14.25
ESTHER	$25
ELIZA	$55
Isac	$7
Bradley	$76
Henry [HENNY]	$13.62 ¼
Jackson	$0
Capy	$25
Viney	$0
Jesdon	$15.12 ½

APPENDIX C

Money Paid to Retreat Plantation Slaves for the following Items: [*]

Item	Categories	cont.	cont.	cont.	cont.	cont.
Corn	corn bushels					
Eggs						
Chickens	small chicks	Ducks	Fowls	Cocks	English ducks	Miocorva ducks
Birds	Tarpins	Quails	swans	turkey	capons (cast/rooster)	
Basket						
Box						
Grain						
Fodder	Poultry fodder					
Making buckets						
Oranges						
"A Present"						
Fanner						
Payment in full	pay for work	Cash	due him/ due her		a/c (account)	over- payment
Loan	to purchase hog	old debt	to purchase chickens			expenses
Fish	tuna					
Church						
Proggan? Freight	freight					
Cloth						
Molasses	honey					
Salt						
Sundries						
Straw Hats						

---

[*]This chart was created by the author based on information in the King Day Book.
Anna Matilda Page King Day Book, 1842–1864, Georgia Archives, Morrow, Georgia.

Item	Categories	cont.	cont.	cont.	cont.	cont.
Shoes	boot brushes				mending shoes	
"For a net"						
Mat						
Bridle						
1843 crop						
Wooden nepels ?						
Tub						
"Taming"						
Tobacco						
Bread/curd board						
Butter						
Music						
People	pmt to Pussy to Mrs. Gale				in full for all demands	

APPENDIX D

Anna Page King Payments 1822–1864

Name (of slave)	Cost	Items	Amount $ Paid
A. McIntosh	$5.00	for a net	$5.00
Abbott	0.25	cash?	0.25
Abby	0.25	?	0.25
Abel	$1.00	?	$1.00
Aberdeem	0.75	5 fowls	
Aberdeem	$1.00	8 chickens	$1.75
Abraham	$1.00	8 fowls	
Abraham	$2.50I	9 chickens	$3.50
Alfred	0.35?		
Alfred	0.5	a loan	0.85
Alic	0.25		
Alic	$1.00	a loan	
Alic	$1.75	pmt. in full	
Alic	$7.80	in full	
Alic	$1.67½	corn	12.4 & ½
Alic Armstrong	0.75	2 hats	
Alic Armstrong	$2.25	15 ducks	$3.00

*This table was created by the author based on information found in the King Day Book. Dates of payment are not included and all illegible items are replaced with a question mark. Anna Matilda Page King Day Book, 1842–1864, Georgia Archives, Morrow, Georgia.

Name (of slave)	Cost	Items	Amount $ Paid
Alic Boyd	0.5	?	
Alic Boyd	0.5	loan	
Alic Boyd	0.62	5 chickens	
Alic Boyd	0.75	6 fowls	
Alic Boyd	$1.55	chickens	
Alic Boyd	$2.15	bal on corn	
Alic Boyd	$2.50	making 5 buckets	
Alic Boyd	$6.50	a/c	
Alic Boyd	65cts	?	
Alic Boyd	$1.37	11 chickens	$17.09
Alic Hamilton	.62½	4 fowls	
Alic Hamilton	$1.00	4 English ducks	
Alic Hamilton	$1.35	8 fowls	
Alic Hamilton	$2.75	?	
Alic Hamilton	.93¾	chickens	
Alic Hamilton	.87½	7 fowls	
Alic Hamilton	$1.06¼	6 fowls	
Alic Hamilton's negro	$4.25	6 ducks 10 chic 9 quail	$14.83
Alic Jun	0.75	fowls	
Alic Jun	$2.00	?	$2.75
Alice	$1.50	loan to purchase hog	$1.50
Amy	0.25	cash?	
Amy	$1.00	8 fowl	
Amy	$1.00	due her	
Amy	$1.25	9 chickens	
Amy	$2.00	2 ducks	
Amy	$2.75	5 ducks & fowls	
Amy Hamilton	$6.00	in full	$14.25
Anne	$0.75	birds	
Anne	0.25	2 chickens	
Anne	.62 & ½	5 chickens	$1.62 & ½
Anthony	$1.00	8 fowls	
Anthony	$1.50	12 chickens	
Anthony	2 & 12½cts	fowls and ducks	
Anthony Hamilton	$1.75	14 chickens	$6.25 & 12½

Name (of slave)	Cost	Items	Amount $ Paid
Armstrong	0.5	tobacco	
Armstrong	$1.00	?	
Armstrong	$1.00	tobacco	$2.50
Balaam	$8.00	1843 crop	
Balaam	$7.68¾	7 bushels of corn	15.66 & ¾
Ben Couper	$3.25	4 fowls	$3.25
Bep	0.5	cash?	0.5
Betty	0.25		
Betty	0.75	3 baskets	$1.00
Betty Couper	$1.13	9 chickens	$1.13
Betty Gould	0.25	baskets	0.25
Billy	$1.501	2 fowls	$1.50
Binah	0.25	2 doz eggs	
Binah	$1.00	cash?	
Binah	$2.50	?	$3.75
Bob Gould	$1.25	10 chickens	
Bob Gould	$2.00	16 chickens	
Bob Gould	$2.00	16 fowls	
Bob Gould	$2.75	22 chickens	
Bob Gould	$3.12 & ½	25 chickens	
Bob Gould	$2.37 & ½	19 chickens	
Bob Gould	$8.12 & ½	65 chickens	$22.11 & ½
Butler	0.25	?	
Butler	0.4	?	
Butler	0.5	shoes?	
Butler	0.5		
Butler	0.75	sundries	
Butler	$1.25	none given	
Butler	$2.18¾	bal on a/c	$5.833 & ¾
Butler & Lord	$2.00	?	$2.00
Butler negro Jacob	$10.50	Poultry	$10.50

Name (of slave)	Cost	Items	Amount $ Paid
Butler's negro	$1.50	ducks	
Butler's negro	$14.62½	Poultry	$15.82 & ½
Cater boy	$2.00	16 chickens	$2.00
Cater Gould	$1.00	8 fowls	$1.00
Cater negro	.81¼	6 fowls	.81¼
Cater's Marcia	.62½	5 chickens	
Cater's Marcia	.62½	5 chickens	$1.25
Caters negro	0.75	6 fowls	
Caters negro	$1.50	?	$2.25
Cates Nancy	$1.75	17 fowls	$1.75
Ceasar	0.3	tarapins?	0.3
Celia	$1.25	in full corn	$1.25
Charles	$1.25	in full	
Charles	$2.37½	19 fowls	$3.62 & ½
Chloe	$6.50	16 ducks	$6.50
Clementine	0.25	2 fowls	
Clementine	0.25	2 fowls	
Clementine	0.25	molasses	
Clementine	0.5	fowls & eggs	
Clementine	0.6	cloth?	
Clementine	0.62	5 chickens	
Clementine	$1.75	pmt. to Pussy	
Clementine	$2.75	?	
Clementine	$3.75	cash?	
Clementine	$13.40	in full to date	
Clementine	.12½	2 chickens	
Clementine	$1.87½	bal on old a/c	
Clementine	.87 & ½	7 fowls	
Clementine	$7.31 & ½	corn & poultry	$34.34
Cooney	0.25	?	
Cooney & Johnny	$1.90	?	$2.15

Name (of slave)	Cost	Items	Amount $ Paid
Couper Charles	$1.00?	tuna?	$1.00?
Couper Negro	$1.50	12 chickens	$1.50
Coyler	$1.25	?	$1.25
Cupid	$2.50 in full	for poultry	
Cupid	$3.00	cash?	
Cupid	$1.45½	5 bushels	
Cupid & Couper	$1.501	2 fowls	$8.45 & ½
Cuyler King	$1.50	?	$1.50
Damian's Patty	$1.157	fowls	$1.15
Daphney	$6.37 & ½ 16 fowls	14 ducks	$6.37 & ½
Darian	$1.00	?	
Darian	$1.50	chickens	
Darian	$1.50	fowls	
Darian	$4.00	Sundries	
Darian	$0.75	???	$8.75
Davy	$1.25	10 fowls	
Davy	$2.75	22 fowls	
Davy	0.5	cocks	
Davy	$1.00	expenses	
Davy	$1.00	old debt	
Davy	$1.00	to purchase chickens	
Davy	$1.50	?	
Davy	$1.75	1 hog	
Davy	$2.50	salt	
Davy	$4.75	?	
Davy	$2.37½	tobacco & ducks	
Davy	.37½	3 chickens	$20.75
Deanna	0.5	sundries	0.5
Delia	$2.37	16 qts corn	$2.37

Name (of slave)	Cost	Items	Amount $ Paid
Dembo	$1.25	9 chics & 1 doz eggs	
Dembo	$1.55	6 fowls & 1 doz eggs	
Dembo	.87½	7 chickens	
Dembo?	$1.50	6 chics 1 duck	$4.17 & ½
Demere negro	0.25	eggs	
Demere Johnson	0.75	6 fowls	
Demere negro	0.5	5 chickens	
Demere's major	0.5	5 chickens	
Demere's negro	$0.60	2 fowls & 1 doz eggs	
Demere negro	$1.00	8 fowl	
Demere negro	$1.00	8 fowls	
Dewey	$2.00	cash?	$2.00
Dianna	$1.25	for Mrs. Gale	$1.25
Duncan	0.25	cash?	
Duncan	0.25	cash?	0.5
Ellen	0.5	eggs	
Ellen	?	0.5	
Emily	.37 & ½	3 chickens	.37 & ½
Florence	0.5	none given	
Florence	$1.50	fowls	
Florence	$1.50	pay for work	
Florence for Tella	$1.00	?	$4.00
Floyd	$1.00	tarapins	$1.00
Frank	0.25	1 basket	0.25
Gent Floyd's servant	$1.00	?	$1.00
George	0.25	2 chickens	
George	$1.00?	?	$1.25

Name (of slave)	Cost	Items	Amount $ Paid
George Gould	0.35	?	
George Gould	0.5	?	
George Gould	$1.84 & ½	3 ducks & 6 fowl	
George Gould	$1.87½	9 fowls	
George Gould	$2.37 & ½	14 fowls	
George Gould	$5.37 & ½	43 chickens	
George Gould	1.87 & ½	15 chickens	$14.19 & ½
George M.	0.25	2 chickens	0.25
Georgia	0.12	none given	
Georgia	0.4	1 chicken	
Georgia	$1.00	?	
Georgia	$1.00	bread/curd board	
Georgia	$1.00	church	
Georgia	$1.10	fowls & ducks	$4.62
Georgia Gould	0.5	4 fowls	
Georgia Gould	.87½	7 fowls	$1.37 & ½
Georgianne	0.25	2 chickens	0.25
Germain	0.5	4 mats	0.5
Gery	$1.10	due him	$1.10
Gop?	$1.00	eggs	$1.00
Gould's negro	$1.12½	cash?	
Guy Hamilton	0.5	chickens	0.5
H. Page	$1.00	?	$1.00
Hamilton	0.5	3 chickens	
Hamilton	$1.75	14 chickens?	
Hamilton	$5.25	ducks & fowls	$7.50
Hamilton Ben	0.5	4 chickens	0.5
Hamilton Charles	$0.75	6 chickens	
Hamilton Charles	$1.12	9 chickens	$1.87
Hamilton Patty	$2.10	7 Miocorva ducks	$2.10

Name (of slave)	Cost	Items	Amount $ Paid
Hamilton's Alic	0.75	6 fowls	
Hamilton's Alic	$2.00	cash?	
Hamilton's Alic	$2.50	?	$5.25
Hamilton's Andre	$1.25	10 fowls	$1.25
Hamilton's boy	0.25	2½ doz eggs	
Hamilton's boy	0.5	2 chics & eggs	
Hamilton's boy	0.5	4 fowls	
Hamilton's boy	0.5	4 fowls	$1.75
Hamilton's Nancy	$1.00	8 fowls	$1.00
Hamilton's Negro	0.96	18 tarapins	
Hamilton's negro	$1.00	2 ?	
Hamilton's negro	$1.12	fowls	
Hamilton's negro	.12½	?	
Hamilton's negro	.37½	cash?	
Hamilton's negro	$1.87 & ½	15 chickens	
Hamilton's negro	10 fowls		
Hamilton's Negro	$2.00	16 chickens	
Hamilton'sNegro	$1.50	12 fowls	$8.83 & ½
Hamilton's old woman	0.6	3 fowls	0.6
Hannah	0.5	4 chickens	
Hannah	$1.00	given	
Hannah	.77½	chickens	
Hannah	.37½	3 chickens	
Hannah	.62½	5 chickens	$3.277½
Hannah Page	0.5	?	
Harriet Abbott	$1.25	10 chickens	
Harriet Abbott	$1.70	14 fowls	$2.95
Harriet Armstrong	$1.88	?	$1.88
Harriet Cater	$1.00	8 chickens	$1.00
Henry	0.62	5 chickens	
Henry	.62 & ½	5 chickens	$1.24 & ½

Name (of slave)	Cost	Items	Amount $ Paid
Henry Demere	$1.87	1.87½	$1.87
Hercules	$1.00	loan	
Hercules	.37&½	3 chickens	$1.37 & ½
Hetty	0.15		
Hetty	$1.00	8 chickens	$1.15
Hopeton Negro	$2.40	poultry $2.40 & fowls	
Ishmael	0.75	100 cts fodder	0.75
Issac Hamilton	0.6		0.6
Jacob	2.12 & ½	tarapins	2.12 & ½
Jacob, Amy, William	$2.06	24 tarapins & 9 boxes?	$2.06
James	$1.50	10 fowls	
James	$1.12 & ½	9 chickens	$2.62 & ½
Jennifer		4 chickens	0.5
Jeremy	.87 & ½	?	.87 & ½
Jerry	0.1	Mr. King	
Jerry	0.25	2 chickens	0.35
Jessica &	$5.75	poultry	
Jessica &	$7.82 & ½	poultry	$13.57 & ½
Jim Cater	.87½	7 fowls	.87½
Jim Wright	$1.00	9 fowls	
Jim Wright	$2.00	9 chickens	$3.00
Jimmy	$1.00	8 chickens	$1.00
Jimpa	$2.25	in full	$2.25
John	0.5	a loan	
John	0.8	7 chickens	12 & ½ (overpaid)

Name (of slave)	Cost	Items	Amount $ Paid
John	$1.50	in full	
John	$2.75	bal for corn	
John	$4.00	corn and eggs	
John		8 chickens	$9.55
John Haggard	$1.00	?	
John Haggard	$1.50	mending shoes	
John Haggard	$2.00	16 chickens	
John Haggard	$2.50	fowls	
John Haggard	.93¾	5 fowls	$7.933 & ¾
Johnnie	0.25	?	
Johnny	0.5	4 chickens	
Johnny Couper	0.65	eggs	$1.15
Julianna	0.25	?	
Julianna	$1.25	honey & fowls	
Julianna	.25½	2 chickens	
Julianna	.62 & ½	5 chickens	
Julianna	0.5	4 fowls	$2.88
Juniper	$1.25	10 chickens	
Juniper	.37 ½	3 chickens	$1.62 & ½
Katy	0.25	cash?	0.25
Kent	0.5	4 chickens	0.5
Lady	0.5	?	
Lady	$1.00	8 chickens	
Lady	$1.00	chickens	$3.50
Lavinia	$2.50	cash?	$2.50
Lewis	0.25	2 fowls	
Lewis	$2.75	fish	
Lewis Hamilton	.18 ½	?	$3.18 & ½
Lord	$1.12 & ½	5 fowls	
Lord Nye?	0.25		$1.37 & ½
Lucinda	.93 & ⅗	?	.93 & ⅗

Name (of slave)	Cost	Items	Amount $ Paid
Major & Gracie Demere	$4.12 & ½	33 fowls	
Major Demere	$1.25	9 fowls	$5.37 & ½
Malley	0.25	?	
Malley	$2.50	? clams	$2.75
March	0.25	2 chickens	
March	0.75	?	
March	$1.00	161 lbs fodder	
March	.62 ½	bal on a/c	
March hamilton	0.5	?	$3.12 & ½
Marcia	0.5	2 chickens/ a loan	
Marcia	$1.87 ½	corn and chics	
Marcia	.12 ½	?	$2.50
Margaret Hamilton	0.75	fowls	0.75
Maria	0.75	6 fowls	
Maria	$2.87	bal for corn	
Maria	.37 ½	?	
Maria	?	corn	$3.99 & ½
Mary Carter	$1.25	10 chickens	$1.25
Mary Suckie	$2.10	21 fowls	$2.10
May Hamilton	0.25	2 doz eggs	
May Hamilton	$1.50	10 fowls	$1.75
Miky	0.5	cash?	0.5
Mitchell	$1.00	8 chickens	$1.00
Molbrook	0.75	cash?	0.75
Mr Cates negro	$1.75	14 chickens	$1.75
Mr. Couper's man	$1.002	straw hats	$1.00
Mr. Gould	$1.15	straw hat	

Name (of slave)	Cost	Items	Amount $ Paid
Mr. Gould	$1.25	10 fowls	
Mr. Gould's boy	$2.001	6 fowls	$4.35
Mr. Grants negro	$2.75	full for fowls	$2.75
Mr. Haggard	$9.00	butter	$9.00
Mr. Highsmith	$1.00	8 chickens	$1.00
Mr. McIntosh	$1.00	bridle?	$1.00
Mr. Tison	$1.00?	salt	$1.00?
Mr. Woolley	$12.13	poultry	$12.13
Mrs. Abbott's William	.62 & ½	5 chickens	.62 & ½
Mrs. Cater's Robbin	$2.001	6 fowls	
Mrs. Cater	$1.50	12 chickens	
Mrs. Cater	$5.00	5 turkeys 4 ducks	
Mrs. Cater	$?	fowls	$8.50
Mrs. Davis	$10.55	17 Turkeys	$10.55
Mumford	$3.76	sundries	$3.76
Nancy	.56¼	3 fowls	.56¼
Nantro	0.25	2 chickens	
Nantro	0.5	fowls	
Nantro	$1.00	8 fowls	
Nantro	$1.25	4 English ducks	
Nantro	$1.18¾	9 chickens	
Nantro?	0.75	6 chickens	$4.93 & ¾
Ned	0.25	2 chickens	
Ned	0.25		
Ned	$1.88	1 basket & fodder?	
Ned	.37½	3 chickens	
Ned	.87½	7 fowls	
Ned	0.25	?	

Name (of slave)	Cost	Items	Amount $ Paid
Ned H	$1.75	18 chickens	
Ned Hamilton	0.5	4 chickens	$6.12 & ½
Negro Bud	$1.00	8 fowl	$1.00
Negro@Hamilton	$1.25	10 chickens	$1.25
Neptune	0.5	eggs	
Neptune	0.75	6 chickens	
Neptune	$0.75	6 chickens	
Neptune	0.75	6 chickens	
Neptune	0.87	7 fowls	
Neptune	0.9	poultry	
Neptune	$1.00	in full	
Neptune	$1.00	poultry	
Neptune	$1.25	10 fowls	
Neptune	$1.25	8 chickens	
Neptune	$2.50	work	
Neptune	$3.00	3 gals honey	
Neptune	$5.87 & ½	corn & poultry	
Neptune	.62 & ½	?	
Neptune	.87 ½	7 chickens	$21.89 & ½
Old Amy	0.68	cash?	
Old Amy	$4.25	fowls 6 turkey 11 ducks	
Old Amy	1.62½	12 chickens	
Old Anthony	$1.25	10 chickens	
Old Anthony	$1.62 ½	13 fowls	$1.87 & ½
Old Charles Couper	$3.30	28 fowls	$3.30
Old Cupid	$1.25	10 fowls	
Old Cupid	$3.15	?	
Old Cupid	$4.50	corn and poultry	
Old Cupid	$3.12½	16 chickens	
Old Cupid	$4.37½	corn	
Old Cupid	.37 & ½	3 chickens	$16.77 & ½
Old Dembo	0.45	1 fowl 1 duck	
Old Dembo	$1.00	8 chickens	
Old Dembo	$5.00	capons?	$6.45

Name (of slave)	Cost	Items	Amount $ Paid
Old Hickey	$7.00	taming	$7.00
Old Jacob	$12.62½	poultry in full	
Old Jacob Butler	$5.70	20 ducks	$18.12 & ½
Old Jane	$4.25	honey	
Old Jane	.12½		
Old Jane	.37 & ½	2½ gal honey	
Old Jane	$7.58	swans, honey & chickens	
Old Katy	.62½	5 fowls	
Old Katy	$1.00	9 fowls	
Old Katy	.37½	3 fowls	$2.00
Old man?	0.75	cash?	0.75
Old Nancy Hamilton	.62½	chickens	.62½
Old Negro	$1.00	2 baskets	$1.00
Old Peter	$1.00	8 fowls	
Old Peter	.87 & ½	7 chickens	$1.87 & ½
Old Whiskey	$2.56	3 baskets	$2.56
Other man	0.65	5 fowls	0.65
Page family	$1.87½	chickens	$1.87½
Patience	0.25	?	
Patience	$1.75	?	$2.00
Patty	$1.75	ducks	
Patty	$2.00	16 chickens	
Patty	$2.25	1 duck & 10 fowls	
Patty	$4.00	ducks & fowls	
Patty	$1.0?	Ducks	
Patty	$2.95¾	7 ducks & fowls	
Patty Hamilton	$1.25	fowls	$15.2 & ¾
Peggy	0.55	fowls	
Peggy	0.5	cash?	

Name (of slave)	Cost	Items	Amount $ Paid
Peggy	$1.00	corn	
Peggy	.37½	3 chickens	$2.37 & ½
Peter	0.54	fowls	
Peter	0.5	eggs	
Peter	0.75	6 dozen eggs	
Peter	0.75	on a/c	
Peter	$1.00	6 chickens & ?	
Peter	$1.00	8 fowls	
Peter	$2.00	17 chickens	
Peter	$2.00	a/c	
Peter	$3.00	18 chics & 5 doz eggs	
Peter	$3.00	cash?	
Peter	$3.00	fowls	
Peter	$3.50	corn	
Peter	$3.65	145 oranges	
Peter	$4.00	a present	
Peter	$1.12½	7 chickens	
Peter	$1.60?	2 doz eggs	
Peter	$1.66¾		
Peter	$2.43¾	pmt in full	
Peter	$3.12½	corn and fowls	
Peter	.12 & ½	11 eggs	
Peter	.31 & ¼	30 eggs	
Peter	.68¾	6 fowls	
Peter	?	6 chickens	$39.69 & ½
Peter Couper	.62 & ½	5 chickens	.62 & ½
Peter Hamilton	$1.50	12 chickens	$1.50
Peter Jun	0.25	?	
Peter Jun	$1.50	12 chickens	
Peter Jun	$1.60	13 chickens	$3.35
Poter	$1.50	9 fowls	$1.50
Prince	0.75	?	0.75
Prince Hamilton	$1.62 & ½	13 fowls	$1.62 & ½
Pussy	0.35	9 eggs 1 chic	
Pussy	0.5	4 chickens	

Name (of slave)	Cost	Items	Amount $ Paid
Pussy	0.5	4 chickens	
Pussy	0.5	4 fowls	
Pussy	0.62	5 chickens	
Pussy	0.85	6 fowls & eggs	
Pussy	$1.00	?	
Pussy	$1.00	8 chickens	
Pussy	$1.00	8 fowls	
Pussy	$1.25	10 chickens	
Pussy	$1.25	9 chickens	
Pussy	$1.42	pmt. in full	
Pussy	$1.62	14 chickens	
Pussy	$3.25	?	
Pussy	$3.33	in full	
Pussy	$3.75	5 bushels corn	
Pussy	$17.05	old debt	
Pussy	$.87 & ½	7 chickens	
Pussy	$1.37 & ½	11 chickens	
Pussy	.56½	chickens	
Pussy	.62½	Damian negro	
Pussy	.87½	7 chickens	
Pussy	2.12 & ½	17 chickens	$45.68
Quamina	0.5	cash?	
Quamina	0.25	1 fowl	
Quamina	0.75	6 chickens	
Quamina	$1.00	?	
Quamina	$1.43	a/c	
Quamina	$2.00	16 fowls	
Quamina	$2.00	a/c fowls	
Quamina	$2.62	7 chickens & eggs	
Quamina	$3.00	corn and eggs	
Quamina	$6.90	poultry & corn	
Quamina	$8.25	corn & poultry	$28.70
Quanamina	0.25	2 doz eggs	
Quanamina	0.37	cash?	
Quanamina	$1.50	9 fowls	
Quanamina	.12½	2 fowls	
Quanamina	$1.29	?	
Quanamina	$2.63	8 fowls & fodder	
Quanamina	$3.00	4 & ½ corn bushels	$9.16 & ½
Rachel	0.25	bal due	0.25

Name (of slave)	Cost	Items	Amount $ Paid
Rhina	0.31	?	
Rhina	0.75	6 fowls	
Rhina	0.75		
Rhina	$1.00	?	
Rhina	.12½	1 chicken	$2.93 & ½
Richard	$0.15	3 tarapins	
Richard	0.5	4 chickens	
Richard	0.75	chickens	
Richard	$1.48	in full	
Richard	$5.20	old debt	
Richard	$6.50	bal for corn	
Richard	$2.00?	16 fowls 1 duck	
Richard	[not legible]	?	
Richard & Nancy	$5.50	corn	$5.50
Richard Demere	$1.25	10 chickens	$1.25
Richard Haggard	$1.50	4 wooden nepels?	$1.50
Robert	0.1	tarapins?	
Robert	0.65	13 tarapins	
Robert	0.75	poultry fodder	
Robert	$1.00	8 fowls	
Robert	$2.00	16 chickens	
Robert Cater	$1.00	8 chics, 1 duck	
Rose	$1.50	12 chickens	$1.50
Ruthy	$1.00	?	
Ruthy	$1.12½	1 chicken	
Ruthy Cater	0.75	6 chickens	
Ruthy Cater	$2.50	20 chickens	$6.25
Sally	0.25	cash?	0.25
Sam	0.2	freight	
Sam	$1.75	2 quails, 1 proggan	
Sam	$2.00	16 chickens	
Sam	$2.00	tub	

Name (of slave)	Cost	Items	Amount $ Paid
Sam	$2.50	purchase hog	
Sam	.62 & ½	?	$9.07 & ½
Sam Carter	$1.25	5 fowls & chics	$1.25
Sam H.	$1.00	2 quails	
Sam Hamilton	$1.00	basket	
Sam Hamilton	$1.25	?	$3.25
Sam McIntosh	0.35	3 chickens	
Sam McIntosh	$1.00	eggs & fowls	
Sam McIntosh	$1.50	8 fowls 1 basket, eggs	
Sam McIntosh	$2.00	15 chickens	
Sam McIntosh	$4.00	corn & chics	
Sam McIntosh	$4.12	33 fowls	$12.97
Sanders	$1.45	pmt. in full	
Sanders	0.5	4 chickens	
Sanders	0.7	corn in full	
Sanders	$2.25	18 chickens	
Sanders	$2.50	fowls	
Sanders	$4.50	in full for corn	
Sanders	$5.25	in full for corn	
Sanders	$2.14 & ½	1 fanner, 3 baskets	$19.29 & ½
Sandra	0.5	4 chickens	0.5
Sarah	0.25	cash?	
Sarah	0.5	4 fowls	
Sarah	.12½	?	
Savannah	0.6		
Savannah	$2.00	cash?	$2.60
Shance Demen	$1.75	18 fowls	$1.75
Stafford's negro	$3.00	23 fowl	$3.00
Stephen King's negro	0.75	1 pair ducks	0.75

Name (of slave)	Cost	Items	Amount $ Paid
Sue Demer	$1.00	8 fowls	$1.00
Sukey	0.5	1 pig?	
Sukey	$3.00	9 ducks	
Sukey	$4.05	in full for all	
Sukey	$5.50	corn	
Sukey	$1.67½	fowls & ducks in full	$14.72 & ½
Sukey & Neptune	$3.57	?	$3.57
Summer	$2.12½	17 chickens	
Summer	$1.00	7 chickens	$3.12 & ½
Sye Wylly	$1.12½	1 duck 7 fowls	$1.12½
Sylvester	0.75	3 boot brushes	0.75
T. Bond	0.5	cash?	0.5
Tella	0.5	4 chickens	0.5
Tim Wright	$1.00	8 chickens	
Tim Wright	$1.26	corn	
Tim Wright	$1.50	11 fowls	
Tim Wright	$4.00	cash?	
Tim Wright	.62½	fowls	$8.38 & ½
Tom Hamilton	$1.50	4 mats	$1.50
Tomas	$1.25	6 fowls	$1.25
Toney	0.5	chickens	
Toney	$1.50	2 bushels corn	
Toney	$2.00	bal for corn	
Toney	$3.00	7 ducks	$7.00
Toney & Julia	$3.50	in full	$3.50
Toney Wylly	$2.75	fowls & ducks	$2.75
Virginia	0.5	none given	
Virginia	$1.50	? grain	$2.00

Name (of slave)	Cost	Items	Amount $ Paid
Virginia & Florence	$2.65	?	$2.65
Whiskey	0.5	3 fowls	
Whiskey	0.75	?	
Whiskey	$1.50	cash	
Whiskey	$1.70 & ½	7 baskets	
Will	$1.57½	5 straw hats	$1.57½
Will Hamilton	.37½	3 fowls	.37½
William	0.1	tarapins?	
William	0.5	8 tarapins	0.6
William & Alfred	.87 & ½	tarapins	
William & Alfred	$1.68	?	$2.55 & ½
William Abbott	$1.47	12 fowls	
William Abbott	$1.75	?	
William Abbott	$3.00	24 fowls	
William Abbott	.62½	4 fowls	
Wylly's boy	.68 & ¾	5 & ½ dozen eggs	.68 & ¾
Wylly's man	$1.00	music	$1.00
Wylly's Negro	0.75	6 fowls	
Wylly's Negro	$1.00	8 chickens	
Wylly's Negro	$1.00	8 chickens	
Wylly's Negro	$1.50	3 ducks & 6 chics	
Wylly's Negro	$1.12 & ½	6 baskets	
Wylly's Sye	$3.701	5 ducks	$3.70

NOTES

Introduction

1. Emily Burke, *Pleasure and Pain: Reminiscences of Georgia in the 1840s* (Savannah, Ga.: Beehive Press, 1978, originally published in 1850), 88–90.

2. Ibid., emphasis added.

3. See Ralph V. Anderson and Robert Gallman, "Slaves as Fixed Capital: Slave Labor and Southern Economic Development," *Journal of American History* 64, no. 1 (June 1977): 24–46; Ira Berlin and Philip D. Morgan, eds., *Cultivation and Culture: Labor and the Shaping of Slave Life in the Americas* (Charlottesville, Va.: University of Virginia Press, 1993); Judith Carney, *Black Rice: The African Origins of Rice Cultivation in the Americas* (Cambridge, Mass.: Harvard University Press, 2001); Joyce Chaplin, "Tidal Rice Cultivation and the Problem of Slavery in South Carolina and Georgia, 1760–1815," *William and Mary Quarterly* 49, no. 1 (January 1992): 29–61; Sharla Fett, *Working Cures: Healing, Health, and Power on Southern Slave Plantations* (Chapel Hill: University of North Carolina Press, 2002); Michael P. Johnson, "Work, Culture, and the Slave Community: Slave Occupations in the Cotton Belt in 1860," *Labor History* 27 (Summer 1986): 325–55; Jennifer L. Morgan, *Laboring Women: Gender and Reproduction in the Making of New World Slavery* (Philadelphia: University of Pennsylvania Press, 2004); Philip D. Morgan, "Task and Gang Systems: The Organization of Labor on New World Plantations," in *Work and Labor in Early America*, ed. Stephen Innes (Chapel Hill: University of North Carolina Press, 1988), 189–220; Leslie A. Schwalm, *'A Hard Fight for We': Women's Transition from Slavery to Freedom in South Carolina* (Urbana: University of Illinois Press, 1997); and William L. Van Deburg, *The Slave Drivers: Black Agricultural Labor Supervisors in the Antebellum South* (Westport, Conn.: Greenwood Press, 1979).

4. I prefer to use the term "enslaved" rather than "slave" because it forces us to consider that bondpeople did not let anyone "own" them. They were enslaved against their will. In most cases, I use the terms "bondmen," "bondwomen," or "bondpeople" in place of "slave(s)"; these terms are used interchangeably throughout the book.

It is also my preference to use the term "slaveholders" rather than "slave owners," "owners," or "masters" because we cannot assume that bondpeople allowed themselves to be owned or mastered by someone else. Instead, I use the terms "slaveholders" and "planters" interchangeably. My use of the term "planters" does not correlate with the size or net worth of their property.

5. See Daina L. Ramey, "A Place of Our Own: Labor, Family, and Community among Female Slaves in Piedmont and Tidewater Georgia, 1820–1860," (Ph.D.

diss., University of California, Los Angeles, 1998), 34–37, and "'A Heap of Us Slaves': Family and Community Life among Slave Women in Georgia," *Atlanta History: A Journal of Georgia and the South* 44, no. 3 (Fall 2000): 21–38.

6. Searching for the enslaved viewpoint is an arduous task. Most records offer only the planters' perceptions; these planters did not see the world from the point of view of bondpeople. In their personal papers, for example, slaveholders commented on slaves based on circumstances relevant to their financial investment in them and economic return from them. Because planters did not write much at all about topics such as slave relationships, resistance strategies, and coping mechanisms, it is necessary for the historian to infer bondpeople's views from what they did write. We can also get the enslaved perspective from planter records by asking strategic questions and considering how planters' decisions affected the enslaved. For a recent discussion of enslaved humanity, see Walter Johnson, "On Agency," *Journal of Social History*, 37, no. 1 (Fall 2003): 113–24.

7. See John Blassingame, *The Slave Community: Plantation Life in the Antebellum South* (New York: Oxford University Press, 1972); Orville Vernon Burton, *"In My Father's House Are Many Mansions": Family and Community in Edgefield, South Carolina* (Chapel Hill: University of North Carolina Press, 1985); Stephanie M. H. Camp, *Closer to Freedom: Enslaved Women and Everyday Resistance in the Plantation South* (Chapel Hill: University of North Carolina Press, 2004); Wilma A. Dunaway, *The African American Family in Slavery and Emancipation* (Cambridge: Cambridge University Press, 2003); Eugene D. Genovese, *Roll Jordan Roll: The World the Slaves Made* (New York: Vintage Books, 1974); Herbert G. Gutman, *The Black Family in Slavery and Freedom, 1750–1925* (New York: Vintage Books, 1976); Larry E. Hudson Jr., *To Have and to Hold: Slave Work and Family Life in Antebellum South Carolina* (Athens: University of Georgia Press, 1997); Charles Joyner, *Down by the Riverside: A South Carolina Slave Community* (Urbana: University of Illinois Press, 1984); Wilma King, *Stolen Childhood: Slave Youth in Nineteenth Century America* (Bloomington: Indiana University Press, 1995); Lawrence W. Levine, *Black Culture and Black Consciousness: Afro-American Folk Thought from Slavery to Freedom* (New York: Oxford University Press, 1977); Ann Patton Malone, *Sweet Chariot: Slave Family and Household Structure in Nineteenth-Century Louisiana* (Chapel Hill: University of North Carolina Press, 1992); Albert Raboteau, *Slave Religion: The "Invisible Institution" in the Antebellum South* (New York: Oxford University Press, 1978); Machel Sobel, *The World They Made Together: Black and White Values in Eighteenth-Century Virginia* (Princeton, N.J.: Princeton University Press, 1987); Brenda E. Stevenson, *Life in Black and White: Family and Community in the Slave South* (New York: Oxford University Press, 1996); Sterling Stuckey, *Slave Culture: Nationalist Theory and the Foundations of Black America* (New York: Oxford University Press, 1987); Thomas L. Webber, *Deep Like the Rivers: Education in the Slave Quarter Community, 1831–1865* (New York: W. W. Norton and Company, 1978); and Deborah Gray White, *Ar'n't I a Woman?: Female Slaves in the Plantation South* (New York: W. W. Norton and Company, 1985).

8. Sources play an important role in determining the questions posed and the topics examined. I analyzed primary documents relating to Glynn and Wilkes Counties, including miscellaneous private papers, plantation records, scrapbooks, medical journals, slave narratives, letters, and other correspondence. Poring over

importation records, court cases, traveler's journals, probate records, agricultural literature, and periodicals, I discovered the intricate ways that gender affected slave life and influenced slaveholders' decisions.

9. See Stanley Elkins, *Slavery: A Problem in American Institutional and Intellectual Life* (Chicago: University of Chicago Press, 1976; 1959), and James L. Watson, "Slavery as an Institution: Open and Closed Systems," in Watson, *Asian and African Systems of Slavery* (Berkeley: University of California Press, 1980), 1–15.

10. In order to develop a solid analysis of these representative regions, I relied heavily on slave narratives from Glynn and Wilkes Counties published in the Works Progress Administration (WPA) collection and cross-checked my findings with the originals housed at the Library of Congress. In the 1930s the Work Projects Administration sent a team of interviewers, predominantly whites, to various southern regions to interview the last generation of former slaves. These interviews represent one of the few extant sources from the enslaved perspective. Like any source, scholars should exercise caution when using these testimonies because of racial bias evidenced by the questions asked as well as the method, dialect, and tone of these edited narratives. For a discussion of the strengths and weaknesses of enslaved narratives, see John Blassingame, "Using the Testimony of Ex-Slaves: Approaches and Problems," *Journal of Southern History* 41, no. 4 (November 1975): 473–92. See also Walter Johnson, *Soul by Soul: Life in the Antebellum Slave Market* (Cambridge, Mass.: Harvard University Press, 1999), 9–11; and Stephanie J. Shaw, "Using the WPA Ex-Slave Narratives to Study the Impact of the Great Depression," *Journal of Southern History* 69, no. 3 (August 2003): 623–58.

Fifteen former slaves stated that they resided in Wilkes County and only one said that she lived in Glynn County. Wilkes County narratives found in the WPA collection include the following individuals: Arrie Binns, Alice Bradley, Marshal Butler, Mrs. Mariah Callaway, Willis Cofer, Wheeler Gresham, Jane Smith Hill Harmon, Robert Henry, Emma Hurly, and Manuel Johnson, vol. 12; and Henry Rogers, Jane Mickens Toombs, and Adeline Willis, vol. 13. J. E. Filer and Mollie Kinsey appear in vol. 8 and supplementary series vol. 4, respectively. The narrative of Mrs. Julia Rush is the only WPA narrative that represents the enslaved experience in Glynn County; see vol. 13. In addition to the WPA collection, the testimonies found in *Drums and Shadows* offer rich firsthand accounts of enslaved life in Glynn County along with published plantation journals and letters. See the Savannah Unit of the Georgia Writers' Project, *Drums and Shadows: Survival Studies among the Georgia Coastal Negroes* (Athens: University of Georgia Press, 1940); Frances Anne Kemble, *Journal of a Residence on a Georgian Plantation in 1838–1839* (Athens: University of Georgia Press, 1984); Melanie Pavich-Lindsay, ed., *Anna: The Letters of a St. Simons Island Plantation Mistress, 1817–1859* (Athens: University of Georgia Press, 2002); and Elizabeth W. Allston Pringle, *A Woman Rice Planter, by Patience Pennington* [pseud.] (Cambridge, Mass.: Harvard University Press, 1961).

11. On occasion, in order to make connections and links to larger arguments (macro approach), I use published slave narratives such as those found in James Mellon, ed., *Bullwhip Days: The Slaves Remember, An Oral History* (New York: Avon Books, 1988); Andrew Waters, ed., *On Jordan's Stormy Banks: Personal*

Accounts of Slavery in Georgia (Winston-Salem, N.C.: John F. Blair, 2000); and Donna Wyant Howell, comp., *I Was a Slave: True Life Stories Told by Former American Slaves in the 1930's* (Washington: American Legacy Books, 1995).

I also make references to the more well-known narratives of Harriet Jacobs, Charles Ball, and John Brown. See Harriet Jacobs, *Incidents in the Life of a Slave Girl Written by Herself*, Jean Fagan Yellin, ed., (Cambridge, Mass.: Harvard University Press, 1987); Charles Ball, *Fifty Years in Chains: Or the Life of An American Slave* (New York: H. Dayton, 1859); John Brown, *Slave Life in Georgia: A Narrative of the Life, Sufferings, and Escape of John Brown, a Fugitive Slave Now in England* (1855, reprint, Freeport, N.Y.: Books for Libraries Press, 1971).

I also draw upon work songs on the theory that singing provided a natural metronome for the rhythm of work, religious expression, and dance. All songs or portions of them come from Wilkes and Glynn County sources. Fortunately, the work of Lydia Parrish in coastal Georgia provided several examples for Glynn County. See Parrish, *Slave Songs of the Georgia Sea Islands* (1942, reprint, Athens: University of Georgia Press, 1992). The other songs appear in a variety of places including books written by descendants of slaveholders, regional studies with passing reference to music, plantation scrapbooks, letters, travel accounts, and other published and unpublished documents.

12. According to Works Progress Administration officers, "Brunswick became second in importance to Savannah as a port." It contained "numerous wharves and docks accommodating vessels of 30–foot draft." See WPA Collection, Glynn County, Library of Congress.

13. The six counties made from Wilkes include Elbert (1790), Oglethorpe (1793), Warren (1793), Lincoln (1796), Madison (1811), and Taliaferro (1825).

14. "Many farmers possessed a single family of Negroes," explains James C. Bonner, "and a few had acquired from 20 to 50, denoting the rise of a class of upcountry plantation masters." Bonner, *A History of Georgia Agriculture, 1732–1860* (Athens: University of Georgia Press, 1964), 50.

15. Julia Floyd Smith, *Slavery and Rice Cultivation in Low Country Georgia 1750–1860* (Knoxville: University of Tennessee Press, 1985), 9.

16. The specific numbers for these years are 8.4 and 16.17 slaves per plantation. For additional antebellum years, Flanders estimated that the average size slaveholding was 10.8 for 1830, 11.7 for 1840, and 13.0 for 1850. See Ralph B. Flanders, *Plantation Slavery in Georgia*, (Chapel Hill: University of North Carolina Press, 1933), 70. The statistics for 1830 are confirmed by George Bolten Ellenberg, "Wilkes County, Georgia, Beginnings to 1830: The Growth of Slavery and Its Impact on Class Structure," (M.A. thesis, Clemson University, 1988), 120.

17. Scholars at the Harvard University Inter-university Consortium for Political and Social Research calculated the total number of male and female slaves in the population based on federal census statistics; I calculated the percentages. Note that the Harvard figures for 1850 are slightly higher than my estimates. For 1820 the total slave population for Wilkes County was 9,705; female slaves totaled 4,809 (49.55 percent) and male slaves totaled 4,896 (50.44 percent). For 1850 the total slave population decreased to 8,281; female slaves totaled 4,216 (50.91 percent) and male slaves totaled 4,065 (49.26 percent). Again, in 1860, the slave population decreased to 7,953 slaves; 4,052 females (50.94 percent) and

3,901 males (49.05 percent). For the Harvard University statistics, see their Web site at http://icg.fas.harvard.edu/census/.

18. St. Simons Island is eighteen miles east of Brunswick, Georgia, and is approximately thirteen miles long and two miles wide. Jekyll Island is south of St. Simons and is approximately ten miles long and consists of 11,000 acres.

19. U.S. Department of Commerce, Bureau of the Census, Federal Manuscript Census (Population and Slave Schedules), Glynn County, Georgia, 1820–1860 (microfilm). See also John Solomon Otto, "Slavery in a Coastal Community–Glynn County (1790–1860)," *Georgia Historical Quarterly* 63 (1970): 460–80, especially 462 and 468. He also estimated that sixty-four was the median number of slaves per plantation. See Otto, *Cannon's Point Plantation 1794–1860: Living Conditions and Status Patterns in the Old South* (Orlando, Fla.: Academic Press, Inc., 1984), 34. United States Bureau of the Census, 1820–1860: Population Schedules, Glynn County, Georgia (microfilm). For specific figures for Glynn County and for Wilkes County, see Ramey, "A Place of Our Own," 24–28. See also Otto, "Slavery in a Coastal Community."

20. Smith, *Slavery and Rice Cultivation*, 7, 11. Their annual removal to inland counties such as Appaling, Ware, and Wayne protected slaveholding families from the sweltering heat and humidity of the summer months.

21. The exact figure was 41.67 slaves per holding. U.S. Department of Commerce, Bureau of the Census, Federal Manuscript Census (Population and Slave Schedules) Glynn County, Georgia, 1850 (microfilm). I calculated this figure by dividing the total number of slaves (4,209) by the total number of slaveholders (101) for this particular year.

22. Wilkes County slaves averaged 8,280 in number while Glynn County slaves averaged 3,641 throughout the antebellum period. In 1820 the total slave population for Glynn County was 2,760; female slaves totaled 1,417 (51.34 percent) and male slaves totaled 1,343 (48.65 percent). For 1850 the total slave population increased to 4,232; female slaves totaled 2,256 (53.3 percent) and male slaves totaled 1,976 (46.69 percent). In 1860, the slave population decreased to 2,839 slaves; females totaled 1,493 (52.58 percent) and males totaled 1,346 (47.41 percent). See also table 1.1, p. 14. For the Harvard University statistics, see the Web site: http://icg.fas.harvard.edu/census/.

23. See Deborah Gray White, "Female Slaves: Sex Roles and Status in the Antebellum Plantation South," *Journal of Family History* 8 (Fall 1983): 248–61; White, *Ar'n't I a Woman?*; Brenda E. Stevenson, "Distress and Discord in Virginia Slave Families, 1830–1860," in *In Joy and In Sorrow: Women, Family, and Marriage in the Victorian South, 1830–1900,* ed. Carol Blesser (New York: Oxford University Press, 1991), 103–24; Nell Irvin Painter, "Soul Murder and Slavery: Toward a Fully Loaded Cost Accounting," in *U.S. History as Women's History: New Feminists Essays,* ed. Linda K. Kerber, Alice Kessler-Harris, and Kathryn Kish Sklar (Chapel Hill: University of North Carolina Press, 1995), 125–46; Christie Farnham, "Sapphire? The Issue of Dominance in the Slave Family, 1830–1865," in *"To Toil the Livelong Day": America's Women at Work, 1780–1980,* ed. Carol Groneman and Mary Beth Norton (Ithaca, N.Y.: Cornell University Press, 1987), 68–83; Thelma Jennings, "'Us Colored Women Had to Go Through a Plenty': Sexual Exploitation of African American Slave Women," *Journal of Women's History* 1, no. 3 (Winter 1990): 45–72; Darlene Clark Hine, "Rape and the Inner Lives of Black Women in

the Middle West: Preliminary Thoughts on the Culture of Dissemblance, *Signs* 14 (Summer 1989): 912–20; Diane Miller Sommerville, "The Rape Myth in the Old South Reconsidered," *Journal of Southern History* 61, no. 5 (1993): 481–509; "Rape," in *Black Women in America: An Historical Encyclopedia*, 2nd ed., ed. Darlene Clark Hine, et al. (New York: Oxford University Press, 2005), and *Rape and Race in the Nineteenth-Century South* (Chapel Hill: University of North Carolina Press, 2004); Sharon Block, "Rape without Women: Print Culture and the Politicalization of Rape, 1765–1850," *Journal of American History* 89, no. 3 (2002): 849–96; and Christopher Morris, "Within the Slave Cabin: Violence in Mississippi Slave Families," in *Over the Threshold: Intimate Violence in Early America*, ed. Christine Daniels and Michael V. Kennedy (New York: Routledge, 1999), 268–85.

24. See the first book-length study by Jonathan D. Martin, *Divided Mastery: Slave Hiring in the American South* (Cambridge, Mass.: Harvard University Press, 2004). Aside from Martin, only a handful of scholars have written on the subject of slave hiring. See, for example, Ira Berlin, *Many Thousands Gone: The First Two Centuries of Slavery in North America* (Cambridge, Mass.: Harvard University Press, 1998); Camp, *Closer to Freedom*, 96–99; Robert Fogel and Stanley L. Engerman, *Time on the Cross: The Economics of American Negro Slavery* (Boston: Little, Brown, 1974), 52–57, 103, 107, and 177; Clement Eaton, "Slave Hiring in the Upper South: A Step toward Freedom," *Mississippi Valley Historical Review* 48 (March 1960): 663–78; Keith Barton, "'Good Cooks and Washers': Slave Hiring, Domestic Labor, and the Market in Bourbon County, Kentucky," *Journal of American History* 84 no. 2 (September 1997): 436–60; Loren Schweninger, "The Underside of Slavery: The Internal Economy, Self-Hire, and Quasi-Freedom in Virginia, 1780–1865," *Slavery & Abolition* 12, no. 2 (September 1991): 1–22; and Sarah S. Hughes, "Slaves for Hire: The Allocation of Black Labor in Elizabeth City County, Virginia, 1782–1810," *William & Mary Quarterly* 35 (April 1978): 260–86. See also Frederic Bancroft, *Slave Trading in the Old South* (Columbia: University of South Carolina Press, 1996), 145–64; Robert S. Starobin, *Industrial Slavery in the Old South* (New York: Oxford University Press, 1970), 128–37; Robert Olwell, *Masters, Slaves, and Subjects: The Culture of Power in the South Carolina Low Country, 1740–1790* (Ithaca, N.Y.: Cornell University Press, 1998), 158–66; Joyce Chaplin, *An Anxious Pursuit: Agricultural Innovation and Modernity in the Lower South, 1730–1815* (Chapel Hill: University of North Carolina Press, 1993), 122–24 and 326–327; John Hope Franklin and Loren Schweninger, *Runaway Slaves: Rebels on the Plantation* (New York: Oxford University Press, 1999), 4–6, 26–38, and 134–40; and T. Stephen Whitman, *The Price of Freedom Slavery and Manumission in Baltimore and Early National Maryland* (New York: Routledge, 2000).

25. Historian Betty Wood published a well-documented study of gender and informal economies in coastal Georgia. See Betty Wood, *Men's Work, Women's Work: The Informal Slave Economies of Lowcountry Georgia* (Athens: University of Georgia Press, 1995). However, Ira Berlin and Philip D. Morgan spearheaded the discussion of informal economies by responding to the 1960 publication of Sidney Mintz and Douglas Hall's "The Origins of the Jamaican Internal Marketing System," in *Anthropology* 57 (1960). See also Berlin and Morgan, *The Slave's Economy: Independent Production by Slaves in the Americas* (London: Frank

Cass, 1991); and their later work *Cultivation and Culture* (Charlottesville: University Press of Virginia, 1993); Larry Hudson in *Working toward Freedom: Slave Society and the Domestic Economy in the American South* (Rochester, N.Y.: University of Rochester Press, 1994); Dylan C. Penningroth, "Slavery, Freedom, and Social Claims to Property among African Americans in Liberty County, Georgia, 1850–1880," *Journal of American History* 84 (September 1997): 405–35; and *The Claims of Kinfolk: African American Property and Community in the Nineteenth-Century South* (Chapel Hill: University of North Carolina Press, 2003); and William Dusinberre, *Them Dark Days: Slavery in the American Rice Swamps* (New York: Oxford University Press, 1996).

Chapter 1: "I Had to Work Hard, Plow, and Go and Split Wood Jus' Like a Man"

The chapter title is derived from the narrative of Nancy Boudry, an enslaved female from Columbia County. See *Georgia Narratives* IV, pt. 1, Library of Congress, Manuscript Division, 113. Portions of this chapter appeared in a previously published article. See Daina L. Ramey, "'She Do a Heap of Work': Female Slave Labor on Glynn County Rice and Cotton Plantations," *Georgia Historical Quarterly* 82, no. 4 (Winter 1998): 707–34.

1. George P. Rawick, ed., *The American Slave: A Composite Autobiography* (Westport, Conn.: Greenwood Press, 1977) (hereafter *AS*), vol. 13, pt. 4, 163. Marli F. Weiner describes the variety in slave women's work as "cross-training." See Marli F. Weiner, *Mistresses and Slaves: Plantation Women in South Carolina* (Urbana: University of Illinois Press, 1998), 14.

2. Rawick, *AS*, vol. 12, pt. 1, 75.

3. Bonner, *A History of Georgia Agriculture*, 87.

4. Kemble, *Journal of a Residence*, 229–30.

5. For work on the female majority in agricultural labor, see Carney, *Black Rice*; Leigh Ann Pruneau, "All the Time Is Work Time: Gender and the Task System on Antebellum Low Country Rice Plantations" (Ph.D. dissertation, University of Arizona, 1997); Schwalm, *A Hard Fight for We*; and Ramey, "'She Do a Heap of Work.'" For the importance of enslaved women's reproductive labor, see Morgan, *Laboring Women*.

6. Kemble, *Journal of a Residence*, 234.

7. "Elizafield Plantation Journal, 1838–1861," *Southern Historical Collection* #3213–z, Wilson Library, University of North Carolina, Chapel Hill. A microfilmed copy of the original journal is available through *Records of Ante-Bellum Southern Plantations from the Revolution through the Civil War*. See series J, pt. 4, reel 21. See also Albert Virgil House, ed., *Planter Management and Capitalism in Ante-Bellum Georgia: The Journal of Hugh Fraser Grant, Ricegrower* (New York: Columbia University Press, 1954), 118 and 127.

8. Grant recorded information about the weather, economy, slaves, crops, financial debts and credits, as well as deaths and births in his family and the families of his enslaved laborers from 1832 to 1864. See "Elizafield Plantation Journal, 1838–1861"; and House, *Planter Management and Capitalism*, 103, 252–60, and passim.

9. "Elizafield Plantation Journal, 1838–1861"; and House, *Planter Management and Capitalism*, 99 and 107.

10. At Cannon's Point Plantation on St. Simons Island, for example, "women usually picked more [cotton] than men." See Otto, *Cannon's Point Plantation 1794–1860*, 35.

11. See J. D. Legare, "Account of an Agricultural Excursion Made into the South of Georgia in the Winter of 1832," *Southern Agriculturist* 6 (June–August 1833): 160; and Jacqueline Jones, *Labor of Love, Labor of Sorrow: Black Women, Work, and the Family, From Slavery to the Present* (New York: Vintage Books, 1985), 17.

12. L. A. Chamerovzow, ed., *Slave Life in Georgia: A Narrative of the Life, Sufferings, and Escape of John Brown, a Fugitive Slave Now in England* (London, 1855), 129.

13. Carney, *Black Rice*, chapter 4 and passim.

14. Dr. Daniel Lee, "Agricultural Apprentices and Laborers," *Southern Cultivator* 12, no. 6 (June 1854): 169–70.

15. For general population demographics in Glynn and Wilkes Counties, see Ramey, "A Place of Our Own," 24–28. Scholars of colonial and antebellum South Carolina found similar female majorities in the fields. See Carney, *Black Rice*; Morgan, *Laboring Women*; and Schwalm, *A Hard Fight for We*.

16. Historian Kenneth M. Stampp found that "unskilled" was a relative term. See Stampp, *The Peculiar Institution: Slavery in the Antebellum South* (1956, reprint, New York: Vintage Books, 1989), 59–60. Historian Charles Joyner notes "that one could plausibly argue that virtually all the field hands on a rice plantation should be classified as skilled laborers, in view of the level of competence required in rice culture." See Joyner, *Down by the Riverside*, 59–65, quote, 59–60.

17. Fogel and Engerman, *Time on the Cross*, 43 (emphasis added); Morgan, *Laboring Women*, 150; and Schwalm, *A Hard Fight for We*, 21.

18. See "skill," *Webster's New World Dictionary* (New York: Warner Books, 1990), and Philip D. Morgan, *Slave Counterpoint: Black Culture in the Eighteenth-Century Chesapeake and Lowcountry* (Chapel Hill: University of North Carolina Press, 1998), 204, n. 1.

19. Berlin and Morgan, "Introduction," in *Cultivation and Culture*, 14–15. See also Morgan, *Slave Counterpoint*, 179–94. In hoeing corn, Emily Burke found that "three tasks are considered a good day's work for a man, two for a woman, and one and a half for a boy or girl fourteen or fifteen years old." Burke, *Pleasure and Pain*, 38.

20. Morgan, "Task and Gang Systems," 191–92, 199, and *passim*. See also Morgan, *Slave Counterpoint*, 9.

21. Charles Spaulding Wylly, *Annals and Statistics of Glynn County, Georgia* (Brunswick, Ga.: H. A. Wrench & Sons, 1897), 57. For scattered references to William Page's guardianship of Benjamin Franklin Cater, see William Page Papers #1254, Southern Historical Collection, Wilson Library, University of North Carolina, Chapel Hill.

22. James P. Postell, "Kelvin Grove Plantation Book 1853," Margaret Davis Cate Collection, Hargrett Library, University of Georgia, Athens, Georgia (microfilm).

23. William W. Hazzard, *St. Simons Island, Georgia, Brunswick and Vicinity: Description and Travel 1825* (1825, reprint, Virginia Steele Wood, ed., Belmont, Mass.: Oak Hill Press, 1974), 15.

24. Postell, "Kelvin Grove Plantation Book." In 1857, Postell attempted to sell the plantation along with seventy slaves (thirty-nine women and thirty-one men).

25. "Elizafield Plantation Journal, 1838–1861"; and House, *Planter Management and Capitalism*, 53. See also Frederick Law Olmsted, *The Cotton Kingdom: A Traveller's Observations on Cotton and Slavery in the American Slave States, 1853–1861* (1861, reprint, New York: Da Capo Press, 1996), 191; and Otto, *Cannon's Point Plantation*, 35.

26. The female full hands included Nancy, Betty, Ally, Hamit, Hesta, Hanna, Ruthy, Sarah, Jane, Jinny, Big Nancy, and Elsy. Female three-quarter hands included Molly, Nelly, Eve, and Nanny. Phillis was the only half hand, and Amelia, Patience, Venus, Flora, O. Elsy, and Lindy were one-quarter hands. The male full hands included Summer, Robin, Hanible, Robert, and Tony. Morris was the only three-quarter hand, and October, Willima, Jim, Henry, and Jupiter were the one-quarter hands. See "Kelvin Grove Plantation Book," 4.

27. James P. Postell letter to a Mr. Benton sometime in 1857, "Kelvin Grove Plantation Book," Margaret Davis Cate Collection (Athens: University of Georgia). Finally, Margaret Davis Cate noted that the Armstrongs were prominent planters from the Bahamas in "Plantations of St. Simons Island," typescript in *Margaret Davis Cate Collection*, MSS 997, folder 147, courtesy of the Georgia Historical Society, Savannah.

28. See Ellis Merton Coulter, *Old Petersburg and the Broad River Valley of Georgia: Their Rise and Decline* (Milledgeville, Ga.: Boyd Publishing Company, 1994), 108–14, quote on 109. Early use of cotton gins required as many as "20 men to do the work that 6–8 do now." See "Early Cotton Production," http://sweetmamapam.tripod.com/printproduction.html, 28 June 2001.

29. Charles Lyell, *A Second Visit to the United States of North America I* (New York: Harper & Brothers, 1849), 255.

30. Angela Lakwete, *Inventing the Cotton Gin: Machine and Myth in Antebellum America* (Baltimore: Johns Hopkins University Press, 2004), 3.

31. The outturn was dependent on how fast the laborer "supplied the seed cotton, not on how fast the rollers turned." See Lakwete, *Inventing the Cotton Gin*, 38–40.

32. Ibid., 40.

33. Otto, *Cannon's Point Plantation*, 25.

34. Legare, "Account of an Agricultural Excursion," 246.

35. Average provided by Whitemarsh B. Seabrook, *A Memoir on the Origin, Cultivation and Uses of Cotton: From the Earliest Ages to the Present Time with Special Reference to the Sea-Island Cotton Plant* (Charleston, S.C.: Miller & Browne, 1844). For descriptions of Eve's gin, see Legare, "Account of an Agricultural Excursion," 161, 169, and 244–46; Otto, *Cannon's Point Plantation*, 23, 25, and 135–36; and Mark Stewart, *'What Nature Suffers to Groe': Life, Labor, and Landscape on the Georgia Coast, 1680–1920* (Athens: University of Georgia Press, 1996), 126. For a more recent discussion of cotton gins, see Lakwete, *Inventing the Cotton Gin*.

36. See "Kelvin Grove Plantation Book."

37. Legare, "Account of an Agricultural Excursion," 169 and 247.

38. Nanny, age forty-five, is listed as a three-quarter hand. See "List of Field hands at Kelvin Grove, January 1st, 1853."

39. Jane and Sarah were in their twenties, Hester was nineteen, and Hamit's age was unknown but most likely around the same as the others. "List of Field hands at Kelvin Grove."

40. Seabrook, *A Memoir on the Origin*, 32. See also "Kelvin Grove Plantation Book."

41. Outside of the 1853 and 1857 slave lists, the names of these women are the only ones mentioned in the field journal.

42. See "Elizafield Plantation Journal, 1838–1861"; House, *Planter Management and Capitalism*, 7–9; and Smith, *Slavery and Rice Cultivation*, 35.

43. Smith, *Slavery and Rice Cultivation*, 35. This property consisted of sixteen different fields ranging from five to twenty-five acres. See "Elizafield Plantation Journal"; and House, "Planter Management and Capitalism," 128.

44. The specific dates of these returns are 1845, 1848–1850, and 1854–1856. "Elizafield Plantation Journal"; and House, *Planter Management and Capitalism*, 275–76 (my calculations).

45. It is worth noting that Grant owned more women than men. These figures are slightly different from House's estimate of "119 Negroes." Such findings are the result of calculations drawn from the U.S. Department of Commerce, Bureau of the Census, Federal Manuscript Seventh Census, 1850, Glynn County, Georgia. See also "Elizafield Plantation Journal."

46. Albert V. House, "The Management of a Rice Plantation in Georgia, 1834–1861, As Revealed in the Journal of Hugh Fraser Grant," *Agricultural History* 13 (October 1939): 211.

47. U.S. Department of Commerce, Bureau of Census, Federal Manuscript Census (Population and Slave Schedules), Glynn County, Georgia, 1850. See also "Elizafield Plantation Journal"; and House, *Planter Management and Capitalism*, 258–60.

48. "Elizafield Plantation Journal"; and House, *Planter Management and Capitalism*, 99, 120, 123, and passim.

49. "Elizafield Plantation Journal"; and House, *Planter Management and Capitalism*, 159. However, on the 16th and 17th of that month, Grant indicates that a total of eighteen women worked at Point Fields "chopping."

50. Quote taken from Lewis Cecil Gray, *History of Agriculture in the Southern United States to 1860*, 2 vols. (Washington, D.C.: Carnegie Institution of Washington, 1933), 551, emphasis added. Regarding his discussion of the gradations of strength with respect to nearby Hopeton Plantation, Gray found that planter Thomas Couper made this comment about his slaves. For information pertaining to South Carolina slavewomen's work in ditches, see Leslie A. Schwalm, "The Meaning of Freedom: African-American Women and Their Transition from Slavery to Freedom in Lowcountry South Carolina" (Ph.D. diss. University of Wisconsin, 1991), 36; and Schwalm, *A Hard Fight for We*, 22–23.

51. "Plantation Supplies Issued," in "Elizafield Plantation Journal"; and in House, *Planter Management and Capitalism*, 286.

52. See "Elizafield Plantation Journal"; and House, *Planter Management and Capitalism*, 95, 99, and 116.

53. Morgan, *Laboring Women*, passim, quote on 146.

54. Burke, *Pleasure and Pain*, 88.

55. The list of oxen included, Ben*, John*, Buck, Lemon, Wooly, Prince*, Brandy, Bright, Darly, Harry*, O Luke & Two strays, Mary Ann*, Mira*, Char-

lotte*, Julatta*, Sabrinna*, Phoebe*, Lear*, Dido*, Sissy*, Susy*, Strawberry, and Delia*. Those with an asterisk were also the names of field hands. See "Elizafield Plantation Journal"; and House, *Planter Management and Capitalism*, 278.

56. Burke, *Pleasure and Pain*, 63.

57. J. William Harris, *Plain Folk and Gentry in a Slave Society: White Liberty and Black Slavery in Augusta's Hinterlands* (Middletown, Conn.: Wesleyan University Press, 1985), 13.

58. Ibid., 24. However, in his study of a small planter in Washington County, Georgia, Harris found that Benton Miller worked two of his male slaves 285 and 286 days during 1858. See J. William Harris, "The Organization of Work on a Yeoman Slaveholder's Farm," *Agricultural History* 64, no. 1 (Winter 1990): 39–52, particularly 42.

59. Seabrook, *A Memoir on the Origin*, 31. For a description of the type of plows used in southern agriculture, see Gray, *History of Agriculture*, 195–96 and 795–96.

60. Ursula Scott, Louisiana cotton picker, interview with the author, 5 November 2002.

61. Stuart Bruchey, ed., *Cotton and the Growth of the American Economy: 1790–1860* (New York: Harcourt, Brace & World, Inc., 1967), 172, emphasis in original.

62. Gray, *History of Agriculture*, 735.

63. For vivid descriptions of this process, see Legare, "Account of an Agricultural Excursion," 160–69; Otto, *Cannon's Point Plantation*, 35; and Seabrook, *A Memoir on the Origin*, 735–37. For a general discussion of cotton processing such as ginning and market preparation, see Burke, *Pleasure and Pain*, 38; and J. A. Turner, *The Cotton Planter's Manual: Being a Compilation of Facts From the Best Authorities on the Culture of Cotton* (1857, reprint. New York: Negro Universities Press, 1969).

64. Burke, *Pleasure and Pain*, 38.

65. Harris, *Plain Folk and Gentry*, 33. See also *Southern Cultivator* 13 no. 6 (June 1855): 171–74; Burke, *Pleasure and Pain*, 87; and James Holmes, *"Dr. Bullie's" Notes: Reminiscences of Early Georgia and of Philadelphia and New Haven in the 1800s* (Atlanta: Cherokee Publishing Company, 1976), 142.

66. "Rules of the Plantation," *The News*, Washington, Georgia, 9 April 1840.

67. Rawick, *AS*, vol. 13, pt. 3, 220.

68. Ibid., vol. 12, pt. 2, 196.

69. Ibid., vol. 12, pt. 1, 163.

70. Dorothy Brown, North Carolina cotton picker, interview with the author, 4 November 2002.

71. Coulter, *Old Petersburg and the Broad River Valley*, 116.

72. "Agricola," "Management of Negroes," *Southern Cultivator* 13, no. 6 (June 1855): 171–74, quote on 171.

73. Brown, interview.

74. Victoria Morris, Louisiana and Georgia cotton picker, interview with the author, 4 November 2002.

75. Brown, interview.

76. Rawick, *AS*, vol. 12, pt. 1, 174.

77. Scott, interview.

78. Morris, interview.

79. See Daina Ramey Berry, "'We Sho Was Dressed Up': Slave Women, Material Culture and Decorative Arts in Wilkes County, Georgia," in *The Savannah River Valley up to 1865: Fine Arts, Architecture, and Decorative Arts*, ed. Ashley Callahan (Athens: Georgia Museum of Art, 2003), 73–83.

80. "Dr. F. Ficklen Ledger book, 1834–1842," Mrs. Marion H. Barnett Collection, Georgia Archives, Morrow, Georgia, quote dated 30 June 1839.

81. A few sentences following this passage, Ficklen defines his business as the management of "negroes, horses & etc." Ibid.

82. John Couper, "On the Origin of Sea-Island Cotton," *Southern Agriculturist* (May 1831): 242–45; Seabrook, *A Memoir on the Origin*, 18; Thomas Spalding, "Brief Notes on the Cultivation of Cotton, Rice, Sugar Cane, and the Grape Vine," *Southern Agriculturist* (February 1828): 132; and Turner, *The Cotton Planter's Manual*, 96, 128–36, and 278–83.

83. See Bonner, *History of Georgia Agriculture*, 52; and Seabrook, *A Memoir on the Origin*, 14.

84. Bonner, *History of Georgia Agriculture*, 53. See also Seabrook, *A Memoir on the Origin*, 35–36.

85. Anna Page King to Thomas Butler King, Sr., 23–24 December 1855, Thomas Butler King Papers #1252, Southern Historical Collection, Wilson Library, University of North Carolina, Chapel Hill.

86. Thomas Butler King, "Plantation Day Book, 1842–1864," Georgia Archives, Morrow, Georgia. See also Margaret Davis Cate, "Retreat Plantation," in *Flags of Five Nations: A Collection of Sketches and Stories of the Golden Isles of Guale* (Brunswick, Ga.: Glynn County Chamber of Commerce, n.d.), 53–62; George Alexander Heard, "St. Simons Island During the War Between the States," *Georgia Historical Quarterly* 22, no. 3 (September 1938): 249–72, especially 251; Bessie Lewis, *Patriarchal Plantations of St. Simons Island, Georgia* (Brunswick, Ga.: Glover Printing Company, 1974); and Bessie Lewis, *King's Retreat Plantation: Today and Yesterday* (Brunswick, Ga.: Coastal Printing Company, 1980).

87. Otto, *Cannon's Point Plantation*, 23.

88. Gray, *History of Agriculture*, 731–33.

89. Ibid., 680.

90. See Seabrook, *A Memoir on the Origin*, 23.

91. See Legare "Account of an Agricultural Excursion," 168–69, and 243; and Otto, *Cannon's Point Plantation*, 25 and 35.

92. *Southern Cultivator* 13, no. 6 (June 1855): 182.

93. Worm fences were fences that used crossed rails to make a zigzag pattern around a field or piece of land. See *American Heritage Dictionary of American Language*, 4th ed., (Boston: Houghton Mifflin, 2000).

94. *Southern Cultivator* 13, no. 6 (June 1855): 182.

95. Ibid.

96. Burke, *Pleasure and Pain*, 38.

97. "Rules of the Plantation," *The News*, Washington, Georgia, 9 April 1840.

98. Parrish, *Slave Songs*, 247.

99. Smith, *Slavery and Rice Cultivation*, 49.

100. For ex-planters and agricultural historians describing this process, see Margaret Davis Cate, typescript on Georgia rice cultivation, *Margaret Davis Cate Collection*, MSS 997, box 5, folder 105, Georgia Historical Society, Savannah; James M. Clifton, ed., *Life and Labor on Argyle Island: Letters and Documents*

of a Savannah Rice Plantation, 1833–1867 (Savannah, Ga.: Beehive Press, 1978),
102–8; James C. Darby, "On Planting and Managing a Rice Crop," *Southern Agri-
culturist* (June 1829): 247–54; David Doar, *Rice and Rice Planting in the South
Carolina Low County* (Charleston, S.C.: The Charleston Museum, 1936); Gray,
History of Agriculture II, 726–31; Duncan C. Heyward, *Seed from Madagas-
car* (1937, reprint, Columbia: University of South Carolina Press, 1993); House,
Planter Management and Capitalism, 24–37; and Spalding, "Brief Notes on the
Cultivation of Cotton," 60.

101. Doar, *Rice and Rice Planting*, 9.

102. Heyward, *Seed from Madagascar*, 28–29. Schwalm found that this task
was executed exclusively by women and cites Heyward's example. See Schwalm,
A Hard Fight for We, 19–20; and Schwalm, "The Meaning of Freedom," 32–33.

103. "Elizafield Plantation Journal, 1838–1861"; and House, *Planter Management and Capitalism*, 29.

104. Heyward, *Seed from Madagascar*, 31. See also Carney, *Black Rice*, 107–
41.

105. Amey appears to be the only female in this group not listed with a husband. See "Elizafield Plantation Journal, 1838–1861" and House, "List of Negroes
Belonging to Elizafield Plantation," *Planter Management and Capitalism*, 252–60,
and 29. The wooden bats were lightweight farm instruments with a wide base
used to cover seeds with soil after a recent planting.

106. Heyward, *Seed from Madagascar*, 36; House, *Planter Management and
Capitalism*, 31; and Smith, *Slavery and Rice Cultivation*, 49.

107. Smith, *Slavery and Rice Cultivation*, 50.

108. Parrish, *Slave Songs*, 225.

109. Gray, *History of Agriculture*, 729; Smith, *Slavery and Rice Cultivation*,
55.

110. Heyward, *Seed from Madagascar*, 40.

111. Gray, *History of Agriculture*, 729.

112. Judith Carney, "Rice Milling, Gender and Slave Labour in Colonial South
Carolina," *Past & Present* 153, no. 1 (November 1996): 117–18; and Carney, *Black
Rice*, 116–32.

113. Parrish, *Slave Songs*, 225.

114. Ibid., 236.

115. "Elizafield Plantation Journal"; and House, *Planter Management and Capi-
talism*, 88. Anna Page King of Retreat Plantation also felt better when her slaves
were in good health, and she complained when they were ill. See Daina Ramey
Berry and Melanie Pavich-Lindsay, "'On Saturday Her Fever Returned and We
Could Do Nothing to Save Her': Women, Disease, and Death on a Georgia Sea
Island Plantation," paper presented at the Sixth Southern Conference on Women's
History, Athens, Ga., 7 June 2003.

116. "Elizafield Plantation Journal"; and House, *Planter Management and Capitalism*, 111.

Chapter 2: *"Dey S'lected Me Out to Be a Housegirl"*

1. Anna Page King to daughter Florence Barclay King, 24 February 1852, Thomas
Butler King Papers #1252, Southern Historical Collection, Wilson Library, Uni-

versity of North Carolina at Chapel Hill. See also Pavich-Lindsay, ed., *Anna: The Letters of a St. Simons Island Plantation Mistress.*

2. Anna Page King to daughter "Tootee" [Hannah Matilda King Couper,] 28 February 1856, William Audley Couper Papers #3687, Southern Historical Collection, Wilson Library, University of North Carolina, Chapel Hill. King does not identify who the "others" are—bondpeople or members of the planter family.

3. See Anna Page King to "My own dear child [Hannah Matilda King Couper]," 2 August 1852, William Audley Couper Papers #3687, Southern Historical Collection, Wilson Library, University of North Carolina, Chapel Hill. On 24 February 1852, King made the following remark to her daughter Florence: "Rhina is better—I have not yet asked her about the letter in French." Thomas Butler King Papers #1252, Southern Historical Collection, Wilson Library, University of North Carolina, Chapel Hill.

4. See Frederick Douglass, *Narrative of the Life of Frederick Douglass an American Slave Written by Himself* (Boston: Anti-Slavery Office, 1845); and Webber, *Deep Like the Rivers.*

5. Rawick, *AS,* vol. 12, part I, pp. 201–11.

6. Weiner, *Mistresses and Slaves,* 13. Weiner adds that enslaved women in South Carolina "never did men's work in the Big House," reinforcing the need to establish clear definitions of labor.

7. Jones, *Labor of Love,* 27.

8. Genovese, *Roll Jordan Roll,* 344. See also Wilma King, "The Mistress and Her Maids: White and Black Women in a Louisiana Household, 1858–1868," in *Discovering the Women in Slavery: Emancipating Perspectives on the American Past,* ed. Patricia Morton (Athens: University of Georgia Press, 1996), 82–106; Fett, *Working Cures;* and Weiner, *Mistresses and Slaves.*

9. The narrative of Harriet Jacobs is the most notable example. See Jacobs, *Incidents in the Life of a Slave Girl.*

10. Burke, *Pleasure and Pain,* 33.

11. Rawick, *AS,* vol. 13, pt. 4, 32.

12. Wylly, *Annals and Statistics of Glynn County,* 13. See also the 1849 "Inventory and Appraisement of the Estate of Capt. John Butler, dec'd," Butler Collection, Historical Society of Pennsylvania (HSP). I would like to thank Sue Mullins Moore for sharing her transcription of this document and William Dusinberre for our conversation about the Butler slaves at the Southern Historical Association meeting in November 2003.

13. These elderly bondwomen include Molly (age 80), Nanny (age 64), Judy (age 65), Dicy (age 75), Rosa (age 80), Caroline (age 68), Sally (age 61), Mary (age 71), Libby (age 66), Charity (age 68), Lester's Molly (age 63), Phoebe (age 70), May (age 68), and Amy (age 87). See McIntosh County Court of Ordinary, 21 February 1859, "Division of slaves belonging to the Estate of John Butler, dec'd" (HSP, Courtesy of Sue Mullins Moore, Georgia Southern University).

14. Jones, *Labor of Love,* 24.

15. Burke, *Pleasure and Pain,* 47–48.

16. Rawick, *AS,* vol. 12, pt. 2, 99.

17. Ibid., vol. 12, pt. 2, 100.

18. Ibid., vol. 12, pt. 1, 174.

19. Kemble, *Journal of a Residence,* 360, emphasis in original.

20. Anna Matilda Page King to Anna Rebecca Couper, 22 August 1852, William Audley Couper Papers #3687, Southern Historical Collection, Wilson Library, University of North Carolina, Chapel Hill.

21. Rawick, *AS*, vol. 12, pt. 2, 195–96.

22. See 13 February 1849, "Inventory and Appraisement of the Estate of Capt. John Butler, dec'd," Butler Collection, Historical Society of Pennsylvania (HSP). For a complete list of all bondmen with skilled jobs on the Butler estates, see Appendix A.

23. See McIntosh County Court of Ordinary, 21 February 1859, "Division of slaves belonging to the Estate of John Butler, dec'd." See also Dusinberre, *Them Dark Days*, 213–81, and Malcolm Bell Jr., *Major Butler's Legacy: Five Generations of a Slaveholding Family* (Athens: University of Georgia Press, 1987).

24. Flanders, *Plantation Slavery in Georgia*, 144–45. Genovese explains that "double duty" was more common on small estates. Genovese, *Roll Jordan Roll*, 339.

25. Rawick, *AS*, vol. 12, pt. 1, 74 (emphasis added).

26. Burnette Vanstory, *Georgia's Land of the Golden Isles* (Athens: University of Georgia Press, 1956), 75–76 and 97–98.

27. "Kelvin Grove Plantation Book: Statement of Negroes," Margaret Davis Cate Collection, Hargrett Library, University of Georgia, Athens (microfilm).

28. Ibid.

29. Burke, *Pleasure and Pain*, 27.

30. "Kelvin Grove Plantation Book: Statement of Negroes," Margaret Davis Cate Collection, Hargrett Library, University of Georgia, Athens (microfilm). See Anna Page King to "Lordy," 3 July and 25 November 1854, Thomas Butler King Papers #1252, Southern Historical Collection, Wilson Library, University of North Carolina at Chapel Hill.

31. "Kelvin Grove Plantation Book: Statement of Negroes," Margaret Davis Cate Collection, Hargrett Library, University of Georgia, Athens (microfilm).

32. Genovese, *Roll Jordan Roll*, 334.

33. Ophelia B. Troup, "Memoirs, 1902–1904," Hofwyl Plantation Records, 22, Georgia Archives, Morrow, Georgia.

34. Ibid., 22.

35. Ibid., 28.

36. Rawick, *AS*, vol. 12, pt. 2, 100.

37. Flanders, *Plantation Slavery in Georgia*, 152.

38. Rawick, *AS*, vol. 12, pt. 2, 104–05.

39. Heard submitted the ad on 17 November but it did not appear in print until the 24th. See *Washington News*, Washington, Georgia, 24 November 1829.

40. *The News*, Washington, Georgia, 28 April 1834 (emphasis added).

41. Ibid.

42. Ibid.

43. For a discussion of bondwomen and material culture, see Berry, "'We Sho Was Dressed Up.'"

44. Margaret Davis Cate, "Retreat Plantation Notes," MSS 997, folder 135, typescript in *Margaret Davis Cate Collection*, courtesy of the Georgia Historical Society, Savannah, Georgia; Cate, *Our Today's and Yesterdays: A Story of Brunswick and the Coastal Islands* (Brunswick, Ga.: Clover Brothers, rev. ed., 1930),

127; Will of William Page, 6 February 1827, MSS 997, folder 245, *Margaret Davis Cate Collection*, courtesy of the Georgia Historical Society, Savannah; and Anna Matilda Page King Will, 7 March 1859, Court of Ordinary, Glynn County Ordinary Estate Records, Inventories and Appraisals, Book E (Morrow, Ga.: Georgia Archives).

45. "Inventory of the Personal Property & Estate of William Page, 1827," Glynn County Ordinary Estate Records, Inventories and Appraisals, Book D (Morrow, Ga.: Georgia Archives); William Page Will, 6 February 1827, *Margaret Davis Cate Collection*, MSS 997, courtesy of the Georgia Historical Society, Savannah; and Caroline Couper Lovell, *The Golden Isles of Georgia* (1932, reprint, Atlanta: Cherokee Publishing Company, 1970), 248–49.

46. When the King population reached 352, it is likely that this figure included bondpeople on Retreat, New Field (the tract of land adjacent to Retreat on St. Simons Island), Waverly, and Monticello. King received 140 slaves in 1827 upon the death of his father-in-law, William Page, and acquired additional bondpeople in 1830 and 1837. However, decreasing cotton prices, the Panic of 1837, and other financial losses forced King to place his property in Camden and Wayne Counties along with 100 slaves up for sale in January 1842. When he could not get fair prices for his human property, he placed an advertisement in the *Savannah Republican* for the sale of 246 bondpeople on 5 March 1842. See, for example, King-Wilder Papers, Georgia Historical Society, Savannah Georgia; William Page Will, Georgia Archives, Morrow, Georgia; the William Page Papers #1254, the James Hamilton Couper Plantation Records #185z, the Thomas Butler King Papers #1252, and the Couper Family Papers #186z, *Southern Historical Collection*, Wilson Library, University of North Carolina, Chapel Hill. For discussions of Thomas Butler King's financial troubles in secondary sources, see Edward M. Steel Jr., *T. Butler King of Georgia* (Athens: University of Georgia Press, 1964); Florence Marye and Edwin R. MacKethan III, ed., *The Story of the Page-King Family of Retreat Plantation, St. Simons Island and the Golden Isles of Georgia* (Darien, Ga.: Edwin R. MacKethan Publisher, 2000); and Stephen Berry, "More Alluring at a Distance: Absentee Patriarchy and the Thomas Butler King Family," *Georgia Historical Quarterly* 81, no. 4 (Winter 1997): 863–96.

47. U.S. Department of Commerce, Bureau of the Census, Federal Manuscript Census (Slave Schedules), Glynn County, Georgia, 1850.

48. Anna Page King Will, 7 March 1859, Court of Ordinary, Glynn County Ordinary Estate Records, Inventories and Appraisals, Book E (Morrow, Ga.: Georgia Archives).

49. William Page Will, 6 February 1827, Court of Ordinary, Glynn County Ordinary Estate Records, Inventories and Appraisals, Book D (Morrow, Ga.: Georgia Archives). The only legible names are Cupid, the fifty-year-old driver, and Edward, the twenty-five-year-old carpenter. Other names with comments in the margins include two elderly bondpeople, Hannah and Old August, both listed as sixty years old.

50. Anna Page King to "My dearly beloved Lord" [Henry Lord King], 4 July 1854, Thomas Butler King Papers #1252, Southern Historical Collection, Wilson Library, University of North Carolina, Chapel Hill.

51. Anna Page King to her "dearly beloved child & cousin Amanda," 21 April

1857, William Audley Couper Papers #3687, *Southern Historical Collection*, Wilson Library, University of North Carolina, Chapel Hill.

52. Anna Page King to Mrs. William Audley Couper, 27 April 1857, William Audley Couper Papers #3687, *Southern Historical Collection*, Wilson Library, University of North Carolina, Chapel Hill.

53. Anna Page King to Miss Florence B. King, 22 November 1851, Thomas Butler King Papers #1252, Southern Historical Collection, Wilson Library, University of North Carolina, Chapel Hill.

54. For a recent discussion of enslaved naming patterns, see Daina Ramey Berry, "They Called her 'Pussy': Naming Patterns of Enslaved Women, 1794–1865," unpublished essay presented at the Seminar on the Black Atlantic, Rutgers University Center for Historical Analysis, 22–23 October 2004.

55. Anna Page King to her "dearly beloved child," 28 September 1851, William Audley Couper Papers #3687, *Southern Historical Collection*, Wilson Library, University of North Carolina, Chapel Hill.

56. Anna Page King to Thomas Butler King, 11 July 1848, Thomas Butler King Papers #1252, Southern Historical Collection, Wilson Library, University of North Carolina, Chapel Hill. For a discussion of enslaved and free health on Retreat Plantation, see Berry and Pavich-Lindsay, "'On Saturday Her Fever Returned.'"

57. Ophelia B. Troup, "Memoirs, 1902–1904," Hofwyl Plantation Records, 22, Georgia Archives, Morrow, Georgia.

58. See Camp, *Closer to Freedom*, especially chapter 1.

59. Anna Page King to Florence Barclay King, 22 August 1837, Thomas Butler King Papers #1252, Southern Historical Collection, Wilson Library, University of North Carolina, Chapel Hill.

60. Anna Page King to Miss Jane Johnston, 31 December 1839, William Audley Couper Papers #3687, *Southern Historical Collection*, Wilson Library, University of North Carolina, Chapel Hill.

61. Anna Page King to daughter Florence Barclay King, 16 May 1852, Thomas Butler King Papers #1252, Southern Historical Collection, Wilson Library, University of North Carolina, Chapel Hill. Amanda was Anna King's cousin.

62. Anna Page King to her son, "Lordy" [Henry Lord King], 7 June 1852, Thomas Butler King Papers #1252, Southern Historical Collection, Wilson Library, University of North Carolina, Chapel Hill.

63. Anna Page King to "Tootee," 18 August 1852, William Audley Couper Papers #3687, Southern Historical Collection, Wilson Library, University of North Carolina, Chapel Hill.

64. Anna Page King to "Tootee," 21 August 1852, William Audley Couper Papers #3687, Southern Historical Collection, Wilson Library, University of North Carolina, Chapel Hill, emphasis in the original.

65. Anna Page King to her "Beloved children," 12 April 1857, #3687, Southern Historical Collection, Wilson Library, University of North Carolina, Chapel Hill.

66. Anna Page King to Mrs. William Audley Couper, 27 April 1857, #3687, Southern Historical Collection, Wilson Library, University of North Carolina, Chapel Hill.

67. Anna Page King to her son Mallery King, 23 June 1851, Thomas Butler

King Papers #1252, Southern Historical Collection, Wilson Library, University of North Carolina, Chapel Hill.

68. Parrish, *Slave Songs*, 243.

69. Anna Page King to Thomas Butler King, 6 August 1854, Thomas Butler King Papers #1252, Southern Historical Collection, Wilson Library, University of North Carolina, Chapel Hill.

70. Anna Page King to her "dearly beloved child," 2 April 1857, Thomas Butler King Papers #1252, Southern Historical Collection, Wilson Library, University of North Carolina, Chapel Hill.

Chapter 3: "There Sho' Was a Sight of Us"

1. *The News and Planter's Gazette*, 26 November 1840, emphasis added.

2. Larry E. Hudson, Wilma King, and Philip D. Morgan are exceptions in that their studies emphasized labor as a central part of the slave familial experience. See Hudson, *To Have and to Hold*; Morgan, *Slave Counterpoint*; and King, *Stolen Childhood*. For other work relating to enslaved family and community life, see Blassingame, *The Slave Community*; Camp, *Closer to Freedom*; Genovese, *Roll Jordan Roll*; Stevenson, *Life in Black and White*; and White, *Ar'n't I a Woman?*

3. See Malone, *Sweet Chariot*; Emily West, *Chains of Love: Slave Couples in Antebellum South Carolina* (Urbana: University of Illinois Press, 2004); and Stevenson, *Life in Black and White*.

4. Blassingame, *The Slave Community*, 159.

5. Balanced sex ratios did not guarantee the presence of cohesive families since age differentials played a significant role in mate availability. See Ramey, "A Place of Our Own"; and Ramey, "'A Heap of Us Slaves.'"

6. Flanders, *Plantation Slavery in Georgia*, 173.

7. For a vivid description of the courting process, see Blassingame, *The Slave Community*, 156–61.

8. Rawick, *AS*, vol. 13, pt. 4, 166.

9. Jones, *Labor of Love*, 33.

10. Rawick, *AS*, vol. 12, pt. 1, 175.

11. Blassingame, *The Slave Community*, 159.

12. Rawick, *AS*, vol. 12, pt. 2, 69 (emphasis added).

13. Ibid., vol. 12, pt, 1, 162.

14. Ibid., vol. 12, pt. 1, 164.

15. Ibid., vol. 13, pt. 4, 165.

16. "The Farm Journal of Benton Miller," 10 October 1858, Georgia Archives, Morrow, Georgia (microfilm).

17. Rawick, *AS*, vol. 12, pt. 2, 341.

18. Ibid., 180.

19. Ibid., vol. 12, pt. 1, 175 (emphasis added).

20. "The Farm Journal of Benton Miller," Georgia Archives, Morrow, Georgia.

21. Rawick, *AS*, vol. 12, pt. 1, 207.

22. Ibid., vol. 13, pt. 3, 165.

23. Ibid., vol. 12, pt. 2, 176. For evidence in South Carolina, see Hudson, *To*

Have and to Hold, 159; for Virginia, see Stevenson, *Life in Black and White,* 228–30; and for Louisiana, see Malone, *Sweet Chariot,* 224.

24. This visitation pattern was fairly common throughout the South as slaves in Louisiana, South Carolina, and Virginia testified to similar options. See, for example, Stevenson, *Life in Black and White,* 208–12, and 230–34. For evidence on abroad marriages in Louisiana and South Carolina, see Malone, *Sweet Chariot,* 166–68, 227–28, 262, and 269, and Hudson, *To Have and to Hold,* 142–49, and 160.

25. Rawick, *AS,* vol. 13, pt. 4, 16, 165 (emphasis added).

26. Ibid., vol. 13, pt. 4, 165.

27. Ibid., vol. 13, pt. 3, 30, and vol. 12, pt. 1, 67.

28. Ibid., vol. 12, pt. 1, 160.

29. Clarence L. Mohr, "Slavery in Oglethorpe County, Georgia 1773–1865," *Phylon* 32, no. 1 (Spring 1972): 4–21, quote on 7. For commentary on the Wilkes County pass system, see Charles Danforth Saggus, "A Social and Economic History of the Danburg Community in Wilkes County, Georgia" (M.A. thesis, University of Georgia, 1951), 128.

30. Georgia Writers' Project, *Drums and Shadows,* 176. Perhaps lowcountry slaves offered no testimony on courtship and marriage because they spent the majority of their time working on their home plantations.

31. See Genovese, *Roll Jordan Roll,* 473–75; Hudson, *To Have and to Hold,* 141–45; Stevenson, *Life in Black and White,* 230–33; and White, *Ar'n't I a Woman!* 153–55.

32. Genovese, *Roll Jordan Roll,* 472–73.

33. Carole Elaine Merritt, "Slave Family and Household Arrangements in Piedmont Georgia" (Ph.D. diss., Emory University, 1986), 173.

34. Ibid., 129.

35. Mary married Starobin on 10 October 1858. See "Journal of Benton Miller," Georgia Archives, Morrow, Georgia.

36. Merritt, "Slave Family and Household Arrangements," 173.

37. Genovese, *Roll Jordan Roll,* 315 and 319. See also Weiner, *Mistresses and Slaves,* 22.

38. Rawick, *AS,* vol. 12, pt. 2, 69–70. For an extensive study of corn shuckings and other aspects of plantation culture, see Roger D. Abrahams, *Singing the Master: The Emergence of African American Culture in the Plantation South* (New York: Pantheon Books, 1992). See also Burke, *Pleasure and Pain,* 40–41.

39. Georgia Writers' Project, *Drums and Shadows,* 222.

40. Georgia Writers' Project, *Drums and Shadows,* 174.

41. Rawick, *AS,* vol. 13, pt. 3, 223–24.

42. See White, *Ar'n't I a Woman!* 119–41, especially 119, and Genovese, *Roll Jordan Roll,* 319.

43. Genovese, *Roll Jordan Roll,* 316–17.

44. Burke, *Pleasure and Pain,* 41, and Camp, *Closer to Freedom,* 60–92.

45. Burke, *Pleasure and Pain,* 49–50.

46. Rawick, *AS,* vol. 12, pt. 1, 206.

47. Ibid., vol. 12, pt. 1, 205.

48. Ibid., vol. 12, pt. 1, 76, and vol. 12, pt. 2, 69.

49. Ibid., vol. 12, pt. 2, 2.

50. See Margaret Davis Cate, "Christmas and Other Holidays," typescript in Margaret Davis Cate Collection, University of Georgia.

51. Kemble, *Journal of a Residence*, 92. See also "Inventory and Appraisement of the Estate of Capt. John Butler, dec'd"; and McIntosh County Court of Ordinary, 21 February 1859, "Division of slaves belonging to the Estate of John Butler, dec'd," Butler Collection, HSP.

52. Eliza Frances Andrews, *The War-Time Journal of a Georgia Girl, 1864–1865* (1908, reprint. Lincoln: University of Nebraska Press, 1997), 90–91.

53. Kemble, *Journal of a Residence*, 106.

54. *Ibid.*, 125–26, quote on 186. See also Charles C. Jones, *Religious Instruction of the Negroes in the United States* (Savannah, Ga.: T. Purse, 1842).

55. Kemble, *Journal of a Residence*, 118–19.

56. Holmes, *"Dr. Bullie's" Notes*, 194–96.

57. Kemble, *Journal of a Residence*, 261–62.

58. Ibid., 262.

59. Ibid., 261–63.

60. Marion Alexander Boggs, ed., *The Alexander Letters, 1787–1900: The Moving and Absorbing Saga of a Georgia Family* (Athens: University of Georgia Press, 1980), 106. I wish to thank Dale Couch of the Georgia Archives for identifying this source and the University of Georgia Press for lending me this out-of-print book.

61. Georgia Writers' Project, *Drums and Shadows*, 180.

62. Rawick, *AS*, vol. 12, pt. 1, 77.

63. Ibid., vol. 12, pt. 1, 77.

64. Ibid., vol. 13, pt. 4, 33. Benton Miller's three slaves regularly attended church on Sundays. See the Benton Miller Farm Journal, Georgia Archives, Morrow, Georgia.

65. Rawick, *AS*, vol. 13, pt. 4, 33.

66. Ibid., vol. 13, pt. 4, 33.

67. Andrews, *The War-Time Journal*, quote on 101, song on 90.

68. Ibid., 89.

69. Frances Butler Leigh, *Ten Years on a Georgia Plantation since the War, 1866–1876* (1883, reprint, Savannah, Ga.: Beehive Press, 1992), 147. Leigh was equally impressed with "boat songs."

70. Ibid., 147.

71. Waters, *On Jordan's Stormy Banks*, 22–25.

72. Berry, "'We Sho Was Dressed Up.'"

73. Waters, *On Jordan's Stormy Banks*, 129.

74. Ibid., 9–10. Other slaves such as Alice Bradley expressed great pride in the fact that her family owned a Bible. Bradley proudly testified that she knew her parents' birth and death dates because of the list printed in her family Bible. "I knows dem years is right" she explained after reciting the exact dates to her interviewer in the 1930s, "'cause I got 'em from dat old fambly Bible." Rawick, *AS*, vol. 12, pt. 1, 118.

75. Leigh, *Ten Years on a Georgia Plantation*, 148.

76. Waters, *On Jordan's Stormy Banks*, 114.

77. Ibid.

78. Georgia Writers' Project, *Drums and Shadows*, 180.

79. Holmes, *"Dr. Bullie's" Notes*, 133.

80. Ibid.

81. Johnson's reference to being young indicates that her memories of slavery occurred during childhood. Johnson shared her recollections in the 1930s as part of a federally sponsored project. See Georgia Writer's Project, *Drums and Shadows*, 176. See similar testimony by Floyd White, 182.

82. See Stuckey, *Slave Culture*, 12–17; and the Georgia Writers' Project, *Drums and Shadows*, 208.

83. Rawick, *AS*, vol. 12, pt. 2, 197.

84. Ibid., vol. 12, pt. 1, 163.

85. Ibid., vol. 12, pt. 2, 99.

86. Ibid., vol. 12, pt. 1, 163.

87. "The Negroe Caller," Dubose Family Papers, MS 1738, Hargrett Library, University of Georgia.

88. Rawick, *AS*, vol. 12, pt. 2, 279.

89. Alice O. Walker, ed., *Registers of Signatures of Depositors in the Augusta, Georgia, Branch of the Freedman's Savings and Trust Company*, vol. 1 (Augusta, Ga.: Richmond County Public Library, 1998). Hereafter cited as FS&T.

90. Ibid., 123.

91. Ibid., 282.

92. Ibid., passim.

93. Ibid., 469.

94. Georgia Writers' Project, *Drums and Shadows*, 177.

95. Ibid., 178.

96. Legare, "Account of an Agricultural Excursion," 359.

97. T. Reed Ferguson, *The John Couper Family at Cannon's Point* (Macon, Ga.: Mercer University Press, 1994), 159.

98. Legare, "Account of an Agricultural Excursion," 360–65.

99. "An Inventory of the Goods and Chattels at Hopeton Plantation," Glynn County Court of Ordinary, Estate Records, Book D 1810–1843, Georgia Archives, Morrow, Georgia (microfilm).

100. See, for example, Elizafield Plantation where Hugh Fraser Grant identified the following twenty couples: Driver John and wife [Fortune], Old Harry and L Dinah, March and Amaretta, Emperor and Haigar, Stephen and Hannah, Caesar and Biney, Abraham and Nancy, April and Phillis, Brister and Lear, London and Sary, Prince and Nancy, M John and Matilla, Scipio and Dido, Andrew and Mira, Alec and Flora, Harry and Catherine, Nat and Betty, John Stake and Bess, Jack and Cumsey, and Ben and Nann. For the original journal, see "Elizafield Plantation Journal, 1838–1861," *Southern Historical Collection* #3213-z, Wilson Library, University of North Carolina, Chapel Hill. A microfilmed copy of the original journal is available through the *Records of Ante-Bellum Southern Plantations From the Revolution Through the Civil War*. See series J, pt. 4, reel 21.

101. William Page Will, 6 February 1827, *Margaret Davis Cate Collection*, courtesy of the Georgia Historical Society, Savannah, Georgia; "Inventory of the Personal Property & Estate of William Page, 1827," Glynn County Ordinary Estate Records, Inventories and Appraisals, Book D (Georgia Archives, Morrow, Ga.); U.S. Department of Commerce, Bureau of the Census, Federal Manuscript Census, Glynn County, Georgia, 1850–1860 (microfilm); Anna Page King Will, 7

March 1859, Court of Ordinary, Glynn County Ordinary Estate Records, Inventories and Appraisals, Book E (Georgia Archives, Morrow, Ga.); "Inventory of the Estate of Mrs. Anna Matilda King, 1860," William Audley Couper Papers #3687, *Southern Historical Collection,* Wilson Library, University of North Carolina, Chapel Hill; and Pavich-Lindsay, ed., *Anna: The Letters of a St. Simons Island Plantation Mistress,* Appendix 2.

102. The total enslaved population in 1827 was 140. Of this group, 66 were female and 74 were male.

103. Of the 142 bondpeople in the population, 125 of them belonged to family units. The remaining seventeen bondwomen and bondmen appear on the lists without designated family members. Enslaved families at Retreat are easily reconstructed by analysis of slave lists from 1827, 1859, and 1860. In addition to the order in which the master and/or mistress placed slaves, personal letters of Anna Page King reveal family groupings as well. Other sources used to derive the seventeen families came from wills and estate inventories.

104. Stevenson, *Life in Black and White,* 234.

105. Flanders, *Plantation Slavery in Georgia,* 152–54.

106. Rawick, *AS,* vol. 13, pt. 3, 220.

107. Ibid., vol. 13, pt. 4, 162.

108. *The Digest of the Laws of the State of Georgia* (Philadelphia: R. Aitken, 1801), and Betty Wood, *Slavery in Colonial Georgia, 1730–1775* (Athens: University of Georgia Press, 1984).

109. He explained that enslaved fathers contributed to their families by supplying additional meats and fish. Otto, *Cannon's Point Plantation,* 44–45. Also see Merritt, "Slave Family and Household Arrangements," 160–61.

110. House, *Planter Management and Capitalism,* 255.

111. Rawick, *AS,* vol. 13, 33–36.

112. Wilma King explains that although slave parents spent the majority of their time laboring, "many never stopped trying to foster positive relationships" with their children. King, *Stolen Childhood,* 69–90, and passim. Also see King, "'Raise Your Children Up Rite': Parental Guidance and Child Rearing Practices Among Slaves in the Nineteenth Century South," in Hudson, *Working toward Freedom,* 143–62.

113. Rawick, *AS,* vol. 12, pt. 1, 207.

114. Roswell King Jr., "On the Management of the Butler Estate," *Southern Agriculturist* (December 1828): 523–29, especially 526.

115. Rawick, *AS,* vol. 12, pt. 1, 162–63.

116. Ibid., vol. 12, pt. 2, 202–3.

117. Based on this statement, one can assume that Harmon lived on a small plantation. Ibid., vol. 12, pt. 2, 97–102. Former slave Emma Hurly also recalled eating "pig-fashion in the kitchen." Ibid., vol. 12, pt. 2, 275.

Chapter 4: "O, I Never Has Forgot Dat Last Dinner wit My Folks"

1. Inventory and Appraisement of the Estate of Benjamin F. Cater, dec'd [deceased], 1 February 1841, Glynn County Court of Ordinary, Inventories and

Appraisements, Book D 1810–1843, Georgia Archives, Morrow, Georgia (microfilm).

2. Anna Page King to "My own dearly beloved husband," 20 January 1855, Thomas Butler King Papers #1252, Southern Historical Collection, Wilson Library, University of North Carolina, Chapel Hill.

3. Anna Page King to daughter "My own beloved child" [Hannah Matilda King Couper], 27 April 1857, William Audley Couper Papers #3687, Southern Historical Collection, Wilson Library, University of North Carolina, Chapel Hill. For a discussion of naming patterns of enslaved women, in particular those named "Pussy," see Daina Ramey Berry, "They Called her 'Pussy': Naming Patterns of Enslaved Women, 1794–1865," unpublished essay presented at the Seminar on the Black Atlantic, Rutgers University Center for Historical Analysis, 22–23 October 2004.

4. Rawick, *AS*, vol. 13, pt. 4, 30–31.

5. A.S.D., "On Raising Negroes," *Southern Agriculturist* (February 1838): 77–80.

6. "Rules for Breeding," *The Southern Cultivator* 2, no. 16 (August 1844): 126. See also "Rules for Improvement in Breeding Stock," *The Southern Cultivator* 2, no. 23 (November 1844): 179.

7. Richard Sutch, "The Breeding of Slaves for Sale and the Westward Expansion of Slavery, 1850–1860," *Southern Economic History Project Working Paper Number 10* (Berkeley: University of California, 1972): 3. Sutch refined his thesis on breeding again in 1986. See Sutch, "Slave Breeding," *Social Science Working Paper 593* (Pasadena: California Institute of Technology, 1986) prepared for Randall M. Miller and John David Smith, eds., *Dictionary of Afro-American Slavery* (Westport, Conn.: Greenwood Press, 1986). For other supporting and opposing perspectives during the colonial period, see Keith Thomas, *Man and the Natural World: Changing Attitudes in England, 1500–1800* (New York: Oxford University Press, 1986), 41–50 and 135–36; Kristen Fischer, *Suspect Relations: Sex, Race, and Resistance in Colonial North Carolina* (Ithaca, N.Y.: Cornell University Press, 2002), 175–81; and Morgan, *Laboring Women*, 69–104.

8. By this I am referring to incidences of gang rape and master-slave rape.

9. Sommerville, "Rape."

10. Susan Brownmiller, *Against Our Will: Men, Women and Rape* (New York: Simon and Schuster, 1975).

11. As historian Jacqueline Dowd Hall found analogies between lynching and rape, it seems appropriate to note the "significant resonance" between rape and breeding. See Jacquelyn Dowd Hall, "'The Mind That Burns in Each Body': Women, Rape, and Racial Violence," in *Powers of Desire: The Politics of Sexuality*, ed. Ann Snitnow, Christine Stansell, and Sharon Thompson (New York: Monthly Review Press, 1983), 328–49, quote on 331.

12. "Force" *Oxford Dictionary Thesaurus* (Oxford University Press, 2001).

13. Barbara Bush found this true for Caribbean women as well. See Bush, *Slave Women in Caribbean Society, 1650–1838* (Kingston, Jamaica: Heinemann Publishers, 1990), 110–19.

14. Historian Diane Miller Sommerville examines the strength of male culture across the color lines in her recent work. See Sommerville, *Rape and Race.*

15. Kemble, *Journal of a Residence*, 237. For a description of Morris, see "Driver

Morris' Reward," Malcolm Bell Jr. File, Courtesy of the Coastal Georgia Historical Society, St. Simons Island, Georgia.

16. Kemble, *Journal of a Residence*, 238, emphasis added.

17. See White, *Ar'n't I a Woman?*; and Bush, *Slave Women in Caribbean Society*.

18. Colonial Spanish Florida was the exception because some enslaved women
found legal protection when their slaveholders "solicited" sexual intercourse
against their will. See, for example, Jane Landers, "'In Consideration of Her Enor-
mous Crime': Rape and Infanticide in Spanish St. Augustine," in *The Devil's Lane:
Sex and Race in the Early South*, ed. Catherine Clinton and Michele Gillespie
(New York: Oxford University Press, 1997), 205–17.

19. Because of this, several scholars justify the exclusion of bondwomen from
discussions of rape. With the exception of work by Gerda Lerner, Angela Davis,
Darlene Clark Hine, and Thelma Jennings, most studies of rape focus on black
male rapists/accusers and white female victims. For discussions of black female
victims, see Gerda Lerner, *Black Women in White America: A Documentary
History* (1972, reprint, New York: Vintage Books, 1992), 172–93; Hine, "Rape and
the Inner Lives of Black Women," 292–97; Angela Davis, "Rape, Racism, and the
Myth of the Black Rapist," in *Women, Race & Class* (New York: Vintage Books,
1983), 172–201; and Jennings, "'Us Colored Women Had to Go through a Plenty,'"
45–74. For studies of black on white rape and other forms of sexual violence, see
Peter Bardaglio, "Rape and the Law in the Old South: 'Calculated to excite Indignation in Every Heart,'" *Journal of Southern History* 60, no. 4 (November 1994):
749–72; Victoria Bynum, *Unruly Women: The Politics of Social and Sexual Control in the Old South* (Chapel Hill, University of North Carolina Press, 1992);
Laura Edwards, "Sexual Violence, Gender, Reconstruction, and the Extension
of Patriarchy in Granville County, North Carolina," *North Carolina Historical
Review* 68 (July 1991): 237–60; Sommerville, *Rape and Race in the Nineteenth
Century South*; and Lisa Lindquist Dorr, *White Women, Rape, and the Power of
Race in Virginia, 1900–1960* (Chapel Hill: University of North Carolina Press,
2004).

20. Although it is impossible to rewrite nineteenth-century laws, we can change
our interpretations of certain behaviors. One starting point is to analyze the
raping of enslaved women, even if it was not considered a crime. A second area
that needs further examination is the raping of enslaved men and women who
were used as breeders and forced to have intercourse with partners against their
will. These discussions are important for understanding the inner lives of slaves
because forced breeding had a significant impact on enslaved families.

21. Chamerovzow, *Slave Life in Georgia*, 18–19, emphasis added.

22. See Mellon, *Bullwhip Days*, 297.

23. Octavia B. Rodgers Albert, *The House of Bondage or Charolette Brooks and
Other Slaves* (New York: Hunt and Eaton, 1890), 108.

24. Howell, *I Was a Slave*, 11. Note that the location (state, county, etc.) of
slaves presented in these narratives is not always provided.

25. Mellon, *Bullwhip Days*, 149.

26. Kemble noted that Maria had a "fine child" in one sentence, and then
referred to that same child as a "bonny baby." Kemble, *Journal of a Residence*,
169–70.

27. Ibid., 235–36.

28. Some planters implied that slaves who came from West African societies practiced polygamy. However polygamy may or may not have been part of slaves' past experience for those born in Africa; Christie Farnham and Barbara Bush explain that there is evidence that polygamy did not take root in America. See Farnham, "Sapphire?" 68–83; and Bush, "'The Family Tree Is Not Cut': Women and Cultural Resistance in Slave Family Life in the British Caribbean," in *In Resistance: Studies in African, Caribbean, and Afro-American History*, ed. Gary Y. Okihiro (Amherst: University of Massachusetts Press, 1986), 117–32, particularly 118 and 121.

Historian Patrick Manning provides some compelling information about *polygyny* that suggests further research in this area is warranted. See Manning, *Slavery and African Life: Occidental, Oriental, and African Slave Trades* (Cambridge: Cambridge University Press, 1990).

29. The word *polygamy* (the practice of having more than one wife *or* husband at the same time) is used here deliberately and should not be confused with *polygyny* (the practice of having more than one wife at the same time) or *polyandry* (the practice of having more than one husband at the same time). Gendered distinctions such as these help scholars clarify the perspectives of planters and also allow contemporary scholars the opportunity to refine, reject, or revise earlier conclusions about past behaviors.

At a November 1997 Southern Historical Association panel, several historians challenged my use of the term "forced breeding" and suggested that "forced promiscuity" or "encouraged reproduction" was a more useful description of this practice. However, if planters, overseers, and drivers referred to it as breeding and there is clear evidence of force, I maintain that forced breeding is an appropriate term. This discussion followed my paper titled "'A Heap of Us Slaves': Family and Community Life among Slave Women in Georgia," which was later published in *Atlanta History: A Journal of Georgia and the South* 44, no. 3 (Fall 2000): 21–38.

30. Howell, *I Was a Slave*, 11.

31. We cannot assume that black men were willing participants in having multiple partners because making such assumptions compromises our ability to interpret history through multiple lenses. Therefore, I argue that black men were just as much victims as black women in these situations.

32. This assertion challenges scholars to document the frequency or infrequency of such interactions as opposed to altogether dismissing the practice. In an excellent study of the master-slave relationship, for example, historian Christopher Morris writes the following: "They [slaveholders] might have forced men and women into sexual relations. Or they might have regularly and systematically raped women. . . . This is how abolitionists often portrayed slavery, and although such things did happen, they happened rarely and not systematically. Such business would have been impractical due to the energy required to force such conditions on people and socially unacceptable for paternalistic white men." This argument is quite similar to that of Kenneth Stampp, who claimed that "evidence of systematic slave breeding is scarce." See Morris, "The Articulation of Two Worlds: The Master-Slave Relationship Reconsidered," *Journal of American History* 85, no. 3 (December 1998): 982–1007, quote on 992; and Stampp, *The*

Peculiar Institution, 245. I suggest that scholars study breeding, rape, and the evidence of forced unions at the same level of detail and analysis as they study other aspects of the slave experience. For examples of this, see Edward E. Baptist, "'Cuffy,' 'Fancy Maids,' and 'One-Eyed Men': Rape, Commodification, and the Domestic Slave Trade in the United States," *American Historical Review* 106, no. 5 (2001): 1619–50; Morgan, *Laboring Women;* and Johnson, *Soul by Soul.*

33. Orlando Patterson places the discussion of slave unions, rather than forced breeding, at the center of his introduction and explains that slaves always had to sexually submit to their owners. See Patterson, *Slavery and Social Death: A Comparative Study* (Cambridge, Mass.: Harvard University Press, 1982), 6 and passim.

34. Kemble, *Journal of a Residence,* 245–46.

35. Howell, *I Was a Slave,* 12.

36. Domestic abuse and domestic violence are defined broadly to include a variety of offenses—physical, sexual, and psychological. The terms are used interchangeably. These forms of abuse involve physical force, actions, or conduct that inflicts injury on, or causes damage to, people or property; treatment or usage that tends to cause bodily injury or forcibly interfering with personal freedom. The *threat* of violence is also included in this definition to address interference, control, and manipulation.

37. W. W. Hazzard, "On the General Management of a Plantation," *Southern Agriculturist* (July 1831): 351.

38. "Plantation Management" in *The Southern Cultivator* (June 1855): 173, emphasis added.

39. Kemble, *Journal of a Residence,* 95.

40. Ibid., 207, emphasis added.

41. This information is based on several Centers for Disease Control studies of male/male rape victims, but it is applicable here if one considers the discussion of third-party perpetrators. See www.cdc.gov under the topics "Rape," "Sexual Violence," and "Domestic Violence."

42. Painter, "Soul Murder and Slavery."

43. I am indebted to historian Wilma King and literary critic P. Gabrielle Forman for calling this interaction to my attention.

44. Lydia Marie Child, ed., *Incidents in the Life of a Slave Girl Written by Herself* (Boston: Published for the Author, 1860), 288–89. See also P. Gabrielle Forman, "Manifest in Signs: The Politics of Sex and Representation in *Incidents in the Life of a Slave Girl,*" in *Harriet Jacobs and Incidents in the Life of a Slave Girl: New Critical Essays,* ed. Deborah Garfield and Rafia Zafar (Cambridge: Cambridge University Press, 1996).

45. Kemble, *Journal of a Residence,* 127 and 293.

46. Howell, *I Was a Slave,* 15. Note, however, that the average time between births for slave women was two years rather than "ev'y twelve month." See James Trussell and Richard Steckel, "The Age of Slaves at Menarche and their First Birth," *Journal of Interdisciplinary History* 8 (Winter 1978): 477–505.

47. Several scholars confirm that plantation owners implemented an informal system of rewards and punishments. See, for example, Jones, *Labor of Love,* 34–38; Stevenson, *Life in Black and White,* 245; Sutch, "Slave Breeding"; and White, *Ar'n't I a Woman?* 98–106.

48. W. W. Hazzard, "On the General Management of a Plantation," *Southern Agriculturist* (5 April 1831): 353, emphasis added.

49. Kemble, *Journal of a Residence*, 157.

50. Ibid., 95, emphasis added. See also Magnus Morner, *"Buy or Breed?" Alternative Sources of Slave Supply in the Plantation Societies of the New World* (Stockholm: Institute of Latin American Studies, 1980).

51. King, "On the Management of the Butler Estate," 525.

52. Ibid., 524.

53. Anna Page King to "My own dearly beloved husband" [Thomas Butler King], 26 March 1855, Thomas Butler King Papers #1252, *Southern Historical Collection*, Wilson Library, University of North Carolina, Chapel Hill.

54. Kemble, *Journal of a Residence*, 238.

55. Ibid., 268. As noted above, Major Butler owned two plantations in this region, Butler's Island, a rice plantation in McIntosh County, and Hampton Point, a Sea Island cotton plantation on St. Simons Island in Glynn County, Georgia. Many planters had estates in two different locales and/or counties.

56. Rawick, *AS*, vol. 12, 274–80.

57. Ibid., 327.

58. Ibid., 136.

59. "Estate of Enoch Callaway," Wilkes County Court of Ordinary, Loose Estate Records, Georgia Archives, Morrow, Georgia. For similar distribution patterns and the use of a hat to draw names, see "Estate of Jimmy A. Tate," Wilkes County Court of Ordinary, Estate Records, Inventories, and Appraisals, 1839–1844, Georgia Archives, Morrow, Georgia.

60. The surviving records for Wilkes County petitions cover the years 1818 through 1822. Wilkes County Court of Ordinary, "Affidavits and Certificates of Persons Introducing Slaves into the State of Georgia, 1818–1822," Superior Court Records (microfilm), Georgia Archives, Morrow, Georgia (hereafter "Introducing Slaves").

61. Ellenberg, "Wilkes County, Georgia," 37.

62. "Introducing Slaves."

63. Ibid.

64. Ibid.

65. Several historians estimate that slave women gave birth to their first child around the age of nineteen. Their ideas about the age in which slaves first "married" one another are often intertwined with the discussion of birthing patterns. Perhaps Thurman was aware that he owned any future "increase," which would explain his desire to preserve the union between Moody and Polete. Fogel and Engerman projected that slave women gave birth for the first time at age twenty-two, but their projections are incorrect according to several scholars (e.g., Gutman and Sutch). In a detailed analysis of plantation records, slave birth patterns, and other primary documents, Gutman and Sutch found that nineteen seemed the more likely age. Therefore, if slave women gave birth to their first child around the age of nineteen, they probably "married" or began having intercourse around sixteen. If these statistics are correct, then Thurman made a good investment in preserving the union between Moody and Polete.

66. *Washington News* [New Series—No. 40] Washington, Georgia, 27 March 1828.

67. Survey was conducted by examining a total of seventy-three notices with gender-specific names. Six different newspapers from Wilkes County were used to complete this survey: *The Independent Press* (Washington, Ga., 1840); *Washington News* (Washington, Ga., 1822–1825); *Washington News* [New Series,] (Washington, Ga., 1827–1831); *Wilkes County Republican* (Washington, Ga., 1827–1831); *The News* (Washington, Ga., 1820s and 1830s); and *Washington News and Miscellaneous Advertiser* (Washington, Ga., 1832–1833).

68. *Washington News*, 22 January 1822.

69. Ibid., 25 July 1823.

70. *Washington News* [New Series], Washington, Georgia, 27 March 1828.

71. *Brunswick Advocate*, 6 July 1837.

72. Ibid., 15 June 1837, emphasis in the original.

73. Ibid., 16 November 1837.

74. Ibid., 30 November 1837.

75. Ibid., 9 February 1839, also advertised on 16 and 25 February, 2 and 30 March, 6 and 13 April, and 4 May 1839.

76. Newspapers such as the *Darien Gazette* (1818–1828), the *McIntosh County Herald and Darien Commercial Register* (1839–1840), and a number of Savannah newspapers are rich sources for slave sales in coastal Georgia, including Glynn County.

77. Those listed for sale were the property of William Piles of Glynn County and included "Bill, Will, Polly, Cila, Peter, Fanny, George, Old George, Eliza and Patty." See typescript in the Work Projects Administration Papers, Glynn County Miscellaneous Files, Library of Congress, MSS A898.

78. Kemble, *Journal of a Residence*, 249.

79. Ibid., 249.

80. Extant documents relating to Kelvin Grove slaves cover scattered dates between 1841 and 1860. See, for example, James P. Postell, "Kelvin Grove Plantation Book, 1 January 1853," Margaret Davis Cate Collection, University of Georgia (microfilm); "Benjamin F. Cater Estate Inventory 1 February 1841," Glynn County Court of Ordinary, Estate Records, Inventories and Appraisals, Book D, 1810–1843 (Georgia Archives, Morrow, Ga.); Margaret Davis Cate, "Plantations of St. Simons Island," typescript in Margaret Davis Cate Collection, courtesy of the Georgia Historical Society, Savannah; Lewis, *Patriarchal Plantations of St. Simons Island*; Hazzard, *St. Simons Island*; U.S. Department of Commerce, Bureau of the Census, Federal Manuscript Census, Slave Schedules 1850–1860 (Glynn County, Ga., microfilm); and Wylly, *Annals and Statistics of Glynn County, Georgia*.

81. Notice the gradual decrease in the population throughout the late antebellum period. See James P. Postell, "Kelvin Grove Plantation Book, 1 January 1853," Margaret Davis Cate Collection, University of Georgia (microfilm); "Benjamin F. Cater Estate Inventory 1 February 1841," Glynn County Court of Ordinary, Estate Records, Inventories and Appraisals, Book D, 1810–1843 (Georgia Archives, Morrow, Ga.); and U.S. Department of Commerce, Bureau of the Census, Federal Manuscript Census, Slave Schedule, 1860 (Glynn County, Ga., microfilm).

82. Ibid., 329–40.

83. Q. K. Philander Doesticks, *Great Auction Sale of Slaves, at Savannah, Georgia, March 2d and 3d, 1859* (New York: American Anti-Slavery Society, 1859), 3.

84. Ibid., 3.

85. Ibid., 4 and 7.

86. Ibid., 7.

87. Ibid., 10.

88. Ibid., 12.

89. Ibid., 20.

90. Ibid., 26, emphasis in original.

91. Stephen G. Pettus Will, 13 June 1854, Wilkes County Court of Ordinary Probate Records Book HH (microfilm, emphasis added), Georgia Archives, Morrow, Georgia.

92. Although the Alek [Jr.] is listed with his mother, "preference for paternal kin names is the frequency with which sons received the names for their fathers." Cheryll Ann Cody, "There Was No 'Absalom' on the Ball Plantations: Slave-Naming Practices in the South Carolina Low Country, 1720–1865," *American Historical Review* 92, no. 3 (June 1987): 563–96, quote on 569. See also Berry, "They Called her 'Pussy'."

93. "Will of Margaret Wylly," 23 December 1846, Glynn County Court of Ordinary, Book E, 1844–1853 (microfilm), emphasis added, Georgia Archives, Morrow, Georgia.

94. Ibid.

95. See U.S. Department of Commerce, Bureau of the Census, Federal Manuscript Census (Slave Census Population Schedules), Glynn County, Georgia, 1850.

96. Young children needed their mother's (and in this case, father's) care. Planters found it beneficial to maintain parental connections when young children were involved. "Young" children, in these cases, may have been breastfeeding infants; therefore, Hill thought it was best to keep them with their mothers (and occasionally fathers). See Lodowick Johnson Hill Sr., *The Hills of Wilkes County, Georgia, and Allied Families* (Atlanta: Johnson-Dallis Company, 1922), 100–101 (emphasis added); and King, *Stolen Childhood*.

97. Anna Page King to "My dearly beloved Tootee" [Hannah Matilda King Couper], 29 February 1856, William Audley Couper Papers #3687, Southern Historical Collection, Wilson Library, University of North Carolina, Chapel Hill. See also Pavich-Lindsay, ed., *Anna: The Letters of a St. Simons Island Plantation Mistress*, 301.

98. Ibid.

99. Stevenson, *Life in Black and White*, 209–11, and 213–15.

100. Alexander Pope Sr. Will, 25 June 1863, Wilkes County Court of Ordinary, Book HH, 1837–1877, Georgia Archives, Morrow, Georgia.

101. John H. Pope Will, 4 November 1859, Wilkes County Court of Ordinary, Book HH, 1837–1877, Georgia Archives, Morrow, Georgia.

102. Quotes taken from the "Last Will and Testament, Anna Matilda King." Anna Page King gave birth to the following children: Hannah Matilda Page Couper (b. 1825), William Page (b. 1825), Thomas Butler King Jr., (b. 1829), Henry Lord Page King (b. 1831), Georgia Page King (b. 1833), Florence Barclay King (b. 1834), Mallory Page King (b. 1836), Virginia Page King (b. 1837), John Floyd King (b. 1839), and Richard Cuyler King (b. 1840). William Audley Couper Papers #3687, Southern Historical Collection, Wilson Library, University of North Carolina, Chapel Hill.

103. See http://www.wordiq.com/terms.html. For more legal definitions of "joint tenancy" and "tenants in common," see *Black's Law Dictionary*, 7th ed., ed. Bryan A. Garner (St. Paul, Minn.: West Group, 1999).

104. "Inventory of the Estate of Mrs. Anna Matilda King," 11 January 1860, William Audley Couper Papers #3687, Southern Historical Collection, Wilson Library, University of North Carolina, Chapel Hill.

105. Only the two oldest sons, William Page King and Thomas Butler King Jr., did not receive slaves.

106. Hill, *The Hills of Wilkes County*, 69, emphasis added.

107. Garland Wingfield Will, 6 July 1865, Wilkes County Court of Ordinary, Book HH, 1837–1877, Georgia Archives, Morrow, Georgia.

108. Hill, *The Hills of Wilkes County*, 102.

109. Hill describes Edward as an "old man," and it is safe to assume that his wife was also elderly.

110. Hill, *The Hills of Wilkes County*, 102 and 103.

111. Kemble, *Journal of a Residence*, 119.

112. Franklin and Schweninger, *Runaway Slaves*, 210.

113. *Washington News*, 27 March 1828. Although William allegedly absconded one month earlier, the Whatleys did not place an advertisement in the newspaper until the end of March.

114. *News and Planter's Gazette*, 27 January 1842.

115. *Washington News*, 9 September 1828.

116. Franklin and Schweninger enter this discussion by examining the escape patterns of hired slaves. See Franklin and Schweninger, *Runaway Slaves*, 4–6 and 136–48.

117. This ad ran for eight weeks. See *Brunswick Advocate*, 30 March 1839. Although R. Towson Jr. sent notice to the newspaper on the 24th, the advertisement first appeared on the 30th.

118. *Brunswick Advocate*, 8 June 1857.

119. *Augusta Chronicle*, 2 July 1821.

120. *Washington News*, 24 July 1824.

121. *The News*, Washington, Georgia, 28 April 1834.

122. Typescript of newspaper advertisements from Glynn County, Georgia, WPA Collection, Library of Congress. This ad appeared in Glynn County papers on 8 March 1821.

123. *Brunswick Advocate*, 15 November 1838. This ad ran for twelve weeks.

124. Ibid., 16 March 1839.

125. Ibid., 11 May 1839.

Chapter 5: "For the Current Year"

1. Holmes, *"Dr. Bullie's" Notes*, 80.

2. Several scholars published works relating to the slave's economy. See, for example, Mintz and Hall, "The Origins of the Jamaican Internal Marketing System," 3–26; Mintz, "The Jamaican Internal Marketing Pattern: Some Notes and Hypotheses," *Social and Economic Studies* 4 (1955): 95–103; Mintz, *Caribbean Transformations* (Chicago: Aldine Publications, 1974); Berlin and Morgan, *The Slave's Economy*; Berlin and Morgan, *Cultivation and Culture*; Wood, *Women's*

Work, Men's Work; Madori Takagi, "Female Slave Participation in the Urban Market Economy: Richmond, Virginia, 1780–1860," in *Southern Women: The Intersection of Race, Class and Gender* Working Paper 8 (Memphis, Tenn.: Center for Research on Women, 1994); and Roderick A. McDonald, *The Economy and Material Culture of Slaves: Goods and Chattels on the Sugar Plantations of Jamaica and Louisiana* (Baton Rouge: Louisiana State University Press, 1993).

3. "Genealogy of the Demere Family," typescript found in the Margaret Davis Cate Collection, Courtesy of the Georgia Historical Society, Savannah, Georgia.

4. Burke, *Pleasure and Pain,* 38.

5. This is not to suggest that women did not go to the market and trade. Scholars of African and West Indian history note that women dominated the marketplace selling various wares.

6. "Ophelia B. Troup Memoirs, 1902–04," Hofwyl Plantation Records, Georgia Archives, Morrow, Georgia (microfilm), 20.

7. Self-hire did occur during the American Revolution and the early national era in other parts of the United States. See Schweninger, "The Underside of Slavery," 1–22. Until the recent publication by Jonathan Martin, slave hiring appeared in general studies of urban and industrial slavery as well. See, for example, Martin, *Divided Mastery;* Claudia Dale Goldin, *Urban Slavery in the American South, 1820–1860* (Chicago: University of Chicago Press, 1976); Richard Wade, *Slavery in the Cities: The South 1820–1860* (New York: Oxford University Press, 1964); Starobin, *Industrial Slavery in the Old South;* and Bancroft, *Slave Trading in the Old South.*

8. However, in other parts of the South, scholars have found that slaves directly participated in the negotiation of their contracts. See Eaton, "Slave Hiring in the Upper South," 663–78; and Schweninger, "The Underside of Slavery."

9. Burke, *Pleasure and Pain,* 84.

10. For a complete description of this law, see "A Compilation of the Patrol Laws of the State of Georgia, in Conformity with a Resolution of General Assembly," in *The Digest of the Laws of the State of Georgia* (Milledgeville, Ga.: S & F Grantland, 1818), 3–9. See also Sally E. Hadden, *Slave Patrols: Law and Violence in Virginia and the Carolinas* (Cambridge, Mass.: Harvard University Press, 2001).

11. For a discussion of slave economies in Georgia, see Wood, *Men's Work, Women's Work.* For a broad discussion of Georgia slave codes, see Wood, *Slavery in Colonial Georgia.* West Indian informal economies were much more extensive, and the presence of women in the marketplace was quite common. See, for example, Hilary McD Beckles, *Centering Women: Gender Discourses in Caribbean Slave Society* (Kingston, Jamaica: Ian Randle Publishers, 1999), especially chapter 9; Mintz and Hall, "The Origins of the Jamaican Internal Marketing System"; M. Morrissey, *Slave Women in the New World* (Lawrence: University Press of Kansas, 1990); Rhoda Reddock, "Women and Slavery in the Caribbean: A Feminist Perspective," *Latin American Perspectives,* vol. 12, no. 1 (1985); and Lorna Simmonds, "Slave Higglering in Jamaica, 1780–1834," *Jamaica Journal* 20, no. 1 (1987).

12. *A General Ordinance to Revise, Amend, and Consolidate the General Ordinances of the Board of Commissioners of the Town of Washington* (Washington, Ga.: P. C. Guieu, 1822), Georgia Archives, Morrow, Georgia.

13. Ibid.

14. "Slave Lore: Ordinances of the City of Washington, Georgia, Section 67," Library of Congress, Works Progress Administration, 11 February 1837, edited by John N. Booth, written by Minnie B. Stonestreet of the Federal Writers' Project, 19 October 1937.

15. Ibid, sec. 69, emphasis added.

16. Ibid, sec. 70.

17. Hazzard, "On the General Management of a Plantation," 350–54, quote on 352–53.

18. King, "On the Management of the Butler Estate," 523–29, quote on 524.

19. Ibid., 525.

20. Ibid.

21. Legare, "Account of an Agricultural Excursion," passim; and Olmsted, *The Cotton Kingdom*, 194–95.

22. Anna Matilda Page King Day Book, 1842–1864, Georgia Archives, Morrow, Georgia.

23. For a complete list of the items Anna Page King paid to slaves and other Glynn County residents, see Appendix C and Appendix D.

24. Several plantation records for this period include $1/2$ and $1/4$ cents as a monetary unit. See A. Barton Hepburn, *A History of Currency in the United States* (Reprint. New York: Augusta M. Kelley Publishers, 1967); Colin R. Chapman, *Weights, Money and Other Measures Used by our Ancestors* (Baltimore: Genealogical Publishing Company, Inc., 1996); and Clifford B. Burgess, *Numis-Film Library of United States Coins Since 1793* (Savannah, Ga.: Burgess Hobby Enterprises, 1975).

25. I use the term suitor deliberately given its gendered connotation. According to the Oxford Dictionary, "suitor" is defined as "a man who wants to marry a woman." Perhaps this term could also identify a woman who wants to marry a man.

26. Works Progress Administration Collection, Library of Congress, "Glynn County Miscellaneous Files."

27. Harriet Cumming to her niece, 1908, in Boggs, *The Alexander Letters*, 107.

28. *The News*, 23 July 1840.

29. Distances based on estimates by Sarah Hillhouse, a Wilkes County resident during the antebellum period. See letter to Col. Elisha Porter, 26 January 1787, in Boggs, *The Alexander Letters*.

30. "Shop Book of Wylie Hill 1820–1843," William A. Pope Collection, Georgia Archives, Morrow, Georgia.

31. *The News*, 11 November 1831.

32. Robert Olwell makes the distinction between the market as a place and the market as a process. See Olwell, *Masters, Slaves, and Subjects*, 143.

33. For the early history of the Georgia railroad, see Richard E. Prince, *Steam Locomotives and History: Georgia Railroad and West Point Route* (Green River: Wyo.: Richard E. Prince, 1962).

34. Brunswick and Florida Rail Road Survey in Georgia 1836–1837 Collection, MS #2806, University of Georgia, Hargrett Library.

35. Quote from an untitled column regarding the Brunswick Canal in *Washington News* on 24 April 1824. See also "Trade of Savannah," *Washington News*, 10 July 1824.

36. *Augusta Chronicle,* 9 November 1847.

37. Loammi Baldwin, *Brunswick Canal and Rail Road, Glynn County, Georgia: Charter and Commissioners Report* (Boston: John H. Lastborn, 1837).

38. Ibid.

39. Kemble, *Journal of a Residence,* 122.

40. Ibid.

41. *Brunswick Advocate,* 18 January 1837.

42. Ibid., emphasis added.

43. Duplicate versions of this ad appeared in the newspaper through 15 April 1838.

44. Ibid., 14 June 1838. It is worth noting that these rates were provided monthly rather than yearly. Such trends indicate that contracts could be renewed or cancelled at the company's discretion.

45. "Ophelia B. Troup Memoirs, 1902–04," Hofwyl Plantation Records, Georgia Archives, Morrow, Georgia (microfilm), 23.

46. *Brunswick Advocate,* 20 September 1838.

47. Ibid. In a footnote at the bottom of this advertisement, the contractors noted that they placed similar ads in two Savannah papers and the *Darien Telegraph,* perhaps to encourage people to send their slaves to work on the canal until all positions were filled.

48. Jennifer L. Morgan notes that colonial planters were well aware of the importance of enslaved women's reproductive value. See Morgan, *Laboring Women.*

49. Note that the railroad company was often the plaintiff in some of these cases. See *Jones v. Railroad Co.,* 18 GA 247 (June 1855); *Railroad Co. v. Winn,* 19 GA 440 (January 1856); *Railroad Co. v. Holt,* 8 GA 157 (February 1850); *Railroad Co. v. Davis,* 13 GA 69 (February 1853); *Railroad Co. v. McElmurry,* 24 GA 75 (January 1858); *Griffin v. Railroad Co.,* 26 GA III (June 1858); *Railroad Co. v. Neal,* 26 GA I 20 (June 1858); *Sims v. Railroad Co.,* 28 GA 93 (March 1859); and *Mitchell v. Railroad Co.* 30 GA 22 (March 1860). Several cases appeared before the Georgia Supreme Court well after the abolition of slavery: *Railroad Co. v. Pickett,* 36 GA 85 (June 1867); *Holmes v. Railroad Co.,* 37 GA 593 (June 1868); and *Berry v. Railroad Co.,* 39 GA 554 (June 1869).

50. Kemble, *Journal of a Residence,* 105.

51. Ibid., 123.

52. Kemble noted that the two groups had to work and live separately in order to avoid riots and violence. Ibid., 123–24.

53. Ibid., 104–5.

54. Olwell, *Masters, Slaves, and Subjects,* 159.

55. Eaton, "Slave Hiring in the Upper South," 663.

56. Barton, "'Good Cooks and Washers,'" 445.

57. U.S. Bureau of the Census, Slave Population Schedules, Wilkes County, 1850, and Wilkes County Court of Ordinary, Inventories, Appraisements, and Wills 1828–1844, Georgia Archives, Morrow, Georgia (microfilm).

58. Wilkes County Court of Ordinary, Inventories, Appraisements, and Wills, 1825–1845, Georgia Archives, Morrow, Georgia.

59. Eaton, "Slave Hiring in the Upper South," 663; and Schweninger, "The Underside of Slavery," 10.

60. Fogel and Engerman, *Time on the Cross,* 103.

61. Estate of Archibald L. Hays, Wilkes County Court of Ordinary, Inventories,

Appraisements, and Wills, 31 December 1839, Georgia Archives, Morrow, Georgia.

62. *Washington News,* 14 December 1824.

63. "Garland W. Darrcott," Wilkes County Court of Ordinary, Inventories, Appraisements & Sales of Estates, 1828–1831, Georgia Archives, Morrow, Georgia.

64. I assume that the $5 rate represented the money paid for the entire year as opposed to payments made monthly.

65. See Wheeler family estate inventories, Wilkes County Court of Ordinary, Inventories, Appraisements, and Wills, 1821–1831, Georgia Archives, Morrow, Georgia and Appendix B.

66. "A list of the hiring of Negroes belonging to John W. Wellborn and Caroline C. Wellborn, minors of Lat. Wellborn deceased on the 11th June 1827 til the 1st January 1828 by Charles Green, their Guardian," Wilkes County Court of Ordinary, Inventories, Appraisements, and Wills, 1828–1831, Georgia Archives, Morrow, Georgia.

67. For discussions of infant mortality, see "Kelvin Grove Plantation Book," Margaret Davis Cate Collection (Athens: University of Georgia); "The Journal and Account Book, 1834–1861, of Hugh Fraser Grant of Elizafield Plantation, Glynn County, Georgia," in House, *Planter Management and Capitalism;* and Kemble, *Journal of a Residence,* 214–31. See also Dusinberre, *Them Dark Days,* 235–47, appendix C and appendix D; and Ramey, "A Place of Our Own," 169–79, n. 39 on 169 and tables 5.1, 5.2, and 5.3.

68. "A list of the hiring of Negroes belonging to John W. Wellborn and Caroline C. Wellborn, minors of Lat. Wellborn deceased on the 11th June 1827 til the 1st January 1828 by Charles Green, their Guardian," Wilkes County Court of Ordinary, Inventories, Appraisements, and Wills, 1828–1831, Georgia Archives, Morrow, Georgia.

69. Ibid.

70. *Washington News,* 4 December 1824.

71. Ibid., 5 January 1830. The *Augusta Chronicle* had similar notices in the four December issues published in 1826.

72. Ibid., 20 December 1827.

73. *Augusta Chronicle,* 30 December 1826.

74. *Augusta Chronicle and Georgia Advertiser,* 23 December 1826. A similar notice appeared in the *Washington News* on 20 December 1827.

75. Kemble, *Journal of a Residence,* 123.

76. "Christmas and Other Holidays," unpublished document, Margaret Davis Cate Collection, University of Georgia, Hargrett Library, Athens, Georgia.

77. *Brunswick Advocate,* 23 November 1837.

78. House, *Planter Management and Capitalism,* 112 and 292.

79. *Brunswick Advocate,* 8 November 1838.

80. Ibid., 3 January 1839, repeated 19 January 1839. The company submitted this advertisement on 13 December 1838.

81. In late nineteenth-century England, the British exploited children's brickyard labor and received widespread opposition from the majority of the public. "Brick-Yard Children," *Harper's Weekly,* 24 June 1871.

82. Colonial Williamsburg, "The Manufacturing of Brick and Tile," http://www.colonialwilliamsburg.org, 22 February 2001.

83. Whitman, *The Price of Freedom*, 19–20.

Epilogue

1. Andrews, *The War-Time Journal*, 347.
2. Ibid., 346.
3. Ibid., 347.
4. Leigh, *Ten Years on a Georgia Plantation*, 135.
5. Andrews, *The War-Time Journal*, 320.
6. Ibid., 306–7.
7. Leigh, *Ten Years on a Georgia Plantation*, 126.
8. Andrews, *The War-Time Journal*, 71.
9. Leigh, *Ten Years on a Georgia Plantation*, 11.
10. Andrews, *The War-Time Journal*, 69.
11. Ibid., 318–19.
12. Ibid., 293, 318–20, and passim.
13. Ibid., 321–22.
14. Leigh, *Ten Years on a Georgia Plantation*, 132.
15. Burke, *Pleasure and Pain*, 89.

BIBLIOGRAPHY

Unpublished Manuscripts

Atlanta History Center, Atlanta, Georgia
  Wilkes County Files
  Glynn County Files
Brunswick—Glynn County Regional Library, Brunswick, Georgia
  Glynn County Collection
The Clements Library, University of Michigan, Ann Arbor, Michigan
  Wilkes County Georgia Collection, 1778–1849
Coastal Georgia Community College, Brunswick,
  Margaret Davis Cate Collection
Coastal Georgia Historical Society, St. Simons Island
  John Couper Collection
  Research Files
  Malcolm Bell Jr. File
  J. K. Williams Collection
Family History Center, The Church of Jesus Christ of Latter-day Saints, Los
  Angeles, California
  Daughters of the American Revolution Collection
  U.S. Department of Commerce, Bureau of the Census, Federal Manuscript
  Census, Glynn County, Georgia, 1820–1860.
  U.S. Department of Commerce, Bureau of the Census, Federal Manuscript
  Census, Wilkes County, Georgia, 1820–1860
  U.S. Department of Commerce, Bureau of the Census, Federal Slave Census,
  Glynn County, Georgia, 1850–1860
  U.S. Department of Commerce, Bureau of the Census, Federal Slave Census,
  Wilkes County, Georgia, 1850–1860
Fort Fredericka National Park, St. Simons Island, Georgia
  Margaret Davis Cate Collection
Georgia Archives, Morrow
  Cecilia Abbott Estate Papers
  Banning/Hinton Family Papers
  Bill of Sale from Solomon C. Patton to Lodowick M. Hill, 18 January 1838
  Marian H. Barnett Collection
  Margaret Davis Cate Collection
  Dr. Ficklen Collection, 1834–1842
  John Couper Papers

Daughters of the American Revolution Papers
Glynn County Church Records
Glynn County Court Records
Glynn County Deed Books
Glynn County Estate Records
Glynn County Land Records
Glynn County Tax Digests
Glynn County Will Books
Glynn County Census Records
Thomas Walton Harris Family Papers
Lodowick M. Hill Ledger Book and Slave Transactions, 1852–1865
Wylie Hill Collection Ledger, 1820–1843
Hofwyl Plantation Records
Hopeton Plantation Records
Drury M. Jackson Family Papers
Henry Rootes Jackson Collection
Anna Matilda Page King Day Book, 1842–1864
Thomas Butler King Papers
James Ladson/Pierce Butler Indentures
Benton Miller Papers
Edward Oxford Papers
William A. Pope Collection
Joseph Toomey Collection
Meshack Turner III Papers
Scrapbook of Wilkes County History (miscellaneous items)
Slave Bills of Sale Project
Vanishing Georgia Collection
Wilkes County Church Records
Wilkes County Court of Ordinary, Loose Estate Papers
Wilkes County Deed Books
Wilkes County Estate Records
Wilkes County Geographical Files
Wilkes County Land Records
Wilkes County Ordinances, 1822
Wilkes County Tax Digests
Wilkes County Will Books
Wilkes County Census Records
Alexander Wright Collection
Georgia Historical Society, Savannah
Margaret Davis Cate Collection
Colonial Dames of America Collection
Garnett Family Papers
Julia King Collection
Thomas Butler King Papers
King/Wilder Family Papers
Robert Augustus Toombs Papers
Wayne/Stiles/Anderson Family Papers

WPA Savannah Writers Project Papers
Hargrett Rare Books and Manuscript Library, University of Georgia, Athens
  Joel Abbott Papers
  Alexander Family Papers
  Brunswick & Florida Rail Road Survey in Georgia 1836–1837 Collection
  James Hamilton Couper Papers
  E. Merton Coulter Collection
  DuBose Family Papers
  Francis R. Goulding Collection
  James Hamilton Papers
  Hillyer Family Papers
  Johnston Family Papers
  Andrew Maybank Jones Papers
  Kemme/Chase Family Papers
  Slavery in Georgia Collection
  Robert Augustus Toombs Papers
  W.P.A. Ex-Slave Interviews
Library of Congress, Washington, D.C.
  Workers Project Administration Papers
  Glynn County, Ga.
  Wilkes County, Ga.
Mary Willis Library, Washington-Wilkes County, Georgia
  J. M. Toomey Collection
  Reese Collection
  Colonel Lodowick Merriweither Hill Slave List
  Plowden Collection
  Callaway Family Collection
  Morgan Callaway Letters, 1855–1863
  Wilkes County Tax Digests
Robert Woodruff Library, Emory University, Atlanta, Georgia
  Oliver Family Papers
  Wanderer Ship Collection
  William Henry Stiles Papers
Southern Historical Collection, Wilson Library, University of North Carolina,
    Chapel Hill
  William Audley Couper Family Papers
  James Hamilton Couper Papers
  John Couper Family Papers
  Elizafield Plantation Book
  Gignilliat Family Papers
  Alexander-Hillhouse Family Papers
  Kelvin Grove Plantation Book
  Thomas Butler King Collection
  William Page Family Papers
University Research Library, University of California, Los Angeles
  "Great Auction Sale of Slaves at Savannah Georgia, March 2d and 3d, 1859"
    (New York: American Anti-Slavery Society, 1859).

Published Works and Dissertations

Abrahams, Roger D. *Singing the Master: The Emergence of African American Culture in the Plantation South.* New York: Pantheon Books, 1992.

"Agricola." "Management of Negroes." *Southern Cultivator* 13, no. 6 (June 1855): 171–74.

Albert, Octavia B. Rodgers. *The House of Bondage or Charolette Brooks and Other Slaves.* New York: Hunt and Eaton, 1890.

Anderson, Ralph V., and Robert Gallman, "Slaves as Fixed Capital: Slave Labor and Southern Economic Development." *The Journal of American History* 64, no. 1 (June 1977): 24–46.

Andrews, Eliza. *The War-Time Journal of a Georgia Girl, 1864–1865.* 1908. Reprint, Lincoln: University Press of Nebraska, 1997.

Armstrong, Thomas F. "From Task Labor to Free Labor: The Transition Along Georgia's Rice Coast, 1820–1880." *Georgia Historical Quarterly* 64, no. 4 (Winter 1980): 432–47.

Ashmore, Otis. "Wilkes County, Its Place in Georgia History." *Georgia Historical Quarterly* 1 (1917): 58–68.

Baldwin, Loammi. *Brunswick Canal and Rail Road, Glynn County, Georgia: Charter and Commissioners Report.* Boston: John H. Lastborn, 1837.

Ball, Charles. *Fifty Years in Chains: Or the Life of An American Slave.* New York: H. Dayton, 1859.

Bancroft, Frederic. *Slave Trading in the Old South.* Columbia: University of South Carolina Press, 1996.

Baptist, Edward E. "'Cuffy,' 'Fancy Maids,' and 'One-Eyed Men': Rape, Commodification, and the Domestic Slave Trade in the United States." *American Historical Review* 106, no. 5 (2001): 1619–50.

Bardaglio, Peter. "Rape and the Law in the Old South: 'Calculated to Excite Indignation in Every Heart.'" *Journal of Southern History* 60, no. 4 (November 1994): 749–72.

Barton, Keith C. "'Good Cooks and Washers': Slave Hiring, Domestic Labor, and the Market in Bourbon County, Kentucky." *Journal of American History* 84, no. 2 (1997): 436–60.

Bartram, William. *Travels in Georgia and Florida, 1773–74.* Philadelphia: American Philosophical Society, 1942.

Beckles, Hilary McD. *Centering Woman: Gender Discourses in Caribbean Slave Society.* Kingston, Jamaica: Ian Randle Publishers, 1999.

———. *Natural Rebels: A Social History of Enslaved Black Women in Barbados.* New Brunswick, N.J.: Rutgers University Press, 1989.

Bell, Malcolm, Jr. *Major Butler's Legacy: Five Generations of a Slaveholding Family.* Athens: University of Georgia Press, 1987.

Berlin, Ira, and Philip D. Morgan, eds. *Cultivation and Culture: Labor and the Shaping of Slave Life in the Americas.* Charlottesville: University Press of Virginia, 1993.

———. *The Slave's Economy: Independent Production by Slaves in the Americas.* London: Frank Cass, 1991.

Berry, Daina Ramey. "'We Sho Was Dressed Up': Slave Women, Material Culture, and Decorative Arts in Wilkes County, Georgia." In *The Savannah River Val-*

ley up to 1865: Fine Arts, Architecture, and Decorative Arts, edited by Ashley Callahan, 73–83. Athens: Georgia Museum of Art, 2003.

Berry, Stephen. "More Alluring at a Distance: Absentee Patriarchy and the Thomas Butler King Family." *Georgia Historical Quarterly* 81, no. 4 (Winter 1997): 863–96.

Biehle, Reba Strickland. "Edward Oxford Pioneer Farmer of Middle Georgia." *Georgia Historical Quarterly* 52, no. 2 (June 1968): 187–98.

Blassingame, John W. *The Slave Community: Plantation Life in the Antebellum South.* 1972. Reprint, New York: Oxford University Press, 1979.

———. "Using the Testimony of Ex-Slaves: Approaches and Problems." *Journal of Southern History* 41, no. 4 (November 1975): 473–92.

Block, Sharon. "Rape without Women: Print Culture and the Politicalization of Rape, 1765–1850." *Journal of American History* 89, no. 3 (2002): 849–89.

Boggs, Marion Alexander, ed. *The Alexander Letters, 1787–1900: The Moving and Absorbing Saga of a Georgia Family.* Athens: University of Georgia Press, 1980.

Boney, F. N., ed. *Slave Life in Georgia: A Narrative of the Life, Sufferings, and Escape of John Brown, A Fugitive Slave.* Savannah, Ga.: Beehive Press, 1972.

Bonner, James C. *A History of Georgia Agriculture, 1732–1860.* Athens: University of Georgia Press, 1964.

———. "Profile of a Late Ante-Bellum Community." *American Historical Review* 49, no. 4 (July 1944): 663–80.

Bowen, Elizabeth A. *The Story of Wilkes County Georgia.* Marietta, Ga.: Continental Books, 1950.

Brown, John. *Slave Life in Georgia: A Narrative of the Life, Sufferings, and Escape of John Brown, a Fugitive Slave Now in England.* 1855. Reprint, Freeport, N.Y.: Books for Libraries Press, 1971.

Brownmiller, Susan. *Against Our Will: Men, Women, and Rape.* New York: Simon and Schuster, 1975.

Bruchey, Stuart, ed. *Cotton and the Growth of the American Economy: 1790–1860.* New York: Harcourt, Brace & World, Inc., 1967.

Burke, Emily. *Pleasure and Pain: Reminiscences of Georgia in the 1840s.* Savannah, Beehive Press, 1978.

Burton, Orville Vernon. *In My Father's House Are Many Mansions: Family and Community in Edgefield, South Carolina.* Chapel Hill: University of North Carolina Press, 1985.

Bush, Barbara. "'The Family Tree Is Not Cut': Women and Cultural Resistance in Slave Family Life in the British Caribbean." In *In Resistance: Studies in African, Caribbean, and Afro-American History*, edited by Gary Y. Okihiro, 117–32. Amherst, Mass.: University of Massachusetts Press, 1986.

Byrne, William A. "The Hiring of Woodson, Slave Carpenter of Savannah." *Georgia Historical Quarterly* 77 (Summer 1993): 245–63.

Camp, Stephanie M. H. *Closer to Freedom: Enslaved Women and Everyday Resistance in the Plantation South.* Chapel Hill: University of North Carolina Press, 2004.

Carney, Judith A. *Black Rice: The African Origins of Rice Cultivation in the Americas.* Cambridge, Mass.: Harvard University Press, 2001.

———. "From Hands to Tutors: African Expertise in the South Carolina Rice Economy." *Agricultural History* 67, no. 3 (Summer 1993): 1–30.

———. "Rice Milling, Gender and Slave Labour in Colonial South Carolina." *Past & Present* (November 1996): 108–34.

Cate, Margaret Davis. *Early Days of Coastal Georgia.* New York: Gallery Press, 1955.

———. "Mistakes in Fanny Kemble's Georgia Journal." *Georgia Historical Quarterly* 54, no. 1 (March 1960): 1–17.

———. *Our Todays and Yesterdays: A Story of Brunswick and the Coastal Islands,* rev. ed. Brunswick, Ga.: Clover Brothers, Inc., 1930.

———. "Retreat Plantation." In *Flags of Five Nations: A Collection of Sketches and Stories of the Golden Isles of Guale,* 53–62. Brunswick, Ga.: Glynn County Chamber of Commerce, n.d.

Catterall, Helen, ed. *Judicial Cases Concerning American Negro Slavery and the Negro.* 5 vols. Washington, D.C.: Carnegie Institution, 1930.

Chamerovzow, L. A., ed. *Slave Life in Georgia: A Narrative of the Life, Sufferings, and Escape of John Brown, a Fugitive Slave Now in England.* London, 1855.

Chaplin, Joyce. *An Anxious Pursuit: Agricultural Innovation and Modernity in the Lower South, 1730–1815.* Chapel Hill: University of North Carolina Press, 1993.

———. "Creating a Cotton South in Georgia and South Carolina, 1760–1815." *Journal of Southern History,* vol. 57, no. 2 (May 1991): 171–200.

———. "Tidal Rice Cultivation and the Problem of Slavery in South Carolina and Georgia 1760–1815." *William and Mary Quarterly* 49, no. 1 (January 1992): 29–61.

Chapman, Colin R. *Weights, Money and Other Measures Used by Our Ancestors.* Baltimore: Genealogical Publishing Company, Inc., 1996.

Child, Lydia Marie, ed. *Incidents in the Life of a Slave Girl Written by Herself.* Boston: Published for the Author, 1860.

Clifton, James M. "Hopeton, Model Plantation of the Antebellum South." *Georgia Historical Quarterly* 66, no. 4 (Winter 1982): 429–49.

———, ed. *Life and Labor on Argyle Island: Letters and Documents of a Savannah River Plantation, 1833–1867.* Savannah, Ga.: Beehive Press, 1978.

Clinton, Catherine. *Fanny Kemble's Civil Wars: The Story of America's Most Unlikely Abolitionist.* New York: Simon & Schuster, 2000.

———. ed. *Fanny Kemble's Journals.* Cambridge, Mass.: Harvard University Press, 2000.

Coastal Georgia Historical Society. *Historic Glimpses of St. Simons Island Georgia 1736–1924.* St. Simons Island, Ga.: Coastal Georgia Historical Society, 1971.

———. *Not Soon Forgotten: Cotton Planters & Plantations of the Golden Isles of Georgia 1784–1812.* St. Simons Island, Ga.: Coastal Georgia Historical Society, 1987.

Cody, Cheryll Ann. "There Was No 'Absalom' on the Ball Plantations: Slave-Naming Practices in the South Carolina Low Country, 1720–1865." *American Historical Review* 92, no. 3 (June 1987): 563–96.

Coulter, E. Merton. *Old Petersburg and the Broad River Valley of Georgia: Their Rise and Decline.* Athens: University of Georgia Press, 1965.

Couper, John. "On the Origin of Sea-Island Cotton." *Southern Agriculturist* (May 1831): 242–45.

Cox, Jack F., ed. *The 1850 Census of Georgia Slave Owners.* Baltimore: Clearfield Publishing Company, 1999.

Creel, Margaret Washington. *'A Peculiar People': Slave Religion and Community-Culture Among the Gullahs.* New York: New York University Press, 1988.

Daniels, Christine, and Michael V. Kennedy, eds. *Over the Threshold: Intimate Violence in Early America, 1640–1865.* New York: Routledge, 1999.

Darby, James C. "On Planting and Managing a Rice Crop." *Southern Agriculturist* (June 1829): 247–54.

Doar, David. *Rice and Rice Planting in the South Carolina Low County.* Charleston, S.C.: The Charleston Museum, 1936.

Doesticks, Q. K. Philander. *Great Auction Sale of Slaves, at Savannah, Georgia, March 2d and 3d, 1859.* New York: American Anti-Slavery Society, 1859.

Douglass, Frederick. *Narrative of the Life of Frederick Douglass an American Slave Written by Himself.* Boston: Anti-Slavery Office, 1845.

Dusinberre, William. *Them Dark Days: Slavery in the American Rice Swamps.* New York: Oxford University Press, 1996.

Eaton, Clement. "Slave Hiring in the Upper South: A Step toward Freedom." *Mississippi Valley Historical Review* 48 (March 1960): 663–78.

Elkins, Stanley M. *Slavery: A Problem in American Institutional and Intellectual Life.* Chicago: University of Chicago Press, 1976; 1959.

Ellenberg, George Bolten. "Wilkes County, Georgia Beginnings to 1830: The Growth of Slavery and Its Impact on Class Structure." M.A. thesis, Clemson University, 1988.

Farnham, Christie. "Sapphire? The Issue of Dominance in the Slave Family, 1830–1865." In *'To Toil the Livelong Day': America's Women at Work, 1780–1980,* edited by Carol Groneman and Mary Beth Norton, 68–83. Ithaca, N.Y.: Cornell University Press, 1987.

Ferguson, T. Reed. *The John Couper Family at Cannon's Point.* Macon, Ga.: Mercer University Press, 1994.

Fett, Sharla. *Working Cures: Healing, Health, and Power on Southern Slave Plantations.* Chapel Hill: University of North Carolina Press, 2002.

Fischer, Kristen. *Suspect Relations: Sex, Race, and Resistance in Colonial North Carolina.* Ithaca, N.Y.: Cornell University Press, 2002.

Flanders, Ralph Betts. *Plantation Slavery in Georgia.* Chapel Hill: University of Carolina Press, 1933.

Fogel, Robert W., and Stanley L. Engerman. *Time on the Cross: The Economics of American Negro Slavery.* Boston: Little, Brown, and Company, 1974.

Foreman, P. Gabrielle. "Manifest in Signs: The Politics of Sex and Representation in *Incidents in the Life of a Slave Girl.*" In *Harriet Jacobs and Incidents in the Life of a Slave Girl: New Critical Essays,* edited by Deborah Garfield and Rafia Zafar, 76–99. Cambridge: Cambridge University Press, 1996.

Franklin, John Hope, and Loren Schweninger. *Runaway Slaves: Rebels on the Plantation.* New York: Oxford University Press, 1999.

Gaspar, David Barry, and Darlene Clark Hine, eds. *More than Chattel: Black Women and Slavery in the Americas.* Bloomington: Indiana University Press, 1996.

Genovese, Eugene D. *Roll Jordan Roll: The World the Slaves Made.* New York: Vintage Books, 1974.

Georgia Writers' Project. *Drums and Shadows: Survival Studies among the Georgia Coastal Negroes.* Athens: University of Georgia Press, 1940.

Goldin, Claudia Dale. *Urban Slavery in the American South, 1820–1860*. Chicago: University of Chicago Press, 1976.

Granger, Mary, ed. *Savannah River Plantations*. Savannah Writers' Project. Savannah: The Georgia Historical Society, 1947.

Gray, Lewis Cecil. *History of Agriculture in the Southern United States*. 2 vols. Washington, D.C.: Carnegie Institution of Washington, 1933.

Gross, Ariela J. *Double Character: Slavery and Mastery in the Antebellum Southern Courtroom*. Princeton, N.J.: Princeton University Press, 2000.

Gutman, Herbert. *The Black Family in Slavery and Freedom, 1750–1925*. New York: Vintage Books, 1976.

Gutman, Herbert, and Richard Sutch, eds. *Reckoning with Slavery: A Critical Study in the Quantitative History of American Negro Slavery*. New York: Oxford University Press, 1976.

Hadden, Sally E. *Slave Patrols: Law and Violence in Virginia and the Carolinas*. Cambridge, Mass.: Harvard University Press, 2001.

Hall, Basil. *Travels in North America, 1827–1828*. Edinburgh: Cadell and Co., 1829.

Hall, Jacquelyn Dowd. "'The Mind that Burns in Each Body': Women, Rape, and Racial Violence." In *Powers of Desire: The Politics of Sexuality*, edited by Ann Snitnow, Christine Stansell, and Sharon Thompson, 328–49. New York: Monthly Review Press, 1983.

Hall, Margaret Hunter. *The Aristocratic Journey: Being the Outspoken Letters of Mrs. Basil Hall Written during a Fourteen Months' Sojourn in America 1827–1828*. New York: G. P. Putnam's Sons, 1931.

Harris, J. William. "The Organization of Work on a Yeoman Slaveholder's Farm." *Agricultural History* 64 no. 1 (Winter 1990): 39–52.

———. *Plain Folk and Gentry in a Slave Society: White Liberty and Black Slavery in Augusta's Hinterlands*. Middletown, Conn.: Wesleyan University Press, 1985.

———. "Portrait of a Small Slaveholder: The Journal of Benton Miller." *Georgia Historical Quarterly* 74 no. 1 (Spring 1990): 1–19.

Hazzard, W. W. "On the General Management of a Plantation." *Southern Agriculturist* (July 1831): 350–54.

Hazzard, William. *St. Simons Island, Georgia Brunswick and Vicinity: Description and Travel 1825*. Belmont, Mass.: Oak Hill Press, 1974.

Heard, George Alexander. "St. Simons Island during the War Between the States." *Georgia Historical Quarterly* 22, no. 3 (September 1938): 249–72.

Hepburn, A. Barton. *A History of Currency in the United States*. New York: Macmillan Company, 1924. Reprint, New York: Augusta M. Kelley Publishers, 1967.

Heyward, Duncan Clinch. *Seed from Madagascar*. 1937. Reprint, Columbia: University of South Carolina Press, 1993.

Hill, Lodowick Johnson. *The Hills of Wilkes County Georgia and Allied Families*. Atlanta: Johnson-Dallis Company, 1922.

Hine, Darlene Clark. "Rape and the Inner Lives of Black Women in the Middle West: Preliminary Thoughts on the Culture of Dissemblance." In *Unequal Sisters: A Multicultural Reader in U.S. Women's History*, edited by Ellen DuBois and Vicki Ruiz, 292–97. New York: Routledge, 1990.

Hitz, Alex. "The Earliest Settlements in Wilkes County." *Georgia Historical Quarterly* 40 (September 1956): 260–80.

Holmes, James. *"Dr. Bullie's" Notes: Reminiscences of Early Georgia and of Philadelphia and New Haven in the 1800s,* edited by Delma E. Presley. Atlanta: Cherokee Publishing Company, 1976.

House, Albert V. "The Management of a Rice Plantation in Georgia, 1834–1861, As Revealed in the Journal of Hugh Fraser Grant." *Agricultural History* 13 (October 1939): 208–17.

———, ed. *Planter Management and Capitalism in Antebellum Georgia: The Journal of Hugh Fraser Grant, Ricegrower.* New York: Columbia University Press, 1954.

Howell, Donna Wyant, comp. *I Was a Slave: True Life Stories Told by Former American Slaves in the 1930's.* Washington: American Legacy Books, 1995.

Hudson, Larry E. Jr. *To Have and to Hold: Slave Work and Family Life in Antebellum South Carolina.* Athens: University of Georgia Press, 1997.

———. *Working toward Freedom: Slave Society and Domestic Economy in the American South.* Rochester, N.Y.: University of Rochester Press, 1994.

Hughes, Sarah S. "Slaves for Hire: The Allocation of Black Labor in Elizabeth City County, Virginia, 1782–1810." *William & Mary Quarterly* 3rd Series 35 (April 1978): 260–86.

Jacobs, Harriet, and Lydia Marie Child, eds. *Incidents in the Life of a Slave Girl.* Boston: Published by Jacobs, 1860.

Jennings, Thelma. "'Us Colored Women Had to Go Through a Plenty'" Sexual Exploitation of African American Slave Women." *Journal of Women's History* 1, no. 3 (Winter 1990): 45–72.

Johnson, Guion G. *A Social History of the Sea Islands.* Chapel Hill: University of North Carolina Press, 1930.

Johnson, Michael P. "Work, Culture, and the Slave Community: Slave Occupations in the Cotton Belt in 1860." *Labor History* 27 (Summer 1986): 325–55.

Johnson, Walter. *Soul by Soul: Life Inside the Antebellum Slave Market.* Cambridge. Mass.: Harvard University Press, 1999.

Jones, Charles C. Jr. *Negro Myths from the Georgia Coast.* Detroit: Singing Tree Press, 1969.

———. *The Religious Instruction of Negroes in the United States.* 1930. Reprint, New York: Negro Universities Press, 1969.

Jones, Jacqueline. *American Work: Four Centuries of Black and White Labor.* New York: W. W. Norton, 1998.

———. *Labor of Love, Labor of Sorrow: Black Women, Work, and the Family, From Slavery to the Present.* New York: Vintage Books, 1985.

Joyner, Charles. *Down by the Riverside: A South Carolina Slave Community.* Urbana: University of Illinois Press, 1984.

———. *Remember Me: Slave Life in Coastal Georgia.* Atlanta: Georgia Humanities Council, 1989.

Kemble, Frances Anne. *Journal of a Residence on a Georgian Plantation in 1838–1839.* 1863. Reprint, Athens: University of Georgia Press, 1984.

King, Roswell Jr. "On the Management of the Butler Estate, and the Cultivation of the Sugar Cane." *Southern Agriculturist* (December 1828): 523–29.

King, Wilma. "The Mistress and Her Maids: White and Black Women in a Louisiana Household, 1858–1868." In *Discovering the Women in Slavery: Emancipating Perspectives on the American Past,* edited by Patricia Morton, 82–106. Athens: University of Georgia Press, 1996.

———. "'Raise Your Children Up Rite': Parental Guidance and Child Rearing Practices among Slaves in the Nineteenth-Century South." In *Working toward Freedom: Slave Society and Domestic Economy in the American South*, edited by Larry E. Hudson Jr., 143–62. Rochester, N.Y.: University of Rochester Press, 1994.

———. *Stolen Childhood: Slave Youth in Nineteenth-Century America.* Bloomington: University of Indiana Press, 1995.

Lakwete, Angela. *Inventing the Cotton Gin: Machine and Myth in Antebellum America.* Baltimore: Johns Hopkins University Press, 2004.

Lee, Daniel. "Agricultural Apprentices and Laborers." *Southern Cultivator* 12, no. 6 (June 1854): 169–70.

Legare, J. D. "Account of an Agricultural Excursion Made into the South of Georgia in the Winter of 1832." *Southern Agriculturist* 6 (June–August 1833): 359.

Leigh, Frances Butler. *Ten Years on a Georgia Plantation since the War, 1866–1876.* 1883. Reprint, Savannah, Ga.: Beehive Press, 1992.

Lerner, Gerda. *Black Women in White America: A Documentary History.* 1972. Reprint, New York: Vintage Books, 1992.

Lewis, Bessie. *King's Retreat Plantation: Today and Yesterday.* Brunswick, Ga.: Coastal Printing Company, 1980.

Lewis, Bessie, and Mildred Huie. *Patriarchal Plantations of St. Simons Island, Georgia.* Brunswick, Ga.: Glover Printing Company, 1974.

Lovell, Caroline Couper. *The Golden Isles of Georgia.* 1932. Reprint, Atlanta: Cherokee Publishing Company, 1970.

Lowe, Richard G., and Randolph B. Campbell. "The Slave-Breeding Hypothesis: A Demographic Comment on the 'Buying' and 'Selling' States." *Journal of Southern History* 42, no. 2 (1976): 401–12.

Lyell, Charles. *A Second Visit to the United States of North America.* New York: Harper & Brothers, 1849.

Malone, Anne Patton. *Sweet Chariot: Slave Family and Household Structure in Nineteenth-Century Louisiana.* Chapel Hill: University of North Carolina Press, 1992.

Manning, Patrick. *Slavery and African Life: Occidental, Oriental, and African Slave Trades.* Cambridge, Mass.: Cambridge University Pres, 1990.

Martin, Jonathan D. *Divided Mastery: Slave Hiring in the American South.* Cambridge, Mass.: Harvard University Press, 2004.

Marye, Florence, and Edwin R. MacKethan III, eds. *The Story of the Page-King Family of Retreat Plantation, St. Simons Island and the Golden Isles of Georgia.* Darien, Ga.: Edwin R. MacKethan Publisher, 2000.

McDonald, Roderick A. *The Economy and Material Culture of Slaves: Goods and Chattels on the Sugar Plantations of Jamaica and Louisiana.* Baton Rouge: Louisiana State University Press, 1993.

Mellon, James, ed. *Bullwhip Days: The Slaves Remember, An Oral History.* New York: Avon Books, 1988.

Merritt, Carole. "Slave Family and Household Arrangements in Piedmont Georgia." Ph.D. dissertation, Emory University, 1986.

Mintz, Sidney. "The Jamaican Internal Marketing Pattern: Some Notes and Hypotheses." *Social and Economic Studies* 4 (1955), 95–103.

Mintz, Sidney W., and Douglas Hall. "The Origins of the Jamaican Internal Marketing System." *Anthropology* 57 (1960).

Mohr, Clarence L. "Slavery in Oglethorpe County, Georgia 1773–1865." *Phylon* 32, no. 1 (Spring 1972): 4–18.

Morgan, Jennifer L. *Laboring Women: Gender and Reproduction in the Making of New World Slavery*. Philadelphia: University of Pennsylvania Press, 2004.

Morgan, Philip D. *Slave Counterpoint: Black Culture in the Eighteenth Century Chesapeake and Lowcountry*. Chapel Hill: University of North Carolina Press, 1998.

Morgan, Philip. "The Ownership of Property by Slaves in the Mid-Nineteenth-Century Low Country." *Journal of Southern History* 49, no. 3 (1983): 399–20.

———. "Task and Gang Systems: The Organization of Labor on New World Plantations." In *Work and Labor in Early America*, edited by Stephen Innes, 189–220. Chapel Hill: University of North Carolina Press, 1988.

———. "Three Planters and Their Slaves: Perspectives on Slavery in Virginia, South Carolina, and Jamaica, 1750–1790." In *Race and Family in the Colonial South*, edited by Winthrop D. Jordan and Sheila Skemp, 37–80. Jackson: University Press of Mississippi, 1987.

———. "Work and Culture: The Task System and the World of Lowcountry Blacks, 1700–1800." *William & Mary Quarterly* 39 (October 1982): 563–99.

Morner, Magnus. *"Buy or Breed?" Alternative Sources of Slave Supply in the Plantation Societies of the New World*. Stockholm: Institute of Latin American Studies, 1980.

Morris, Christopher. "The Articulation of Two Worlds: The Master-Slave Relationship Reconsidered." *Journal of American History* 85, no. 3 (December 1998): 982–1007.

Morrissey, M. *Slave Women in the New World*. Lawrence: University Press of Kansas, 1990.

Morton, Patricia, ed. *Discovering the Women in Slavery: Emancipating Perspectives on the American Past*. Athens: University of Georgia Press, 1996.

Myers, Robert Manson, ed. *The Children of Pride: A True Story of Georgia and the Civil War*. New Haven, Conn.: Yale University Press, 1972.

Noble, William Allister. "Sequent Occupance of Hopeton-Atama 1815–1956." M.A. thesis, University of Georgia, 1957.

O'Donovan, Susan Eva. "Transforming Work: Slavery, Free Labor, and the Household in Southwest Georgia." Ph.D. dissertation, University of California, San Diego, 1997.

Olmsted, Frederick Law. *The Cotton Kingdom: A Traveller's Observations on Cotton and Slavery in the American Slave States, 1853–1861*. 1861. Reprint, New York: Da Capo Press, 1996.

Olwell, Robert. *Masters, Slaves, and Subjects: The Culture of Power in the South Carolina Low Country, 1740–1790*. Ithaca, N.Y.: Cornell University Press, 1998.

Otto, John Solomon. *Cannon's Point Plantation 1794–1860: Living Conditions and Status Patterns in the Old South*. Orlando, Fla.: Academic Press, Inc., 1984.

———. "Slavery in a Coastal Community–Glynn County (1790–1860)." *Georgia Historical Quarterly* 63 (1970): 460–80.

Otto, Rhea Cumming. *1850 Census of Georgia Wilkes County*. Savannah: Rhea C. Otto, 1990.

Painter, Nell Irvin. "Soul Murder and Slavery: Toward a Fully Loaded Cost Accounting." In *U.S. History as Women's History: New Feminists Essays*, edited by Linda K. Kerber, Alice Kessler-Harris, and Kathryn Kish Sklar, 125–46. Chapel Hill: University of North Carolina Press, 1995.

Parrish, Lydia. *Slave Songs of the Georgia Sea Islands*. 1942. Reprint, Athens: University of Georgia Press, 1992.

Patterson, Orlando. *Slavery and Social Death: A Comparative Study*. Cambridge, Mass.: Harvard University Press, 1982.

Pavich-Lindsay, Melanie, ed. *Anna: The Letters of a St. Simons Island Plantation Mistress, 1817–1859*. Athens: University of Georgia Press, 2002.

Penningroth, Dylan. *The Claims of Kinfolk: African American Property and Community in the Nineteenth-Century South*. Chapel Hill: University of North Carolina Press, 2003.

———. "Slavery, Freedom, and Social Claims to Property among African Americans in Liberty County, Georgia, 1850–1880." *Journal of American History* 84, no. 2 (September 1997): 405–35.

Prince, Richard E. *Steam Locomotives and History: Georgia Railroad and West Point Route*. Green River, Wyo.: Richard E. Prince, 1962.

Pringle, Elizabeth W. Allston. *A Woman Rice Planter, by Patience Pennington* [pseud.]. Cambridge, Mass.: Harvard University Press, 1961.

Pruneau, Leigh Ann. "All the Time Is Work Time: Gender and the Task System on Antebellum Lowcountry Rice Plantations." Ph.D. dissertation, University of Arizona, 1997.

Raboteau, Albert J. *Slave Religion: The "Invisible Institution" in the Antebellum South*. New York: Oxford University Press, 1978.

Ramey, Daina L. "'A Heap of Us Slaves:' Family and Community Life among Slave Women in Georgia." *Atlanta History: A Journal of Georgia and the South* 44, no. 3 (Fall 2000): 21–38.

———. "A Place of Our Own: Labor, Family and Community among Female Slaves in Piedmont and Tidewater Georgia, 1820–1860." Ph.D. dissertation, University of California, Los Angeles, 1998.

———. "'She Do a Heap of Work': Female Slave Labor on Glynn County Rice and Cotton Plantations." *Georgia Historical Quarterly* 82, no. 4 (Winter 1998): 707–34.

Rawick, George P., ed. *The American Slave: A Composite Autobiography*. Georgia Narratives vols. 12–13, supplement series 1, vols. 3–4. Westport, Conn.: Greenwood Press, 1977.

Reddock, Rhoda E. "Women and Slavery in the Caribbean: A Feminist Perspective." *Latin American Perspectives* vol. 12, no. 1 (Winter 1985): 63–80.

Saggus, Charles Danforth. *Agrarian Arcadia: Anglo-Virginian Planters of Wilkes County, Georgia in the 1850s*. Washington, Ga.: Mary Willis Library, 1996.

———. "A Social and Economic History of the Danburg Community in Wilkes County, Georgia." M.A. thesis, University of Georgia, 1951.

Schwalm, Leslie A. *A Hard Fight for We: Women's Transition from Slavery to Freedom in South Carolina*. Urbana: University of Illinois Press, 1997.

———. "The Meaning of Freedom: African-American Women and Their Transition from Slavery to Freedom in Lowcountry South Carolina." Ph.D. dissertation, University of Wisconsin, 1991.

Schweninger, Loren. "The Underside of Slavery: The Internal Economy, Self-Hire, and Quasi-Freedom in Virginia, 1780–1865." *Slavery & Abolition* 12, no. 2 (September 1991): 1–22.

Seabrook, Whitemarsh B. *Memoir on the Origin, Cultivation and Uses of Cotton: From the Earliest Ages to the Present Time with Special Reference to the Sea-Island Cotton Plant.* Charleston, S.C.: Miller & Browne, 1844.

Shaw, Stephanie J. "Using the WPA Ex-Slave Narratives to Study the Impact of the Great Depression." *Journal of Southern History* 69, no 3 (August 2003): 623–58.

Simmonds, Lorna. "Slave Higglering in Jamaica, 1780–1834." *Jamaica Journal* 20, no. 1 (1987): 31–38.

Singleton, Teresa. "The Archeology of Afro-American Slavery in Coastal Georgia." Ph.D. dissertation, University of Florida, 1980.

Smith, Julia Floyd. *Slavery and Rice Culture in Low Country Georgia 1750–1860.* Knoxville: University of Tennessee Press, 1985.

Sobel, Machel. *The World They Made Together: Black and White Values in Eighteenth-Century Virginia.* Princeton, N.J.: Princeton University Press, 1987.

Sommerville, Diane Miller. "Rape." In *Black Women in America: An Historical Encyclopedia,* 2nd Edition, edited by Darlene Clark Hine, et al., 21–28. New York: Oxford University Press, 2004.

———. "The Rape Myth in the Old South Reconsidered." *Journal of Southern History* 61, no.5 (1993): 481–509.

———. *Rape and Race in the Nineteenth-Century South.* Chapel Hill: University of North Carolina Press, 2004.

Stampp, Kenneth M. *The Peculiar Institution: Slavery in the Antebellum South.* 1956, Reprint, New York: Vintage Books, 1989.

Starobin, Robert S. *Industrial Slavery in the Old South.* New York: Oxford University Press, 1970.

Steel, Edward M. T. *Butler King of Georgia.* Athens: University of Georgia Press, 1964.

Stevenson, Brenda E. "Black Family Structure in Colonial and Antebellum Virginia: Amending the Revisionist Perspective." In *The Decline in Marriage among African Americans: Causes, Consequences, and Policy Implications,* edited by Claudia Mitchell-Kernan and M. Belinda Tucker, 27–56. New York: Russell Sage Foundation, 1995.

———. "Distress and Discord in Virginia Slave Families, 1830–1860." In *In Joy and In Sorrow: Women, Family, and Marriage in the Victorian South, 1830–1900,* edited by Carol Blesser, 103–24. New York: Oxford University Press, 1991.

———. *Life in Black and White: Family and Community in the Slave South.* New York: Oxford University Press, 1996.

———. "'Marsa Never Sot Aunt Rebecca Down': Slave Women, Religion and Social Power in the Antebellum South." Unpublished paper presented at the Southern Historical Association's annual meeting in Atlanta, Georgia, 6 November 1997.

———. "Slavery." In *Black Women in America: An Historical Encyclopedia,* edited by Darlene Clark Hine, Elsa Barkley Brown, and Rosalyn Terborg-Penn, 1045–76. Bloomington: Indiana University Press, 1993.

Stewart, Mark A. "Rice, Water, and Power: Landscapes of Domination and Resistance in the Lowcountry, 1790–1880." *Environmental History Review* 15, no. 3 (Fall 1991): 47–64.

———. *'What Nature Suffers to Groe': Life, Labor, and Landscape on the Georgia Coast, 1680–1920.* Athens: University of Georgia Press, 1996.

Stuckey, Sterling. *Slave Culture: Nationalist Theory and the Foundations of Black America.* New York: Oxford University Press, 1987.

Sutch, Richard. "The Breeding of Slaves for Sale and the Westward Expansion of Slavery, 1850–1860." In *Southern Economic History Project Working Paper Number 10.* Berkeley: University of California, 1972.

———. "Slave Breeding." *Social Science Working Paper #593.* Pasadena: California Institute of Technology, 1986.

Takagi, Madori. "Female Slave Participation in the Urban Market Economy: Richmond, Virginia, 1780–1860." *Southern Women: The Intersection of Race, Class and Gender Working Paper 8.* Pamphlet. Memphis, Tenn.: Center for Research on Women, 1994.

Thomas, Keith. *Man and the Natural World: Changing Attitudes in England, 1500–1800.* New York: Oxford University Press, 1986.

Trussell, James, and Richard Steckel. "The Age of Slaves at Menarche and their First Birth." *Journal of Interdisciplinary History* 8 (Winter 1978): 477–505.

Turner, J. A. *The Cotton Planter's Manual: Being a Compilation of Facts From the Best Authorities on the Culture of Cotton.* 1857. Reprint, New York: Negro Universities Press, 1969.

Vanstory, Burnette. *Georgia's Land of the Golden Isles.* Athens: University of Georgia Press, 1956.

———. *History of Altama Plantation 1763–1969.* n.p., n.d.

Van Deburg, William L. *The Slave Drivers: Black Agricultural Labor Supervisors in the Antebellum South.* Westport, Conn.: Greenwood Press, 1979.

Wade, Richard. *Slavery in the Cities.* New York: Oxford University Press, 1964.

Walker, Alice O., ed. *Registers of Signatures of Depositors in the Augusta, Georgia, Branch of the Freedman's Savings and Trust Company.* Vol. 1. Augusta, Ga.: Richmond County Public Library, 1998.

Waters, Andrew, ed. *On Jordan's Stormy Banks: Personal Accounts of Slavery in Georgia.* Winston-Salem, N.C.: John F. Blair, 2000.

Watson, James L. "Slavery as an Institution: Open and Closed Systems. In *Asian and African Systems of Slavery,* edited by James L. Watson, 1–15. Berkeley: University of California Press, 1980.

Webber, Thomas L. *Deep Like the Rivers: Education in the Slave Quarter Community, 1831–1865.* New York: W. W. Norton, 1978.

Weiner, Marli F. *Mistresses and Slaves: Plantation Women in South Carolina, 1830–1880.* Urbana: University of Illinois Press, 1998.

West, Emily. *Chains of Love: Slave Couples in Antebellum South Carolina.* Urbana: University of Illinois Press, 2004.

White, Deborah Gray. *Ar'n't I a Woman?: Female Slaves in the Plantation South.* New York: W. W. Norton and Company, 1985.

———. "Female Slaves: Sex Roles and Status in the Antebellum Plantation South." *Journal of Family History* 8 (Fall 1983): 248–61.

Whitman, T. Stephen. *The Price of Freedom: Slavery and Manumission in Baltimore and Early National Maryland.* New York: Routledge, 2000.

Wilcox, Irene Stilwell. *The Census Records of Elbert County, 1820–60 and the 1850 Census of Wilkes County.* Easley, S.C.: Southern Historical Press, 1979.

Willingham, Robert M. Jr. *No Jubilee: The Story of Confederate Wilkes.* Washington, Ga.: Wilkes Publishing Company, 1976.

———. *We Have This Heritage: The History of Wilkes County, Georgia Beginnings to 1860.* Washington, Ga.: Wilkes Publishing Company, 1969.

Wood, Betty C. *Slavery in Colonial Georgia, 1730–1775.* Athens: University of Georgia Press, 1984.

———. *Women's Work, Men's Work: The Informal Slave Economies of Lowcountry Georgia.* Athens: University of Georgia Press, 1995.

Work Projects Administration. *Drums and Shadows: Survival Studies among the Georgia Coastal Negroes.* Athens: University of Georgia Press, 1940.

Wylly, Charles S. *Annals and Statistics of Glynn County, Georgia.* Brunswick, Ga.: Press of H. A. Wrench & Sons, 1897.

Periodicals

Augusta Chronicle, 1806–1867, Augusta, Georgia
Augusta Georgia Constitutionalist, Augusta, Georgia
Brunswick Advocate, 1837, Brunswick, Georgia
Darien Gazette, 1818–1828, Darien, Georgia
Georgia Gazette, 1763–1770, Savannah, Georgia
The Independent Press, 1840, Washington, Georgia
The McIntosh County Herald and Darien Commercial Register, 1839–1840, Darien, Georgia
The News, 1820s and 1830s, Washington, Georgia
The News and Planter's Gazette, 1840–1844, Washington, Georgia
The Savannah Republican, 1858–1865, Savannah, Georgia
Southern Agriculturist, 1828–1840, Macon, Georgia
The Southern Cultivator, 1844–1858 Augusta, Georgia
The Southern Spy, 1829–1830, Washington, Georgia
Washington Gazette, 1849, Washington, Georgia
Washington News, 1816–44, Washington, Georgia
The Washington News and Miscellaneous Advertiser, 1832, Washington, Georgia
Wilkes Republican, 1853, Washington, Georgia

INDEX

DAINA RAMEY BERRY is an associate professor of history at Michigan State University. She has contributed chapters to *The Chattel Principle: Internal Slave Trades in the Americas, 1808–1888* and other edited volumes. She is on the editorial board of *Black Women in America: An Historical Encyclopedia,* second edition. She has articles in *Atlanta History: A Journal of Georgia and the South,* the *Journal of African American History,* the *Georgia Historical Quarterly,* and the *Journal of Women's History.*

The University of Illinois Press
is a founding member of the
Association of American University Presses.

University of Illinois Press
1325 South Oak Street
Champaign, IL 61820-6903
www.press.uillinois.edu